Marxist theories of imperialism

Marxist theories
of imperialism
A critical survey

Anthony Brewer

Department of Economics, University of Bristol

Routledge & Kegan Paul

London, Boston, Melbourne and Henley

First published in 1980
by Routledge & Kegan Paul plc
14 Leicester Square, London WC2H 7PH
9 Park Street, Boston, Mass. 02108, USA
464 St Kilda Road, Melbourne,
Victoria 3004, Australia and
Broadway House, Newtown Road
Henley-on-Thames, Oxon RG9 1EN

Reprinted in 1982 and 1984

Set in 10/12 Compugraphic Garamond
and printed in Great Britain by
Ebenezer Baylis and Son Limited
The Trinity Press, Worcester, and London

British Library Cataloguing in Publication Data
Brewer, Anthony
Marxist theories of imperialism.
1. Imperialism
2. Communism
I. Title
321.03   JC359   80 41000

ISBN 0 7100 0531 8
ISBN 0 7100 0621 7 Pbk.

To Alan and Iris Brewer

Contents

Preface

My aim in this book is to survey Marxist writings on imperialism and, more broadly, on the emergence and development of the world capitalist economy. A great deal has been written in this field, but I think there is a place for a survey that is not intended to replace the existing literature, but rather to provide a guide to it, to establish what the main writers have to say, how their theories relate to each other, and how far they make sense. I have tried to maintain a sympathetic but critical position; critical because I think that Marxist theories have often suffered from being accepted or rejected wholesale rather than being subjected to detailed scrutiny and constructive criticism, and sympathetic because there is a great deal to be learned from them.

I have, in turn, benefited greatly from the constructive criticism of others. I would like to thank Martin Browning and Aidan Foster-Carter for helpful comments, and I owe a special debt to Roger Berry and to Andy Friedman who each read the whole first draft and told me where I was going wrong. They should not be blamed for remaining errors. Karen Snodin helped me with translations, Gillian Baker, Pat Shaw and, especially, Marjorie Lunt typed successive drafts with great skill and patience, while Janet, Robert and David Brewer prevented me from becoming too obsessed with the project.

Parts of chapter 10 are based on a forthcoming article in *Capital and Class.*

A.A. Brewer

Abbreviations

Some books that are referred to repeatedly are cited in the text by an abbreviated form of their title rather than in the standard form. They are listed below; for full details see the bibliography.

Accumulation	Luxemburg (1951), *The Accumulation of Capital*
Alliances	Rey (1973), *Les Alliances de classes*
Anti-Critique	Luxemburg (1972), *The Accumulation of Capital – an Anti-Critique*
Capital	Marx (1961, 1957, 1962), *Capital*, vols I–III
Colonialisme	Rey (1971), *Colonialisme, néo-colonialisme et transition au capitalisme*
CULA	Frank (1969a), *Capitalism and Underdevelopment in Latin America*
CWE	Wallerstein (1979), *The Capitalist World Economy*
DAU	Frank (1978), *Dependent Accumulation and Underdevelopment*
EPEA	Arrighi and Saul (1973), *Essays on the Political Economy of Africa*
FC	Hilferding (1970), *Finance Capital*
Imperialism	Lenin (1950), *Imperialism, the Highest Stage of Capitalism*
IWE	Bukharin (1972a), *Imperialism and World Economy*
LAUR	Frank (1969b), *Latin America,: Underdevelopment or Revolution*
LL	Frank (1972), *Lumpenbourgeoisie: Lumpendevelopment*
Manifesto	Marx (n.d.a.), *Manifesto of the Communist Party*
MWS	Wallerstein (1974a), *The Modern World System*
PEG	Baran (1973), *The Political Economy of Growth*
UE	Emmanuel (1972), *Unequal Exchange*

1 · Introduction

I Imperialism: the scope of the book

The last two or three hundred years have seen two interconnected developments that have totally transformed the world. Firstly, production and productivity have increased to levels that would previously have seemed not so much impossible as inconceivable, and the whole nature of industry and of many of the goods produced has altered beyond recognition. How could earlier generations have conceived of live colour television pictures from the moon, broadcast to a mass audience in their own homes? Secondly, inequalities of wealth and power between different parts of the world have grown to an equally unprecedented degree. American workers watch their colour televisions, while their African and Asian counterparts suffer malnutrition. These are facts that everyone knows, but we tend to take them for granted and to ignore the extent to which they determine the whole character of the contemporary world. They can only be understood and analysed by looking at the historical process by which they have evolved, on a world scale and over a period of centuries.

The same period has been marked by a third, less obvious, development: the rise to dominance of the capitalist mode of production. In this form of economic organisation, production is carried out by many distinct, privately owned enterprises that sell their products on the market and employ wage workers. Capitalism has almost completely supplanted earlier forms of organisation (peasant agriculture, feudal estates, slave plantations) in the advanced countries. In the underdeveloped countries peasant agriculture still supports a large part of the population, but these areas have been drawn into a world market and a world-wide system of specialisation that has completely undermined traditional economic and social structures.

The colonial empires hacked out by European powers, and the whole system of European and American military and political dominance over

1

the world, that reached its peak in the early twentieth century, can only be understood in the context of this process of uneven development. The basis for military supremacy was economic. Superior technology meant superior armaments and a capacity to transport armed men to any part of the world. Superior economic organisation made it possible to finance the overhead costs of military forces, and to deploy them to devastating effect. The motives for imperial expansion were also predominantly economic. Some historians now seek to deny this, but the men of the East India Company, the Spanish *Conquistadores*, the investors in South African mines and the slave traders knew very well what they wanted. They wanted to be rich. Colonial empires were exploited ruthlessly for economic gain as sources of cheap raw materials and cheap labour, and as monopolised markets. The romantic image of empire (flags fluttering over distant outposts, etc.) may be appealing, but a serious study must concentrate on more fundamental economic issues.

I am not arguing, nor has any sane Marxist ever argued, that every incident in the history of empire can be explained in directly economic terms. Economic interests are filtered through a political process, policies are implemented by a complex state apparatus, and the whole system generates its own momentum. Much of the history of the British empire, for example, pivots on the need to safeguard the route to India. British policy in, say, the Mediterranean should not be explained in terms of the economic gains to be made in that area alone, but in terms of the maintenance of the empire as a whole. The overall drive to imperial expansion must be explained as one element in the whole process of capitalist development.

Equally, the creation of formal empires, under a single flag and a single political authority, is only a part of the story, and perhaps not the most important part. Formal political independence, with a flag, an airline and a seat at the UN, does not guarantee real equality, though it may be a necessary precondition for real independence and development. Some countries have never been formally annexed, and most Latin American states have been formally independent for a century and a half, but they have been drawn into a system of inequality, exploitation and dominance almost as deeply as have areas subjected to direct colonial rule. Underdeveloped countries still participate on very unequal terms in a world system of trade and investment.

My purpose in this book is to survey the various accounts of the development of the capitalist world economy that have been put forward within the Marxist tradition. I shall not discuss non-Marxist theories, nor will I discuss pre-capitalist empires or Soviet expansionism. This is not to deny the importance of these topics (especially the last); it is simply a matter of drawing a line that will enclose a reasonably coherent subject area.

I have argued that imperialism (in any of several different senses of the word) must be seen in the context of the whole history of capitalism on a world scale. Correspondingly, any theory of imperialism can only make sense when seen as a whole. This dictates the structure of the book. The work of each major writer must be seen as a whole, since it is their 'vision' of the whole system that determines their treatment of particular aspects of it. The main body of this book will, therefore, be devoted to an examination of the work of a succession of major theorists in (approximate) chronological order. The focus, in each case, is on the logical coherence of the economic theory that underlines a particular political position.

II Historical outline

Before discussing the theories, I will give a very brief, selective, and inevitably inadequate outline of the historical record.

The fifteenth century is as good a starting point as any. At this time, Europe was not particularly rich or technically advanced compared with, say, India or China. The Arabic cities dominated what long-distance trade there was, controlling the trading links between Europe and Asia and the main Indian ocean routes. Certain parts of Europe had, however, a crucial lead in weaponry and shipbuilding, together with the ability and incentive to take advantage of it. This was the basis for the explosive expansion of the Spanish and Portuguese seaborne empires at the end of the fifteenth and the beginning of the sixteenth centuries.

During the first part of the 'mercantile period' (1500–1800), Spain and Portugal dominated. The Spanish empire was based on the mining of precious metals in Central America and the Andes; these were funnelled through Panama to Spain, running the gauntlet of piracy in the 'Spanish Main' on the way. The mines, and the agricultural estates that fed them, were worked by forced labour. The Portuguese empire was more a string of trading posts which controlled the traffic in spices and, later, in African slaves, leaving social systems and systems of production relatively untouched. At the same time the expanding mercantile cities of Western Europe came to depend on imports of grain produced by serf labour on the estates of Prussia and Poland, shipped from the Baltic ports.

In the seventeenth century, the emphasis shifted to the production of sugar in slave plantations in the Caribbean and Brazil, while Spain and Portugal progressively lost control of the seas and of key parts of their empires, first to the Dutch and then to the English and French. Labour was scarce in the areas suitable for sugar growing, and the 'Atlantic triangle' was born, with manufactured goods (especially guns) being shipped to Africa, slaves to the Americas, and sugar back to Europe. As the eighteenth century went on, the English, French and Dutch trading posts in Asia were being expanded into territorial possessions, and there were signs of the more profound changes in Europe that developed in the following century.

In the mercantile period, then, European commerce came to dominate much of the world, though the goods exchanged in intercontinental trade were still mainly luxuries (sugar, spices, tobacco, etc.) together with slaves and precious metals. The organisation of society and of production in South and Central America was totally and forcibly transformed, with whole populations being exterminated and replaced, while in Africa and Asia the impact of Europe was in general either superficial or wholly destructive (the slave trade, the looting of India).

How this pattern of trade and production should be described is controversial. Frank and Wallerstein (chapter 7 below) insist that it was a *capitalist* world system, while others such as Banaji, Brenner and Rey (chapters 8 and 11) would describe it as a system of mainly *pre-capitalist* societies, linked by exchange, which contained an evolving capitalist centre in Europe. This disagreement is part of a larger debate over the definition of capitalism.

By the eighteenth century, capitalist relations of production, characterised by the employment of free wage labour in privately owned businesses producing for the market, were well established in England and, to a lesser extent, elsewhere in north-west Europe. Productivity was rising fairly rapidly (though not as rapidly as later), and was already well above levels in the rest of the world. One factor in this general technical advance was the development of science with state support. The seventeenth and eighteenth centuries were the period of the 'scientific revolution', which was very closely linked to military and mercantile needs. Astronomy and the measurement of time were critical to navigation, and these sciences were at the heart of the Newtonian revolution in physics, and thus of a wholly new view of nature.

The decades around 1800 are a critical turning point, separating the mercantile period from the classical epoch of capital development. In the political sphere, the American and, above all, the French revolutions created a new conception of politics. Britain supplanted France as a major colonial power and took effective control of India, which became the lynchpin of the British empire.

Even more significant, the industrial revolution, centred in Britain, marked the start of a new era. It was a protracted affair, but taken as a whole it must surely be regarded as about the most significant breakthrough in human history. Its short-run effects on the mass of the people were probably retrograde, but it was henceforth possible to conceive of the abolition of poverty and drudgery through the mechanisation of production. Marx's vision of the possibilities of socialism is based squarely on the potential created by industrialisation.

The industrial revolution happened when and where it did because of a conjunction of external and internal factors (whose relative importance is a matter of debate). The organisation of production in Britain was by this stage wholly capitalist, based on firms that were relatively large (by previous standards) but numerous, flexible and driven by fierce competition between themselves. These enterprises could recruit workers with the skills they needed from a substantial urban proletariat, and lay them off again equally quickly when market conditions changed or when labour-saving innovations made them redundant. Britain controlled the markets of the world; a vital advantage since the most important raw material, cotton, had to be imported, while a large part of the product was exported to markets abroad. The profits of empire contributed to the ready availability of funds for investment. This was a new kind of society, which the rest of the world regarded with amazement.

In a wider sense, the industrial revolution went on through much of the nineteenth century, a period of sustained capital accumulation and development in the main centres of capitalism. The new industrial methods were introduced into industry after industry, and at the same time they were spreading to other parts of Europe and North America. This was the context in which Marx wrote. By the end of the nineteenth century, Germany and the United States had emerged as major industrial rivals to Britain, and Japan had started on the process of industrialisation.

The case of Japan is important, since it is the only example of complete capitalist development outside Europe and areas of European settlement.

Those who argue that it was subjection to Europe that was the cause of the failure of development elsewhere can point out that Japan was one of the few areas that remained outside European control, while those who argue that the success or failure of capitalist development depends primarily on internal social structures can point out that Japan started from a social structure that had much in common with European feudalism.

The area effectively integrated into the capitalist world economy expanded enormously during the nineteenth century. Most of Latin America achieved formal independence (with some British support), but came under informal British control. Asia, the largest and most populous continent, was opened up for capitalism. The British established effective control of the whole Indian subcontinent, and forced China, at gunpoint, to permit the import of opium. The French got Indo-China and the Dutch already controlled the East Indies. Russia was steadily pushing back its frontiers in Siberia and Central Asia. Parts of Africa were colonised, setting the scene for the scramble for the rest at the end of the century. North America was opened up (gold rushes, cowboys and so on) and so was Australasia.

It was in this period that the world was definitively divided into 'advanced' and 'underdeveloped' areas, and the basic patterns of the present world economy were established. A new pattern of trade emerged, replacing the trade in luxuries that characterised the mercantile period. The advanced capitalist centres exported manufactures in return for imports of food and raw materials. The physical bulk of goods traded expanded colossally, but the means of transport were able to cope, having themselves been revolutionised along with the rest of industry.

The end of the nineteenth century marks another major turning point, the beginning of what Lenin called the 'imperialist stage' of capitalism. Following his lead, many Marxists reserve the term 'imperialism' to describe the twentieth century, using other terms for the expansionism of earlier periods. I will follow the usage of whichever writer is under discussion.

At this time, there was a rapid increase in the size of firms and a very rapid spread of monopoly in the form of cartels, trusts and so on. The twentieth century is the period of 'monopoly capital'. There was also a large increase in the export of capital, augmenting rather than replacing trade in commodities, at first in the form of loans to governments and public utilities, but increasingly as 'direct' investment in productive enterprises. In the early twentieth century investment was mostly in resource-based industries and in related infrastructure. The natural resources of the whole planet were opened up for exploitation by the capitalist firms of the advanced capitalist centres.

At the same time there was a scramble for control of the few remaining areas not already brought under colonial control, especially in Africa. Latin America passed, more gradually, from the British to the American sphere. Once the division of the world was complete, any further territorial expansion had to be at the expense of rival colonial empires. There was a sharp increase in tension between the main powers, especially between Germany (the rising power) and Britain (with the largest empire), which culminated in two world wars.

That the rise of monopoly, the export of capital and the outbreak of inter-imperialist rivalry are connected is generally agreed among Marxists, though the exact nature of the connection is more disputable. This is the subject matter of the 'classical Marxist' theories of imperialism (chapters 4 and 5) worked out at the time by Hilferding, Bukharin and Lenin.

The twentieth century has seen a number of developments. Firstly, the area covered by the world capitalist system has contracted as a result of the subtraction first of Russia, then of China, Cuba, much of south-east Asia and so on. In all cases these areas broke away as a result either of war or of violent internal struggles. The nature of the systems installed in these countries will not be discussed here, but the fact of their existence has had important effects on the world balance of power.

Secondly, international trade has grown more rapidly than total production, and (perhaps more important) international investment by major firms has grown even faster, and made then into 'multi-nationals' operating on a world-wide basis. Markets for liquid money capital have also been internationalised, particularly through the development of 'Euromarkets'. Within its reduced geographical territory, the world capitalist economy is much more tightly integrated than ever before, despite the achievement of formal independence by most underdeveloped countries. The system cannot possibly be understood by looking at particular nation states in isolation.

Thirdly, the capitalist world is very clearly divided into advanced and underdeveloped countries, which differ from each other not only in income levels, but also in almost every other aspect of their economic and social structure. There are, as in all previous periods, a few doubtful cases (semi-developed countries in southern Europe, and special cases like Israel and South Africa), but it is notable how small a fraction of the world's population they contain. In almost all cases there is no difficulty at all in assigning a country to one group or the other. This sharp cleavage is clearly a major structural feature of the world system.

The advanced countries (Europe, North America, Australasia, Japan) went through a bad patch in the two world wars and the depression of the 1930s, but then experienced the 'long boom' of the 1950s and 1960s. Overall, levels of productivity have increased enormously over the century and the capitalist form of organisation has almost completely displaced others. Trade and investment flows within the advanced 'centre' have grown especially rapidly, so that trade with the under-developed 'periphery' is now a relatively small part of the total. The economy of a typical advanced country is dominated by a relatively large industrial sector, with a service sector which is also fairly large and organised on modern capitalist lines. Agriculture only employs a small fraction of the labour force, but uses modern capital intensive techniques. (In some cases, a peasant sector survives with the help of subsidies.) The majority of the population are wage earners, and trades union organisations, if they have not fundamentally altered the nature of capitalism, have at least ensured that the benefits of increased productivity have been shared with the working class. The institutions of 'bourgeois democracy' are well established, with free elections and guarantees of personal freedom. The advanced countries contain the headquarters of the main multi-national companies and are the main centres of technological development.

These countries produce and export a very wide range of manufactured and primary products. Their imports from under-developed areas consist mainly of primary products, produced where natural conditions are most favourable, together with labour intensive products produced by cheap labour.

Turning to the underdeveloped world, there are important differences between the 'three continents' (Latin America, Asia, Africa). In Latin America indigenous societies were almost wholly destroyed centuries ago. White or creole ruling classes with a European culture have been established for an equally long time, and the institutions of the modern state were installed at almost the same time as in Europe. The larger Latin American countries have average income levels which are well above those of Africa and Asia, though equally far below those of Europe. At the same time, they have all the structural features of under-development.

In Asia, major pre-capitalist civilisations were drawn into the capitalist orbit more gradually and at a later date. The larger Asian countries have well-established indigenous ruling classes, a considerable technological capacity, and industrial sectors which are quite large in absolute terms, though small relative to the size of the population. Average income levels, however, are very low, with an enormous mass of peasants and workers reduced to starvation level or below, and massive unemployment. Some smaller Asian countries, on the other hand, are relatively industrialised, and Japan is, of course, in another category altogether.

Africa suffered the destructive effects of the slave trade over several centuries, but actual European penetration into the larger part of the continent did not come until the 'imperialist' stage, much later than in Asia or Latin America. It is, in general, the least developed continent, with tiny industrial sectors and low levels of income.

Despite these differences, one can still talk of a 'typical' under-developed country, characterised by the small proportion of the population employed in modern industry, by permanent large-scale un-employment or underemployment, and by large, low-productivity agricultural and service sectors. Wages and incomes are low (except for a small élite). Agriculture mainly consists of small peasant holdings, except where there are plantations producing for export. These peasant farms are no longer self-sufficient 'subsistence' holdings, but are integrated into the market system. Foreign trade generally accounts for a rather large fraction of total national income, with essential imports of capital goods, intermediate products and raw materials being paid for by exports of primary products or labour intensive manufactures. Export earnings also have to finance outflows of dividends, interest and royalties. Underdeveloped countries generally trade with advanced countries and not with each other. This pattern is clearly quite unlike that of an 'untouched' pre-capitalist economy, and is the result of incorporation into the world capitalist system.

The class structure of underdeveloped countries is also distinctively different both from that of a pre-capitalist society and from that of the advanced countries. The small scale of industry and its domination by foreign firms with labour-saving production methods mean that the industrial working class and local industrial capital, the principal forces in advanced countries, hardly exist. In their absence, the system is dominated by the local representatives and affiliates of multi-national companies, by trading interests and by landlords. The largest popular

classes are the peasantry and the urban 'lumpenproletariat' of unemployed or casually employed workers.

Advanced and underdeveloped countries, then, are complementary
halves of a very unequal world system, which is the product of a process
of development that stretches back centuries. At different stages in its
evolution, and in different areas, it has taken very different forms. A
complete theory of imperialism must account for all of them.

III Historical materialism

The writers surveyed in this book differ from each other on many issues,
but they share a common set of assumptions. All assign a central role to
the evolution of the economic system, and agree that imperialism must
be explained in terms of the development of 'capitalism'. This approach
derives, of course, from Marx, and in this section I will briefly
summarise some of the elements of Marx's method, historical
materialism.

Marx starts from the observation that production is always social;
Robinson Crusoe is a myth. Seen from a technical, physical point of view
(the *forces of production*) or in terms of the actual activity of work (the
labour process), production is the activity of human beings working on
the natural environment to modify it to meet their needs. As a social
process, however, it also involves relations between people, the (*social*)
relations of production, which govern access to the means of production
and the use of the product. These relations are not a matter of deliberate
choice; the organisation of production in, say, Europe today is not the
result of a conscious decision that wage labour in capitalist factories is a
better system than the serfdom of the middle ages or the slave system of
antiquity. It is the product of a long process of historical evolution.

Marx argues that the analysis of society must start from this structure
of social relations, and not from individual choices or motivations:

> In the social production of their existence, men enter into definite,
> necessary relations, which are independent of their will, namely
> relations of production corresponding to a determinate stage of
> development of their material forces of production. The totality of
> these relations of production constitutes the economic structure of
> society, the real foundation on which there arises a legal and
> political superstructure and to which there correspond definite

forms of social consciousness. The mode of production of material life conditions the social, political and intellectual life-process in general. (Marx, 1976, p. 3)*

Marx's assertion that the economic 'foundation' ultimately determines the 'social, political and intellectual life-process in general' is one of the most controversial aspects of his work. It does not seem to me to be useful to discuss it at a general level; the test is whether it can be justified by detailed analysis in particular cases. I propose to treat it throughout as a working hypothesis, adopted for purposes of argument, and to see how far we can get with an analysis which starts from the economic structure.

Marx insisted on the need for abstraction. Society is too complex to be grasped as a totality, an integrated whole, in a single step. Instead, we must isolate the simplest and most fundamental social relations and build up an abstract representation of how they work and how they fit together. The concepts developed in this way can then be used to construct an analysis of the real (or 'concrete') world.

However, a single set of abstract concepts will not serve for the analysis of all societies. Marx praised the 'classical' economists (of the late eighteenth and early nineteenth centuries, notably Smith and Ricardo) for recognising the need for abstraction, but criticised them for applying concepts appropriate to the analysis of the capitalist economies of their time to all periods of history, thus failing to recognise the historical specificity of capitalism. Different stages of development were characterised by particular, different structures, and a separate process of abstraction was necessary for each. A *mode of production*, in the abstract, is a simple, basic structure of social relations that is the starting point for the analysis of a particular stage of history. It is essential to Marx's approach that there are only a limited number of these basic forms.

Each mode of production (except the simplest, the primitive-communal, and the highest, the future communist mode) defines a pair of opposed *classes*, a class of producers and a non-producing class that exploits them. The relation between these two classes is the central, defining feature of the mode of production. At this level of abstraction,

* References are to the bibliography on p. 295. Following the usual convention, the dates given are those of the edition cited, but the date of the original publication is given in the bibliography. Some frequently cited works will be referred to by an abbreviated form of their title; these abbreviations are listed on p. xi. Throughout, any emphasis in quoted extracts is in the original, unless otherwise stated.

classes should not be thought of primarily as groups of people, but as opposing positions within a structure of social relations. In particular, a class cannot be conceived of in isolation, since it only constitutes a class by virtue of its relation to another class; there cannot be employers without employees, slave-owners without slaves, and so on.

Some words of caution are necessary here. Recent 'structuralist' interpretations of Marx seem to me to have lost contact with Marx's materialism. Although Marx places the primary stress on the objective structure of social relations, this does not mean that these structures are ghostly 'essences' manipulating their 'bearers'. They exist only in the relations between real, flesh and blood human beings, and modes of production, in their pure form, exist only in the mind of the analyst. If I say, as I will, that 'capitalism develops the forces of production' (or some similar formula), then this is shorthand for 'a social organisation of the sort described by the concept of the capitalist mode of production induces people to act in such a way as to bring about an increase in output and productivity'.

Marx's original idea was simple and elegant. The various modes of production were successive *stages* in the history of human society. Each had its own structure and was able to 'reproduce' itself, that is to maintain both the forces of production (by replacing used up means of production, etc.) and the relations of production (by perpetuating the subordination of one class to another). The mechanisms of reproduction differ, of course, between different modes. The stability of each mode, however, was only relative; each generated development of the forces of production and, in the process, brought about changes in its own functioning that led in the end to a breakdown of the existing structure and its replacement by the next in the sequence.

> At a certain stage in their development, the material productive
> forces of society come into conflict with the existing relations of
> production. . . . From forms of development of the productive
> forces these relations turn into their fetters. At that point an era of
> social revolution begins. . . . In broad outline, the Asian, ancient,
> feudal and modern bourgeois [capitalist] modes of production may
> be designated as progressive epochs of the socio-economic order.
> (Marx, 1976, pp. 3–4)

Society, according to this account, has evolved from a (rather nebulous) primitive-communal stage, through the ancient and feudal periods, into the capitalist societies of Marx's (and our) time, which will in turn be replaced by communism. The *ancient* mode is defined by the opposition between slaves and free, slave-owning citizens, while the *feudal* mode, in its classic form, involves production for local use by a class of unfree peasants or serfs who control their own subsistence plots, but are compelled, by extra-economic coercion, to support a class of feudal landlords.

The most frequently studied mode of production, and the only one that Marx analysed in detail, is the *capitalist* mode. This is characterised by generalised commodity production, production for the market by many distinct and unco-ordinated units of production, together with a polarisation of wealth, so that a class of owners of the means of production confronts a class of free but propertyless workers. Ownership of the means of production excludes non-owners (the workers) from production, except on terms acceptable to the owners. Workers have to sell their labour power (their capacity to work) to the capitalists in return for wages with which they buy the goods they need to live. Marx's analysis of capitalism will be discussed in more detail in chapter 2.

Marx recognised that non-European history could not be fitted into this 'Eurocentric' succession of stages, and he introduced a distinct mode, the 'Asian' or 'Asiatic' mode (discussed further in chapter 2) to deal with this problem. The point of the Asiatic mode is that it does not develop in a way that leads on to further stages, but tends to persist unless disrupted from outside. He also admitted that the succession of stages could be broken by outside influences, especially by conquest:

> In all conquests there are three possibilities. The conquering nation subjects the conquered nation to its own mode of production . . .; or it allows the old mode to remain and is content with tribute . . .; or interaction takes place, which gives rise to a new system, a synthesis. . . . In all cases the mode of production – whether that of the conqueror or of the conquered nation or the one resulting from the fusion of the two – is the determinant of the new distribution that occurs. (Marx, 1976, p. 27)

What he insists on is the analytical primacy of the mode of production, not the inevitability of a certain succession of stages.

A real society cannot, in any case, be reduced to a single abstract mode of production. Marx argued that: 'In every social formation there is a specific kind of production that predominates over all the others, and whose relations therefore determine their rank and influence. It is a general illuminant tingeing all other colours and modifying their specific features' (1976, p. 39). Relations characteristic of several modes of production may be combined in a 'social formation' with one of them predominating. This interpretation has been revived recently (see chapter 8). Among other advantages, it permits the inclusion of the *petty-commodity* mode of production, a mode which has never predominated, and which therefore does not appear in a list of stages. It is characterised by production for the market by independent producers who own their own means of production.

Once we regard modes of production as basic forms of organisation which can be combined and elaborated upon in many ways in different historical circumstances, the range of possibilities becomes almost infinite. A limited number of modes can be analysed carefully in (conceptual) isolation, and then the complications can be built in to analyse a rich variety of real situations. This is the scientific method; the discovery of simple ideas which can elucidate complex problems.

What Marx left, in short, was not a complete interpretation of history, but a fragmentary outline of European history, an analysis of the capitalist mode of production, and some tantalisingly brief indications as to how his analysis could be extended. It would be foolish to treat Marx's writings as holy writ. In the study of imperialism, a central problem is the analysis of interactions between initially very different societies, characterised by different dominant modes of production. Marx's few writings on India and Ireland (discussed in chapter 2 below) are not particularly helpful. The Marxist method, on the other hand, has proved very fruitful, as I shall try to show.

IV The state

In any analysis of imperialism, the actions of (capitalist) *states* must play an important role. It is almost an axiom of Marxist theory that the state acts to defend the interests of the ruling class (i.e. the dominant exploiting class). There are many statements to this effect in Marx's writing, although he presented very little detailed analysis to support it. The state was one of the (many) topics that he planned to work on and write about at length but which he never managed to reach.

It is fairly easy to see why the state should act to preserve the broad outlines of the existing social system or, in other words, the dominant mode of production. The ruling class is normally well organised to defend its interests, and the higher level personnel of the state apparatuses (politicians, bureaucrats, military officers, etc.) have a clear interest in preserving the existing state organisation, which could hardly hope to survive a wholesale change in the social order. In any case, a failure to meet the essential needs of the dominant mode could only result in chaos and economic regression unless it were coupled with the propagation of a positive alternative. Support for the existing order does not necessarily imply unthinking conservatism. On the contrary, it requires constant adaptation to changing circumstances, and may mean acting against the interests of particular sections of the ruling class. It does not necessarily follow either, that the state will succeed in this task; circumstances may overwhelm it, and the historic role of stupidity and error should not be underrated.

Within this framework, there are still many alternative policies, many degrees of freedom. An assertion here that the state acts to promote the interests of the 'ruling class' is not self-evident, and may not even be meaningful. There are always, in practice, divisions of interest within the capitalist class, so that the interests of that class as a whole are not clearly defined. Some Marxists appear to believe in a special providence that guides the hand of statesmen, so that their actions inevitably coincide with the 'objective requirements of expanded reproduction', or some-thing of the sort. This is surely not an adequate analysis; policies are the outcome of real political practice, of class conflict, and of the conflict of sectional interests both within classes and cutting across class boundaries, all within a given political and ideological structure. The state, it is often said, has a certain 'relative autonomy'. A certain amount of work has been done on these lines, but the construction of general theories is at a very early stage.

This leaves something of a gap in the theory of imperialism. In most of the theories discussed in this book, the focus is on an economic analysis which shows that certain state policies serve the interests of (major sections of) the capitalist class, and this is taken to explain the policies concerned. I shall concentrate on the economics of imperialism, following the general trend of the literature. The economic analysis is, at the least, an important part of the story, even if it is not the whole of it.

V Theories of capitalism as a world system

Marxist theories of the development of capitalism on a world scale tend to fall into two groups. There are those that concentrate on the progressive role of capitalism in developing the forces of production, and conversely those that present capitalism as a system of exploitation of one area by another, so that development in a few places is at the expense of the 'development of underdevelopment' in most of the world. Capitalism, according to the first view, creates the material preconditions for a better (socialist) society, as well as the class forces that will bring it about, while on the second view it is precisely the failure of capitalism to generate economic development that makes revolution necessary. The historical record, however, suggests that there is an element of truth to both of these opposed views; capitalism has generated massive technological and economic advances and also enormous geographical disparities in economic development.

The first of these views is broadly that held by the 'classical' Marxists, from Marx himself to Lenin and his contemporaries. It has been strongly revived in recent years. According to this account, the development of each country is determined primarily by its internal structure, and specifically by the nature of the dominant mode of production. Capitalism, a system in which free wage workers are employed by competing firms, tends to generate economic development, while other modes do not. External forces have their effect primarily by altering the organisation of production.

Competition between capitals is at the heart of a classical Marxist analysis of capitalism. The largest, most efficient firms with the newest capital equipment are the most profitable, and can increase their lead, while weaker firms fall behind and the weakest are eliminated by bankruptcy or takeover. The threat of failure forces all firms to maximise profits, to plough profit back into expansion, and to seek out new methods of production, new markets, new sources of supply, and so on. In pre-capitalist modes of production, by contrast, the exploiting class must, above all, maintain the basis of the extra-economic coercion which they exercise over the producers. The result is relatively static systems dominated by custom, with the (potentially investable) surplus redirected into non-productive channels.

The expansion of capitalism constantly expands the demand for natural resources (minerals, land, etc.) and this is one motive behind the geographical expansion of capitalism. Even with a static demand, development of means of transport together with the search for cheaper sources of goods will tend to draw new areas into the capitalist orbit. Capital accumulation by itself tends to increase the demand for labour power as well, but the adoption of labour-saving methods tends to offset this. The search for cheap labour is another motive for geographical expansion.

In the classical Marxist account, grossly oversimplified, capitalism emerges first in a few centres and generates capital accumulation and development there, opening up a lead over the rest of the world without necessarily taking anything from it (though capital will always take anything it can get). Capitalism spreads, starting the same process in other areas. Different parts of the world can be regarded, very crudely, as runners in the same race, in which some started before others. Any advantage gained by one at the expense of others is incidental.

The alternative view has been developed since the Second World War, notably by Frank and Wallerstein, as a response to the failure of capitalist development in many parts of the world. In this view, the unit of analysis must be a *world system*, in which different geographical areas or nation states are merely component parts. Capitalism is not characterised by a specific relation between classes, but rather by production for profit within a world system of exchange and by the exploitation of some areas by others. The 'metropolis' or 'core' exploits the 'satellites' or 'periphery' by direct extraction of profit or tribute, by 'unequal exchange' (see below) or through monopolistic control over trade. The state machines of the centre play a key role in this. In the periphery, ruling classes emerge which owe their position to their function as inter-mediaries in the system of exploitation, so that they have an interest in preserving it and in preserving the patterns of production that underlie it. Underdevelopment is not a state of original backwardness, but is the result of the imposition of a particular pattern of specialisation and exploitation in the periphery.

Within this world system, different forms of 'labour control' may be used, such as forced labour, wage labour, slavery, and so on. The class structure of different 'nations' and the particular forms of exploitation in production are merely results of the place of the areas concerned in the world system, rather than being the key determining factors (as they are in a classical Marxist analysis).

In this approach, oversimplified, capital accumulation is seen not as a precondition for genuine, qualitative advances in the level and methods of production, but rather as a redivision of a fixed magnitude, a transfer of resources from the exploited periphery to the centre. Development in some areas and the 'development of underdevelopment' in others are opposite sides of the same coin.

These two views involve quite different readings of history. In the classical Marxist view, capitalism started off in a few places and has since spread out geographically in a process of *internationalisation* of capital, and has also evolved through a succession of *stages*, with key turning points in the industrial revolution and at the date when large-scale export of capital (not goods) started (i.e. around 1900). According to Frank and Wallerstein, by contrast, capitalism as a world system dates from the sixteenth century, and the system has persisted essentially unchanged ever since. The classical Marxists see capitalism in dynamic terms, while their opponents see it as a basically static system of exploitation.

The contradictions between these two views should not be over-stressed, though they are very real. The world economy is a complex whole in which relations of production and exploitation exist both within and between 'nations'. It may not matter very much whether we say that underdevelopment is the product of external influences (which also determine a certain class structure and organisation of production), or alternatively that underdevelopment is caused by a certain class structure and organisation of production (which may be in whole or part the result of external influences). When we get to a more detailed level of analysis there are many theories that cut across this simple classification. Never-theless, I think it is a helpful preliminary way of ordering the material.

The definition of the term 'underdevelopment' differs according to the approach adopted. In the classical view, underdevelopment is synonymous with backwardness, with an earlier stage of development. Frank and his followers, on the other hand, would argue that an isolated country could not be called underdeveloped, and that underdevelopment is defined by incorporation into a world system in a subordinate position. Whichever definition is adopted, there is little doubt as to which category to put any particular country in (though there have been half-hearted attempts to label Canada as underdeveloped), so this is not likely to lead to confusion. I shall use the term descriptively; an underdeveloped country is one that shows the general structural features of under-development described in section II above.

Marx (chapter 2), in his main theoretical work, concentrated on a closed and wholly capitalist economy. In a rather less formal way, he analysed the origins and expansion of capitalism within a single nation state. His importance to the theory of imperialism is primarily that he established a basic framework of analysis that other writers have built on. In a series of articles on India, however, Marx made it clear that he regarded British rule, however brutal, as ultimately progressive in that it laid the foundations for subsequent capitalist development.

Rosa Luxemburg (chapter 3) developed Marx's picture of the expansion of capitalism into the pre-capitalist societies that surround it. She advanced two explanations for this expansion. The first is that capitalist economies suffer a chronic problem of 'realisation', that is of selling the products produced for sale, and must therefore seek markets abroad. This idea recurs in a variety of forms in the history of imperialism, and I shall refer to it as 'underconsumptionism' (though Luxemburg's variant of it does not exactly fit the term). I shall argue that underconsumptionism is mistaken. However, Luxemburg also argued that competitive pressures lead to expansionism, in search of raw materials and cheap labour, and here I think she is right. In either case pre-capitalist 'natural' (non-market) economies cannot be penetrated by simple market competition, there being no markets to compete in, and they must therefore be broken open by force.

Rey (chapter 8) has developed this idea recently, giving a more sophisticated account of the workings of the pre-capitalist modes involved and their interaction ('articulation') with capitalism. He argues that (some kinds of) commodity exchange can take place without fundamental alteration in the mode of production, so that incorporation into a world market is not necessarily a key turning point, but that the installation of capitalist production requires forcible penetration and the imposition of a 'colonial' mode of production. Once capitalist relations of production have 'taken root', they can reproduce themselves and expand by primarily economic means, under the aegis of a local state. Even in this 'neo-colonial' stage, however, the persistence of a pre-capitalist mode articulated with capitalism hampers development, and this accounts for slow growth in underdeveloped areas.

Hilferding, Bukharin and Lenin (chapters 4 and 5), the main authors of what I will call the 'classical Marxist theory of imperialism' (since Marx did not discuss 'imperialism' as such), wrote immediately before and during the First World War. In economic life, the main change since Marx's time had been the development of monopoly. This fulfilled Marx's prediction that the competitive process, with its constant elimination of smaller and weaker firms, would generate an inevitable tendency to monopoly. It remained, however, to analyse the results of this development. At the same time, there was a scramble for colonies and intense antagonisms emerged between the main capitalist powers. All three writers stressed the formation of monopolies on a national basis, and the intensification of competition on a world scale between national groupings of capital. At the same time, they predicted an acceleration of capitalist development in backward areas of the world.

Hilferding's main contribution (chapter 4) was the concept of *finance capital*, the product of the fusion of industrial and financial capital into huge interlocking groups which still competed with each other, but not by price cutting. Instead they enlisted state support in their efforts to gain control of whole industries by financial and political means. Most of the elements of a theory of inter-imperialist rivalry were worked out by Hilferding, but his main focus was on the internal development of a single (advanced) capitalist economy.

Bukharin (chapter 5) transformed Hilferding's analysis by setting it in the context of a world economy in which two tendencies were at work. The tendency to monopoly and the formation of groups of finance capital is one, and the other is an acceleration of the geographical spread of capitalism and its integration into a single world capitalist economy. Blocs of finance capital form on a national basis, because of their links with national states. Competition thus becomes competition between 'state capitalist trusts', with annexation and war as means employed in the competitive struggle. One element in Bukharin's theory should be noted; because of the tendency of the rate of profit to fall (Marx's theory, discussed in chapter 2), the profit rate, he argued, tends to be lower in advanced centres than in backward areas, promoting the outflow of capital and the development of underdeveloped areas. This is an argument that recurs in the theory of imperialism, and that is, I shall argue, mistaken. It does not seem essential to Bukharin's theory as a whole.

Lenin's pamphlet on imperialism (also discussed in chapter 5) follows Bukharin in most respects while avoiding the main issues of theory. Lenin's main contribution was to insist that 'imperialism' should be regarded as a *stage* of capitalist development, the monopoly stage, rather than being a policy of capitalist states or an aspect of the relations between capitalist states. This terminology causes some confusion, since other writers (following everyday English usage) use the term to refer specifically to international relations of dominance and exploitation. Another aspect of Lenin's account which has caused confusion is his rather obscure treatment of the reasons for capital export, which could be interpreted in terms of the falling rate of profit or of underconsumptionist theories. Altogether, Lenin's pamphlet has been treated with a reverence that it does not deserve.

The work of Baran (chapter 6) represents a turning point in the theory of capitalist development on a world scale. The main Marxist writers, from Marx to Lenin, had expected full capitalist development to be achieved, in due course, throughout the underdeveloped world. By the 1950s it was clear that this had not (yet) happened. Baran was the first to argue that the destiny of the underdeveloped countries was distinctively different from that of the areas that had experienced capitalist development at an earlier date.

His main arguments related to the effect of monopoly which, he argued, leads to restriction of output and of investment, and hence to low growth (in all parts of the world). In advanced countries output is high, and high monopoly profits depress workers' consumption, so that there is a chronic shortage of demand, which can be (partially) overcome by waste and especially by military spending. In underdeveloped countries, the 'surplus' is partly absorbed by the luxury spending of the ruling class, but much of it is transferred to the advanced countries (as profits), where it contributes to the problem of absorbing the rising surplus. Monopoly thus transforms capitalism from a force for development into a cause of stagnation, in advanced and underdeveloped countries alike. In underdeveloped countries, however, there was no competitive stage, so that they are 'frozen' at a low level of development of production.

Frank (chapter 7) is the central figure in recent debates. He has many followers, many of his arguments have been accepted implicitly even by his opponents, and important developments in theory have emerged from criticisms of his work by Laclau and others. I shall argue that his theories have crucial weaknesses, but that he has performed an enormous service to Marxism by forcing Marxists to confront the issue of underdevelopment, the most important single issue of our time. Frank's conception of capitalism as a world-wide system of monopolistic exchange and exploitation has already been described. The main criticism of this approach is that it ignores the role of relations of production in determining both the dynamics and the class structure of the system.

The 'dependency theorists' are a group of (mainly) Latin American writers whose position is similar to Frank's. They have concentrated on the economic aspects of the problem, arguing that growth in underdeveloped countries has been limited by balance of payments problems and narrow home markets which derive from their position in the world economy. Their work is valuable but limited, since they do not offer an explanation of the pattern of trade which is the basis of their arguments. They are discussed, along with Frank and Wallerstein, in chapter 7.

Emmanuel (chapter 9) stands somewhat outside the main lines of development of Marxist theories of imperialism; his theory of 'unequal exchange' has started a new line of its own. He, too, sees capitalism as a world system of exploitation through exchange, but he provides a mechanism whereby surplus can be transferred through trade in *competitive* markets, not by monopolistic exchange. An essential element in Marx's theory of a closed capitalist economy is the establishment of a single general rate of profit and a corresponding set of 'prices of production'. Marxist theories of the world economy lacked any corresponding linkage between the analysis of production and of exchange, until Emmanuel provided a theory of the determination of prices of production in a world economy. The main assumption is that capital is mobile internationally, while labour is not. The main criticism of his analysis is that certain key variables (the pattern of specialisation, productivity, wages) remain inadequately explained. Emmanuel has made a useful contribution to a theory of the world economy, but he claims too much for it.

Amin (chapter 10) has incorporated the formal analysis of international exchange into an account of accumulation on a world scale. He argues that the impact of already developed capitalism on less developed or pre-capitalist areas imposes a pattern of specialisation that limits future development. His argument has much in common with that of Baran, the 'dependency theorists' and Emmanuel, but he meets many of the objections that I have raised against their work by an explicit treatment of 'unequal specialisation'. Important weaknesses, however, remain. The determinants of the development of productivity in different areas remain unclear, and his 'underconsumptionist' treatment of demand seems to me to be misconceived.

There have also been a number of debates on more specific issues, generally revolving around the differences between the Frank-Wallerstein position and the newly revived classical Marxist approach. One major area of debate surrounds the concept of a mode of production and its application to contemporary underdeveloped countries (chapter 11). The central point at issue here is whether the internal structure of underdeveloped countries can be conceptualised in terms of the persistence of pre-capitalist relations of production, and, if so, whether this is cause or consequence of their backwardness. A second area of debate concerns the trends in the relative standing of different capitalist states (chapter 12). In the post-war period, Marxists tended to assume that the United States would maintain or increase its dominance as the principal imperialist power, and that underdeveloped countries would inevitably become relatively, if not absolutely, poorer and more thoroughly subordinated as long as they remain part of the world capitalist system. Capitalism was seen as a stable, self-reinforcing global system of inequality. This view has now been challenged by a revival of the Lenin-Bukharin prediction of rivalry between relatively equal imperialist centres, together with capitalist development in the underdeveloped world.

Taken together, the writings surveyed in this book seem to me to provide most of the makings of a coherent theory of the evolution of capitalism on a world scale, though such a theory has yet to be worked out in detail. What follows is my guess at the form it might take. It is only a tentative outline; to go further would go beyond the scope of this work.

The 'mercantile' period was characterised by very loose integration of the world economy, so that developments in different parts of the world were determined primarily by the dominant mode of production in each area. Transport costs were high, long-distance trade was mainly in luxuries and both capital and skills were relatively immobile. Europe advanced because Europe was becoming capitalist. Elsewhere, European military power had its effect mainly by transforming the mode of production, either installing new pre-capitalist modes (as in Latin America) or clearing the ground for future capitalist development (as in North America).

The nineteenth century was a period of transition. The emerging world economy was still rather loosely integrated, and the emergence of new centres was still possible where internal conditions were ripe and resolute state support was forthcoming. At the same time, the development of capitalism in Europe and North America was breaking up mercantile monopolies, bringing down transport costs, and inaugurating a new stage of development.

As the world economy became more closely integrated, the more developed industrial centres had a crucial advantage, since productivity levels were rising while wages remained relatively low. As a result, they had a crushing cost advantage in all the main lines of industrial production, and relatively backward areas were confined to natural resource linked activities. The advantages of the more developed areas could not be readily transferred, since skills were mainly in the hands of the workers, and capital tended to flow towards concentrations of skills. The need for a network of specialised services and suppliers had a similar effect. These 'external economies' were especially important in the epoch of competitive capitalism, but remain important up to the present.

Over this long period, development in some areas did tend to produce underdevelopment elsewhere, though it is not clear that the 'development of underdevelopment' in the periphery made much contribution to development at the centre.

Monopoly capital, however, tends to 'internalise' these external economies by taking over external suppliers and by codifying and routinising skills. Modern multi-national firms are able to transfer technology to new locations with relatively low additional costs. At the same time, wage levels in advanced countries have been rising. The cost advantages of established industrial centres have thus been eroded on both counts. There is now a clear tendency for production to be shifted to low-wage areas in underdeveloped countries, although it will take a very long time for this tendency to work its way through the whole range of industries.

It does not follow that the whole of the Third World can look forward to complete capitalist industrialisation, since one would expect the emergence of new poles of development and the elimination of weaker competitors. Equally, the mass of the population in the newly developing areas may not gain very much for a long time. Capital intensive methods of production hold down the demand for labour and the resulting unemployment holds down wages. The prospect is one of uneven development as between different areas, accompanied by working-class poverty – very much what Marx predicted over a century ago.

Part I

Classical Marxist theories of capitalist expansion

2 · Marx

Marx did not use the term imperialism, nor is there anything in his work that corresponds at all exactly to the concepts of imperialism advanced by later writers in the Marxist tradition. He did, of course, have a theory of capitalism, and of its development, and we can find extensive, if rather scattered, coverage in his work of the impact of European capitalism on non-European pre-capitalist societies. Rather than foreseeing the creation of a world capitalist economy necessarily dominated by a few centres, as many subsequent writers have done, Marx saw the relative backwardness of the non-European world and its subjection to European masters as essentially *transitory* phenomena (though perhaps very long-lasting) in the process of the formation of a wholly capitalist world economy.

Later writers in the Marxist tradition have, in general, not based their analysis of imperialism on Marx's writings on colonies. They have drawn both on the central core of Marx's theory, and on particular aspects of it, at first sight unconnected with imperialism. (Rey, for example, starts with Marx's discussion of rent, Emmanuel with the theory of prices of production.)

I will start this chapter by setting out, very briefly, Marx's theory of a wholly capitalist system. Marx argued that capitalism could, in principle, exist on its own and develop without *needing* to expand into surrounding pre-capitalist societies. Capitalism, however, necessarily originated within a wider pre-capitalist world, so the next step will be to look at Marx's theory of the origins of capitalism, and to see why capitalism will, in fact, expand at the expense of other modes of production. Finally, I will survey Marx's writings on colonies, and in particular the famous articles on India. The first two sections, then, deal with the capitalist mode of production in the abstract; the rest of the chapter with the insertion of that mode into social formations that are not wholly capitalist.

A preliminary comment on terminology: Marx did not have a generic

27

term to describe the rule of a more advanced nation state over a more backward area. I have used the term *colonialism*, which has been widely adopted subsequently. When Marx himself uses this term he usually refers to the settlement of uninhabited areas or areas from which the indigenous inhabitants have been driven out (such as Australia and America).

I The capitalist mode of production

The heart of Marx's life work is the analysis of a pure capitalist mode of production, contained in *Capital*, volumes I–III (*Capital* I, Marx, 1961; *Capital* II, Marx, 1957; *Capital* III, Marx, 1962, cited below by title and volume number). The centrepiece is a theory of a closed, homogeneous, capitalist economy. Labour power has a single price, governed by the value of labour power, and, when prices of production are introduced (in the third volume) there is a single general rate of profit which accrues to all capitals. This is an abstraction, of course, and throughout the three volumes Marx offers illustrations which link the abstract theory to a far more complex reality. Within the theory, though, there is no space for any difference in economic conditions between different countries. This conception of the capitalist mode of production is diametrically opposed to that of Frank and Wallerstein for whom the metropolis-satellite or core-periphery relation (respectively) is a defining feature of capitalism.

In this section, I will outline the basic theory very briefly with the focus on introducing key concepts which are used by later writers. This is not a text on Marxist economic theory in general: a substantial literature exists on this subject for those who wish to read more about it (see, for example, Howard and King, 1975).

Capitalism is a particular form of *commodity production*. By 'commodity production', Marx means the production of goods for sale on the market. This form of economy exists where there are many independent producers who produce goods which they do not intend to use themselves, but which they exchange for those they do want. Marx distinguishes between the *use value* of a commodity, that is the use to which it can be put, and its *exchange value*, what can be got in exchange for it. The production of use values is absolutely essential to the survival (*reproduction*) of any society, but in a commodity-producing society this is obscured by the fact that the producer is interested only in the exchange value of his product.

Marx argues that exchange values are explained and determined by (labour) *values*, where the value of a commodity is defined as the *socially necessary labour time* (measured in hours) which is *directly or indirectly required to reproduce it*. The labour theory of value has been the subject of much debate (see Morishima, 1973, 1974, 1976; Steedman, 1975, 1977; Himmelweit and Mohun, 1978; Wright, 1979). The difficulty in using labour values is that goods do not, in fact, exchange at their values in a developed capitalist economy; they exchange at market prices which fluctuate around prices of production (see below). In cases of joint production and in any but the simplest cases involving fixed capital, values are hard to define satisfactorily, and are liable to come out negative, or to fail to add up correctly (Steedman, 1975, 1976, 1977).

In fact, very few theories of imperialism depend heavily on labour values, so we can bypass this debate. For our purposes we can regard values as a convenient tool of analysis introduced by Marx and used by him in the main exposition of his theory, but his main propositions can be restated in terms of other theories of price. In my view, the heart of Marx's theory is his definition of the *social relations* which define capitalism, and we can describe these with or without using the labour theory of value. In this chapter I will use labour values, since that was the method used by Marx.

Marx then moves on to define capitalist production, a special case of commodity production. He asks: what is the source of the *surplus value* (roughly, profit) which accrues to a capitalist?

He finds the source of this in the specific *social relation* which links a wage worker with a capitalist employer. The worker, he says, sells his *labour power*, his capacity to work, rather than his *labour*. The distinction between labour power and labour is crucial to the labour theory of value (the labour value of labour would be a nonsense), but it also expresses a central feature of capitalism; the actual work process, the conversion of labour power (the capacity to work) into actual work itself, is carried out under the authority of the new owner of labour power, its buyer, the capitalist. The capitalist also buys *means of production* (materials, equipment, etc.).

The value created by labour is the number of hours worked in (say) a day (given average conditions of production), but the wage paid by the capitalist corresponds to the *value of labour power*, that is, the labour required to reproduce a day's labour power, which is, in turn, the value of the commodities needed for the subsistence of the worker and his family (since the worker must be reproduced) for a day. If the value created in a day exceeds the value of a day's labour power then there is *surplus value* which the capitalist can pocket when he sells the product.

In terms of the relationship between the workers as a whole and capital as a whole this amounts to saying that profit (or surplus value) exists when the total product exceeds the commodities received by the workers plus the commodities required to replace the means of production used up. Surplus value, in other words, corresponds to a *surplus product*. For an individual capitalist, profit (or surplus value) depends on prices (or values), since the commodities individual workers get will not be the same as those they produce, and where the goods consumed are not produced within the same unit of production we cannot subtract the one from the other unless they can be reduced to a common unit. For an open economy the same problem exists when workers produce export goods and consume, in part, imported goods.

Marx's theory of the wage (or value of labour power) is something of a difficulty. He states that the commodities needed by workers are not determined by purely physiological needs, though these set a minimum, but also contain a 'historical and moral' element. In other parts of his work, notably the pamphlet *Wage, Price and Profit*, there are elements of a theory of the determination of wages by bargaining power. What is clear is that if wages rise so far as to reduce profits below some minimum level, then this will provoke a cessation of production and a crisis. Within capitalism, this sets an upper limit to wages which ensures the existence of profit.

Capital, in this framework, is 'value in process', that is, it is money or commodities being used to extract surplus value from workers in the way we have described. An individual capitalist's wealth will first be in the form of money, then of means of production and labour power, then of the commodities produced, and finally in the form of money, from the sale of the commodities, ready to start the cycle again. (In fact all these stages will overlap.) Capital is defined by the cycle as a whole. In measuring the capitalist's capital (for example, 'a capital of £1 million') we count the value of money, work in progress, means of production and final commodities. This differs from the definition of capital used in bourgeois economics in two ways: the latter is narrower, in only including means of production, but wider in including means of production regardless of the social context. For Marx *wealth is only capital if it is used by capitalists to produce surplus value in a capitalist system*. This is the definition I will use throughout. To put it another way, bourgeois economics views capital as a technical requirement of production, Marx views it as a social relation which defines a specific *mode of production*.

We should pause here to consider the status of the two 'spheres' of *production* and *circulation (exchange)*. Both are integral parts of the *circuit of capital*, the cycle described above. Capitalist production as a whole consists of many different capitals, within each of which the capitalist exercises direct authority, but which are linked together by market exchange; capitalist production is anarchic and is governed by the blind working of economic laws independent of the will of any individual. The circuits of these different capitals intertwine with each other: each must buy means of production from others, and workers must buy means of subsistence from one capital with wages that they are paid by another. Capitalist production as a whole, therefore, includes the many separate production processes and the processes of exchange that link them. Both are integral, necessary parts of production as a social process. Some Marxists have tried to argue that production (narrowly defined) is in some sense the primary element and circulation secondary. In view of the discussion above, this view will not stand up.

The question becomes more difficult when part of production is carried out under capitalist relations of production and part under pre-capitalist relations, with the two linked together by exchange. An example is the relation between the slave plantations producing cotton in America and the cotton textile industry in Lancashire in the industrial revolution for which they supplied the raw material. Some writers would want to describe this as wholly capitalist production (with an unorthodox form of labour discipline), others as a relationship between two different modes of production. I will discuss this issue later (chapters 7, 8, 11), but will comment now that the question seems, at least in part, semantic. The important point is that there is a *social process of production* which encompasses both capitalist and pre-capitalist *relations of production*. This possibility is an important characteristic of systems of commodity production. This, however, is to jump ahead; my concern at the moment is with a wholly capitalist system.

The essential character of a capitalist system comes out most clearly in Marx's discussion of the *reproduction* of the system. He discusses this mainly in the context of *simple reproduction*, i.e. a state of affairs in which the system is reconstituted the same as before after each cycle of production. This device is only for analytical simplicity. The really important case is *reproduction on an extended scale* (also called expanded reproduction, reproduction on a progressively increasing scale, and so on), where part of profit is *accumulated* as new capital, so that the system grows. Note also that the idea of a simple 'period of production' starting with means of production, wage goods for workers' consumption, etc., and ending when these have been used up and replaced by newly produced goods, is another analytical fiction which simplifies the story without affecting the principles involved.

Consider first the relation between workers and capital. At the start of a period of production workers have no wealth, 'nothing to sell but their labour power', and they therefore have no option but to look for a job. They cannot produce on their own account, since they cannot acquire means of production. The capitalist pays them a wage, enough to cover their (socially determined) needs. At the end of the period of production the workers have spent their wages, and are thus back where they started, forced once again to seek a job. Throughout, Marx assumes that there will be a *reserve army of labour*, a pool of unemployed workers competing for jobs and keeping wages down. If expansion of the system absorbs all these unemployed workers so that the threat of unemployment no longer holds down wages and maintains labour discipline, then a crisis will ensue which will reduce production, promote labour-saving investment and reconstitute the reserve army.

The capitalist, on the other hand, starts with purchasing power (*money capital*) sufficient to pay wages (*variable capital*) and buy means of production (*constant capital*). At the end of the process he gets enough revenue to replace his outlay, plus a surplus (profit), which can be used entirely for his own consumption (simple reproduction) or partly for new investment (expanded reproduction).

Starting, then, from a situation in which owners of commodities (capitalists) confront propertyless workers, the cycle of production ends with the reproduction of the same confrontation between the same two classes, ready for the cycle to start again. Marx stresses that this does not explain the origins of capitalism: we shall come to his explanation of that later.

The other defining feature of capitalism is that it is a species of commodity production, so production is carried out by many separate, competing capitals with no central co-ordinating plan. This poses another problem for the reproduction of the system. It is not enough that capitalists should get surplus value, in terms of exchange values. The right mix of use values: means of production, necessities of consumption and so on, must also be produced.

Marx analyses this problem in the final chapters of volume II of

Capital, in terms of the exchange between two *departments* of social production: *department 1*, the industries that produce means of production; and *department 2*, producing consumer goods. He shows, using numerical examples, or *schemas of reproduction*, that there is a certain relation between the scale of these departments which is consistent with simple reproduction, and another relation, depending on the rate of accumulation, which will be consistent with extended reproduction. It is easy to see how this analysis could be pursued in more detail to see the necessary proportions between different branches of production within each department.

One aspect of Marx's analysis of reproduction which has caused endless debate and which is very relevant to the theory of imperialism is the question of markets. How can capitalists hope to sell all the goods that they produce? There is an argument used by many Marxist theorists, which I shall label *underconsumptionism* (see Bleaney, 1976, for fuller discussion). In its simplest form it goes like this: if the workers cannot afford to buy the whole product, then how can the capitalists sell it? In the schema of simple reproduction, Marx answers that the capitalists consume the surplus product themselves. This entails selling to each other, since each specialises in the production of a particular product, but wishes to consume others. However, the idea that capitalists consume their profits is only an analytical fiction necessary to preserve the idea of simple reproduction. In fact the capitalists save and accumulate, and are forced to do so by competition (see below). This does not, however, fundamentally alter things. The capitalists still exchange the surplus product among themselves; they simply buy means of production instead of means of consumption, and the proportions between departments 1 and 2 must be correspondingly different. The argument is slightly complicated by the assumption that wages are advanced to workers; some of the new investment takes the form of wage payments to additional workers, who then spend the money on consumer goods. The money used to carry out these transactions is not a problem either, since it passes from hand to hand without being used up. At the end of each cycle it has returned to its starting point, ready to circulate again.

The core idea of underconsumptionism is that consumer demand is somehow more fundamental than demand for means of production, that the latter only exists to provide for the former. It is often argued (Sweezy, 1942, is a classic case) that if consumption is (say) static, then there will be no incentive to invest. This is simply wrong, since investment can be directed to the investment goods (means of production) industries as well as to the consumer goods industries. In a socialist system, investment would be directed to the satisfaction of human needs, but in a capitalist system all that matters is that the investment be profitable. Consumer demand has no special status in a capitalist framework; the bulk of it is from workers, who will only be employed if they contribute to profits, so that both consumption and investment derive primarily from spending by capitalists which is directed to making profits.

This does raise the possibility that investment will be insufficient if profit prospects are poor. In this case capitalists will cut back on investment and employment, thereby reducing demand and setting off a chain reaction. On the other hand, when high profits are expected, the chain reaction works the other way round. Marx expected capitalism to evolve through a series of booms (which ensure the development of the forces of production) and slumps, or 'periodic crises'. Marx's analysis of these issues is scattered, and it is not easy to refute the suggestion that he was an underconsumptionist since some isolated phrases taken out of context can be interpreted in this way. What is important is that the logic of his analysis is not consistent with underconsumptionism. The schemas of expanded reproduction show that it is possible in principle for demand to expand in line with supply, although it is equally possible for the system to suffer crises as it does, repeatedly, in practice. The reason for these crises must be sought in the determinants of profitability, and not in any inherent problem of demand.

I will discuss some particular variants of underconsumptionism as they arise, notably those of Luxemburg, Baran and Amin; underconsumptionist arguments are important in the theory of imperialism because they can explain a search for external markets to make up for the deficiency of demand at home.

II Competition and the dynamics of capitalism

We have seen that, in Marx's theory, surplus value is generated by the gap between the value produced by a worker, which is simply the length of the working day, and the value of labour power. Marx calls the part of the working day which is equivalent to the value of the commodities the worker can buy with his wage, *necessary labour*, and the rest is *surplus labour*. Surplus value can be increased in two ways: by increasing the working day (Marx calls this *absolute surplus value*) or by reducing necessary labour. This latter can be done by increasing productivity in the industries producing wage goods (or means of production used in the wage goods industries), thus reducing the value of labour power (in hours of labour equivalent) without reducing the actual commodities that the worker receives. Marx calls this *relative surplus value*.

Looking at it another way, the surplus product that workers produce can be increased either by making them work for longer (absolute surplus value) or by improving production methods so that more is produced in the same time (relative surplus value). Absolute surplus value has a limit, set by physical exhaustion, while relative surplus value does not. Absolute surplus value is important in the early stages of capitalist development and in colonies, where working hours are extended to the maximum and wages forced down to a minimum, while relative surplus value is dominant in advanced capitalism.

Both absolute and relative surplus value are forced on capitalists by the pressure of *competition*, which is the primary driving force in capitalism. Any new method of production which reduces costs (whether it be a technical improvement or an 'improvement' in labour discipline) will bring extra profits to those who introduce it quickly, before the general price level has been forced down. Once it is generally adopted, competition will force prices down in line with the lowered costs, and wipe out any remaining high cost producers.

Marx assumes (in general rightly) the large-scale production is more efficient than small-scale. Competition, therefore, forces capitalists to accumulate and reinvest to the maximum possible extent in order to produce on a large scale. This growth through reinvestment of profits, Marx calls *concentration* of capital. Those who get ahead in this race will be better able to survive, especially in slumps, and will be able to buy out smaller firms. The growth of the scale of production by amalgamation of capitals is called *centralisation*.

Despite the constant increase in efficiency produced by these processes, Marx asserts that there is a tendency towards a *falling rate of profit*. This idea is important to us because many Marxists have suggested that imperialism is a response to falling profits. Marx's argument is as follows: let c stand for the value of means of production used, v for the value of labour power and s for the surplus value generated. Then s/v is called the *rate of surplus value*: surplus labour divided by necessary labour. The *rate of profit*, however is: $s/(c + v)$, since the capitalist relates his profit to the total capital invested, in means of production and in the purchase of labour power. Now the profit rate:

$$\frac{s}{c+v} = \frac{s/v}{c/v + 1}$$

dividing top and bottom by v.

The fraction c/v which appears on the bottom of this expression is the *value composition of capital*.

Marx defines the *technical composition of capital* as the ratio of the mass (physical quantity) of means of production to the mass of labour employed. The *value composition of capital* is the ratio between the values of these two. Marx says (*Capital*, I, p. 612): 'I call the value composition of capital, in so far as it is determined by the technical composition and mirrors the changes of the latter, the *organic composition* of capital.' However, he seems to forget this definition and in fact uses the term organic composition interchangeably with value composition.

He asserts that as capital is accumulated c/v will rise, and this will outweigh any rise in s/v (as a result of relative surplus value, i.e. productivity increase) to ensure that the rate of profit will tend to fall. This is the *law of the tendency of the rate of profit to fall*.

He then admits *counter-tendencies*. There are several: s/v may rise, wages may be depressed below the value of labour power, and so on. The most important is the fact that if productivity is rising, the value of any given quantity of means of production will fall, since less labour is required to produce it. Marx calls this the *cheapening of the elements of constant capital*. For this reason, the value of means of production used need not rise even though the mass (physical quantity) does. The 'falling rate of profit' theory depends, essentially, on rapid technical progress in consumer goods industries, using an increasing mass of means of production, without corresponding technical progress in the production of means of production.

Another counter-tendency that we must mention is *foreign trade* (*Capital*, III, p. 232). This is, obviously, of particular interest to us. Marx argues that capital invested in foreign trade may make a higher profit, for several reasons. These include the possibility that the home country is more advanced and thus gains a super profit just as the first firms to produce an innovation do, the possibility that labour may be more productive in the home country without being higher paid (the opposite of

Emmanuel's argument, which I will discuss later), and the high rate of exploitation in colonies. These are a ragbag of reasons with little theoretical backing; without an adequate theory of the world economy they can be nothing more. In any case, the theoretical argument is at the stage of analysing a closed and homogeneous capitalist economy, in which these factors have no place.

The decisive argument is the cheapening of the elements of constant capital discussed above, since this cheapening is inherent in the process of capitalist development, just as a rising technical composition of capital is. There is no special reason to expect the organic (value) composition of capital either to rise or to fall. It can in any case be shown that capitalists will only adopt new techniques that increase the rate of profit at the existing level of wages. Any technical innovation that reduces costs will also raise the general level of profits once it is in general use (Himmelweit, 1974; Hodgson, 1974).

This rejection of the falling rate of profit is still controversial, though the arguments cited above seem decisive to me. It has large implications for Marxist theory, since many Marxists have predicted an automatic collapse of capitalism because of falling profits. This was not, however, the major foundation for Marx's prediction that capitalism was ultimately doomed, which rests on the contradiction between *private appropriation* and increasingly *social production*. Specifically, the tendency to concentration and centralisation concentrates workers into larger and larger masses in an increasingly tightly integrated economic system, thus creating the social conditions for a proletarian revolution. This revolution has not yet occurred in the most advanced countries, while Marxist revolutionaries have had more success in relatively less developed countries. The need to explain this fact is one reason for the study of imperialism.

The falling rate of profit theory has been used to explain capital export and hence imperialism, and this has been regarded as part of a process of 'mobilising the counter-tendencies' to falling profits. The falling rate of profit is quite unnecessary to these arguments, since they amount to saying that capital seeks out cheap labour and high profits, which is sufficient explanation by itself.

Another quite distinct effect of competition is the formation of *prices of production*. (This will be dealt with in more detail in the discussion of Emmanuel's theories, chapter 9.) The basic idea is that competing capitals will move from one industry to another in search of higher profits. Where profits are high, an inflow of capital will lower them by increasing supply and depressing price. This means that prices will deviate from values, since if prices were proportional to values, the rate of profit would be high in industries where the organic composition of capital was low, and vice versa. The effect of competition, then, will be to form a single *general rate of profit*.

This analysis enables Marx to deal with *commercial capital* (or *merchant's capital*). This is a specialised part of capital which takes over functions of buying and selling from *industrial (productive) capital*. According to the labour theory of value, surplus value arises in production and not in exchange, so that commercial capital does not produce any surplus value. It does, however, perform a necessary function, since purchase and sale of commodities are essential parts of the circuit of capital, and must, therefore, receive a profit (from a difference between buying and selling prices) equivalent to the general rate of profit. This profit on commercial capital, plus the costs of commercial operations, is at the expense of the profits of industrial capital. Commercial capital played a much more important role in the origins of capitalism than it does in Marx's analysis of a pure capitalist system.

It is important to note that merchant's capital (commercial capital) is not a particular branch of industrial capital (like, say, the cotton industry, or agricultural capital). It performs a distinct, non-productive function which is common to all branches of industrial capital. Industrial firms can, and do, perform this function themselves, selling direct to each other and, less frequently, to consumers. Since Marx's time, the subordination of commercial capital to industrial capital has proceeded much further.

Another functional fraction of capital is *financial capital* (or *money dealing capital*, as Marx frequently calls it). This performs a rather heterogeneous collection of functions unified by the fact that all involve handling money (as opposed to commodities), and by the fact that they permit a centralisation of money capital. In the cycle of production that defines industrial capital, the capitalist is apt to find himself with idle money balances that have to be held either as reserves or for use at a later date. If a bank can collect together all this idle money it can economise greatly on the actual money held, and put the rest to use by lending it out to other capitalists who are temporarily short of money. The savings of individuals (retired capitalists, members of non-capitalist classes and so on) can also be collected together and put to use.

The importance of these different fractions of capital (industrial, commercial, financial) is that they define different fractions of the capitalist class which may have different interests. There are other divisions within the capitalist class, for example between small and large businesses and between capitals in different branches of production (agriculture, industry, etc.). One of the functions of political activity and of the state is to arbitrate between these different interests.

Summarising the argument so far, Marx has defined the capitalist mode of production in terms of the relation between two classes, wage workers and capitalists, shown how a closed capitalist system can reproduce itself on an expanding scale, and shown that this system has a dynamic, driven by competition, that generates accumulation, increasing productivity and the concentration of capital. The next step is to analyse the emergence and development of capitalism in a world that is initially entirely pre-capitalist, or, in other words, the functioning of the capitalist mode of production in social formations which contain other modes as well.

III Primitive accumulation: the origins of capitalism

The theory of the workings of a capitalist system cannot explain its origins. Capitalism, once in existence, has a logic which can be captured by abstract theory, but its origins are a once for all process that must be explained in terms of the historical circumstances under which it occurred. Since the defining feature of capitalism, for Marx, is the relation between a class of propertyless, free workers and a class of private owners of the means of production, the essence of the problem is to explain how these two classes came into being.

Capitalism first emerged in Europe. It was transplanted, partly grown, to the colonies of European settlement (America, Australia, etc.) and developed on an independent basis in Japan. In the rest of the world, however, capitalism came from outside, as an alien growth introduced, frequently, at the point of a gun. It is obvious that this pattern in the origins of capitalism must play an important part in explaining the different trajectories of these different parts of the world in subsequent periods.

Marx did not regard this geographical pattern as accidental. He argued that the prospects for the development of capitalism depended crucially on the previous structure of society, and that this was different in different parts of the world. Europe (and Japan: see *Capital*, I, chapter 27, p. 718n) was dominated by the *feudal* mode of production, while most of Asia (particularly India and China) was characterised by the *Asiatic* mode of production.

The decay of the feudal mode of production created a fertile environment for the growth of capitalism, he argued, while the Asiatic mode did not. This was primarily because feudalism involved a form of private property in land (the main means of production in a principally agrarian society), while the Asiatic mode of production was based on communal ownership of land. 'Bernier correctly discovers the basic form of all phenomena in the East – he refers to Turkey, Persia, Hindostan [India] – to be the *absence of private property* in land. This is the real key even to the Oriental heaven' (Marx, 1969, p. 451).

Since this aspect of Marx's thought is controversial, I give here some quotations from *Capital* to demonstrate the importance, for Marx, of the pre-existing social structure in determining the prospects for the development of capitalism. This point will be developed further in the discussion of Marx's writings on India.

> Usury has a revolutionary effect in all precapitalist modes of production only in so far as it destroys and dissolves those forms of property on whose solid foundation and continual reproduction in the same form the political organisation is based. Under Asian forms, usury can continue a long time, without producing anything more than economic decay and political corruption. Only where and when the other prerequisites of capitalist production are present does usury become one of the means assisting in establishing the new mode of production by ruining the feudal lord and small scale producer, on the one hand, and centralising the conditions of labour into capital, on the other. (*Capital*, III, chapter 36, pp. 583–4)

> To what extent [commerce] brings about a dissolution of the old mode of production depends on its solidity and internal structure. And whither this process of dissolution will lead, in other words what new mode of production will replace the old, does not depend on commerce, but on the character of the old mode of production itself.

> The obstacles presented by the internal solidity and organisation of pre-capitalistic, national modes of production to the corrosive influence of commerce are strikingly illustrated in the intercourse of the English with India and China. . . . [In India] this work of

dissolution proceeds very gradually. And still more slowly in China, where it is not reinforced by direct political power. (*Capital*, III, chapter 20, pp. 325, 328)

Both the Asiatic and feudal modes of production, in their pure forms, involve production for local use by peasant families producing agricultural and handicraft-manufactured goods for their own subsistence, and also supporting a ruling class who extract a surplus by extra-economic coercion. In the case of the feudal mode of production, the key social relations link individuals (or families; succession to both rights and duties is normally hereditary); an individual lord has rights over a certain territory, and can exploit the peasants of that territory by extracting rent in labour services, in kind or in money. Correspondingly, individual peasants are tied to particular plots of land, having the right to till that land and the corresponding duty to perform surplus labour for the landlord. In the Asiatic mode of production, the link is between a state (representing a ruling class) and the village communities which occupy the land, distribute it among their members according to customary rules, and are exploited by 'tax-rent'. The political organisations corresponding to these two modes of production mirror the difference in their economic organisation; feudalism is characterised by 'parcellized' sovereignty (the phrase is from Anderson, 1974) divided between many semi-independent feudal lords, while Asiatic society is 'despotic'. For a fuller discussion of the concept of the Asiatic mode, recently revived after being ignored since Marx, see Krader (1975) and Anderson (1974).

There are difficulties with both of these concepts. The concept of the feudal mode as applied to Europe is well established, but there are disputes over its definition (see chapters 8 and 11) as there are over the definition of capitalism; these debates derive mainly from the problems of analysis posed by societies outside western Europe. The concept of an Asiatic mode is even less well established; Anderson (1974) rejects it forcefully. Part of the problem is that the distinction between feudal and Asiatic modes is not as clear as it seems at first, since there are many forms of land tenure intermediate between the two. In any case, the real history of forms of economic organisation in Asia before capitalist penetration is both complex and little understood, so the differences between Europe and Asia remain to be explained.

As the feudal order in Europe disintegrated it broke down into a society of independent peasant producers, some paying rent to landlords, who also relied on common lands to graze animals etc. Production was thus a mixture of subsistence peasant production, handicraft production for local use, and small-scale production for the market. Feudal landlords, however, had some claims on the land in the form of rents, and ill-defined rights over common lands.

The crucial stage was the conversion of these (privately owned) feudal rights into full private property in the land, including the right to dispossess the occupiers; a right that generally did not exist in the classic feudal social order.

Capitalism is defined by the relation between propertyless, free workers and the owners of the means of production. By expelling peasants from the land, the means of production were concentrated into the landlords' hands while at the same time the expelled peasants became a proletariat, and the separation of activities previously carried out in self-sufficient units created markets. What follows is Marx's description of the logic of this process in the abstract (*Capital*, I, part VIII, especially chapter 30). Lenin worked through a rather similar analysis (Lenin, 1974) in his polemic against the *Narodniks* to show how capitalism creates an (internal) market. In practice, other changes were occurring at the same time.

To begin with, peasant farmers largely produce their own subsistence (including the products of rural handicrafts) and exchange only a surplus on the market. They trade, on a small scale, with an urban handicrafts sector, while landlords spend their rents on the products of peasant farmers and on the better quality handicraft products, as well as on maintaining servants, etc.

After the expulsion of the peasants, food is produced in much the same quantities, on the same land by a smaller number of agricultural workers, suffering a lower standard of living; the surplus in agriculture has thus increased. A substantial part of the dispossessed peasants are employed as wage workers in urban or rural industry, fed from the agricultural surplus. Their products can be sold (by their employers), because pre-capitalist rural craft industries have been largely destroyed, creating a vacuum into which capitalist producers can move.

This process, as Marx describes it, can, in principle, be carried through without any fundamental changes in the forces of production: much the same goods are produced, in the same way, using the same land and the same means of production. What has happened is that the social relations of production have been completely reorganised. Previously production was largely for direct use. Now, industry and agriculture, urban and rural production have been separated, and production is largely for sale. Previously the producers possessed their own means of production; now they are propertyless wage earners.

This process Marx calls the *primitive accumulation of capital*. It is not accumulation in the sense of the creation of means of production that did not exist before. From the point of view of society as a whole it is not accumulation at all. It is primitive accumulation of capital, because means of production and labour power that were not previously part of capital are transformed into capital. To quote: 'We know that the means of production and subsistence, while they remain the property of the immediate producer, are not capital. They become capital only under circumstances in which they serve at the same time as means of exploitation and subjection of the labourer' (*Capital*, I, chapter 33, p. 767).

In practice, of course, this process occurred over a long period of time during which methods of production were changing, and other forces were at work undermining pre-capitalist forms of organisation. The account given above is an abstraction.

One aspect of the transition that needs more explanation is the origins of the capitalist farmer. Typically, in England, landlords did not operate all of their land as capitalist farmers themselves, but rented it out to capitalist tenant farmers, who employed agricultural wage labour. Marx's account here is rather unclear (as are the historical facts), but it seems that he saw the origins of the capitalist tenant farmers primarily in the better off peasants who allied themselves with the landlords in the struggles over enclosure of common lands, a class that came later to be called by their Russian name, the *kulaks*.

There are other points that we should note. Firstly, the description given by Marx applies mainly to England, the first fully capitalist society. In France, for example, the revolution of 1789 established a system of free peasants mainly owning their own land, and capitalist agriculture was slow to develop. The transition from feudalism to capitalism depends very strongly on specific circumstances.

Secondly, Marx emphasises other factors (while always placing the main stress on the creation of a proletariat): the influx of plunder into England from India and other colonies, the establishment of a world market and the massive growth in mercantile wealth, and so on. The exact role of these is not very clear. The influx of wealth presumably made it easier for prospective capitalists to gather together the means to start businesses and build them up, and it promoted a turnover in the actual personnel of the landowning class with the *nouveau riche* buying out declining and indebted feudal magnates. All of this must have acted as a sort of lubricant for the still very slow progress of the capitalist juggernaut.

Many recent writers, especially Baran and Frank, have reversed Marx's emphasis here, making the flow of plunder into Europe the main factor in the origins of capitalism (and in the failure of capitalism to develop elsewhere). Marx certainly discusses both the internal and the external factors in primitive accumulation, and the interpretation given above is only one possible reading. I think that it accords both with the logic of Marx's argument and with the weight of his arguments. A stress on external factors is consistent with a picture of capitalism in which a centre-periphery division on a world scale is a defining feature, but such a definition of capitalism is not to be found in Marx.

Thirdly, Marx emphasises the role of the state. Its main function during the process of primitive accumulation (apart from providing legal backing for the expulsion of peasants) is to repress the newly forming working class, and keep their wages down.

> The organisation of the capitalist process of production, once fully developed, breaks down all resistance. The dull compulsion of economic relations completes the subjection of the labourer to the capitalist. Direct force, outside economic conditions, is of course still used, but only exceptionally. . . . It is otherwise during the historical genesis of capitalist production. (*Capital*, I, chapter 28, p. 737).

IV Stages of development and the spread of capitalism

Once capitalism is established, capitalists are driven by competition to find new methods of production which raise productivity and lower costs of production. This is in contrast to pre-capitalist modes of production in which a reduction in manpower required generally brings no benefits (since redundant producers cannot be expelled) and in which an increase in output is only of use in so far as it can be consumed by the ruling class or used to maintain unproductive servants, soldiers, etc. Competition in a capitalist system generates cumulative development. Each advance is soon copied, the laggards go bankrupt, and the leader's advantage can only be maintained by repeated expansion and innovation.

As early as 1848, in the *Communist Manifesto* (Marx and Engels, n.d.,a, cited below as *Manifesto*), Marx insisted that it was the development of the forces of production that represented the essential historical function of capitalism:

> The bourgeoisie cannot exist without constantly revolutionising the instruments of production, and thereby the relations of production, and with them the whole relations of society.

> The bourgeoisie, during its rule of scarce one hundred years has created more massive and more colossal productive forces than have all preceding generations together. (*Manifesto*, pp. 51, 54)

At the same time, capitalism expands, and draws all other societies into its orbit.

> The bourgeoisie, by the rapid improvement of all instruments of production, by the immensely facilitated means of communication, draws all, even the most barbarian, nations into civilisation. The cheap prices of its commodities are the heavy artillery with which it batters down all Chinese walls, with which it forces the barbarians' intensely obstinate hatred of foreigners to capitulate. (*Manifesto*, p. 53)

How does this expansion take place? I have argued that Marx was not an underconsumptionist, and that he did not see capitalism as dependent on external markets. He was not wholly consistent in this: in the *Manifesto*, for example, we read: 'The need of a constantly expanding market chases the bourgeoisie over the whole surface of the globe. It must nestle everywhere, settle everywhere, establish connections everywhere.'

The inconsistency is, however, more apparent than real. Firstly, capitalism does not develop evenly; where one industry (such as cotton textiles in the industrial revolution) develops ahead of others, it can find itself hampered by a shortage of demand relative to a greatly expanded supply. Secondly, and this is really the same point seen from another angle, the fact that capitalist production does not require external markets, does not mean that capitalists will ignore external markets where they exist. On the contrary, competition forces capitalist firms to seek out the markets in which they can get the best price for their products, and to seek out the cheapest sources of supply for the goods that they buy. The search for cheap raw materials is particularly important, since their availability depends, in part, on natural conditions (climate, mineral deposits) which are to be found in widely spread parts of the globe. Thirdly, although there is no inevitable shortage of demand, there is, equally, no guarantee that demand will always be adequate. Capitalist economies progress through a sequence of booms and slumps, so that there are always periods in which excess supplies of goods exist and sellers must search desperately for markets.

The other factor that drives the capitalist sector of a national or world economy to expand at the expense of pre-capitalist production is a need for fresh supplies of labour power. It is true that the reserve army of labour is constantly replenished by workers made redundant as a result of the advances in productivity that competition enforces, but Marx always assumed that a healthy capitalist system would tend to expand more rapidly than the growth of productivity in itself would permit, and would thus tend, periodically, to run into shortages of labour. In the absence of any external source of labour power this would cause an increase in the wage (demand exceeding supply in the market for labour power) which would both stimulate labour-saving innovations and provoke a crisis which would reduce demand for labour. Any external sources of labour power would be eagerly raided in order to stave off the crisis.

The competitive process meets both of these needs; the need for markets and the need for labour power, so long as capitalist production is surrounded by pre-capitalist producers of commodities, especially small-scale individual producers. The technical advance enforced by competition enables capitalist firms to undercut the products of pre-capitalist producers, eating into their markets and at the same time ruining the producers and forcing them into the proletariat. Since capitalism emerged in a decaying feudal society in which commodity production was well established already, conditions were favourable for it to expand and dominate economic life in western Europe (though this took a long time).

At the time when capitalism first emerged, which was also the time when the first capitalist empires were established, it had two features worth particular note. Firstly, the dominant form of capital was merchant capital, and, secondly, the methods of production used were still essentially those of pre-capitalist times. There is a long first period in the history of capitalism in which these two special features predominate, variously called the period of merchant capitalism or the period or stages of *simple co-operation* and of *manufacture*. There follows the period which was Marx's main subject, when industrial capital had come to predominate and when methods of production had been revolutionised by the rise of *modern industry*. In England, the leading capitalist centre, modern industry originated in the late eighteenth century, but did not come to dominate until well into the nineteenth.

I have described the role of merchant capital in fully developed capitalism, but all that is necessary for the existence of merchant capital is that exchange of commodities should take place on a sufficient scale, and commodity production pre-dates the rise of specifically capitalist production.

In a pre-capitalist world, it is only the surplus over the needs of reproduction that is sold, and, where this surplus is gathered by a ruling class in the form of rents in kind or as the product of forced labour, its 'cost of production' is not clearly defined. There is thus scope for huge differences in prices between different areas, and great scope for monopoly profits. In addition, natural conditions produce great differences in the costs of production in different areas. With a large enough volume of trade, these differences in prices will be eliminated, but when long distance trade was costly and very risky, there was scope for large profits in trade, and very large profits from monopolising trade. It is for these reasons that Marx says: 'The independent development of merchant's capital, therefore, stands in inverse proportion to the general economic development of society' (*Capital*, III, chapter 20, p. 322).

At the same time, the emergence of commodity exchange and, with the development of merchant capital, large-scale trading, constitutes a basis for the emergence of financial capital. As we shall see in discussing Marx's views on India, he places great stress on the political power of the 'moneyocracy' during the period of transition, a power gained largely by corruption. The period of transition from feudalism to capitalism and the early stages of development of capitalism are thus marked by a massive efflorescence of merchant's capital and financial capital, later to be cut down by the rise of industrial capital.

The commercial empires of the sixteenth to eighteenth centuries were therefore driven mainly by attempts to monopolise trade (though a simple desire for plunder, a motive that is as old as the existence of societies worth plundering, was also an important element). In some cases (the Spanish in America, the Dutch in the East Indies, various nations in the sugar plantations of the West Indies and of the adjacent parts of South America) these essentially commercial activities extended into the organisation of production, where indigenous sources of supply proved inadequate. In general, the production systems set up were not capitalist, for the simple reason that no proletariat existed in the areas concerned.

Marx was, rightly or wrongly, very clear that participation in a world economy dominated by merchant capital did not necessarily make the mode of production capitalist.

> Independent mercantile wealth as a predominant form of capital represents the separation of the circulation process from its extremes, and these extremes are the exchanging producers themselves. They remain independent of the circulation process, just as the latter remains independent of them. . . . Money and commodity circulation can mediate between spheres of production of widely different organisation, whose internal structure is still chiefly adjusted to the output of use values. (*Capital*, III, chapter 20, p. 322)

The whole chapter from which this quotation is taken, entitled 'Historical Facts about Merchant's Capital', is of great importance in understanding Marx's view of the emergence of a capitalist world economy, which clearly differs from that of Frank and Wallerstein.

Where the pre-conditions for capitalist production exist, however, merchant capital tends to move into (capitalist) production. This typically takes the form of the dominance of merchants over small-scale independent producers, which can develop into 'outwork', a system in which the workers work in their own homes with materials and other means of production provided by the merchant. This is, however, according to Marx, only a byway in the development of capitalism:

> The transition from the feudal mode of production is twofold. The producer becomes merchant and capitalist. . . . This is the really revolutionary way. Or else, the merchant establishes direct sway over production. However much this serves historically as a stepping stone . . . it cannot by itself contribute to the overthrow of the old mode of production, but tends rather to preserve and retain it as its precondition. (*Capital*, III, chapter 20, p. 329)

The dominance of merchant capital, therefore, tended to undermine the feudal mode of production to some extent while at the same time hampering the rise of industrial capital and of truly capitalist production. This point is not merely of historical importance. This stage of development persists even now in many rural areas in the Third World, and some recent writers have stressed the dominance of merchant capital as an important factor delaying capitalist development in underdeveloped areas.

At the same time, capitalist production was, to start with, based on older techniques of production. The first stage of capitalist production Marx calls *co-operation*. By this he means that the only change in technique is the massing of large numbers of workers in one place where before, as independent producers, they would all have been working separately. The next stage, Marx calls *manufacturing*. This term has a specific meaning for Marx and his contemporaries, quite different from modern non-Marxist usage. By manufacturing, Marx means a process of production divided between different workers into tiny, repetitive operations (the *detail division of labour*) carried out with specialised tools, but without genuine mechanisation. There are gains in productivity and also a reduction in costs as a result of employing less skilled workers (see *Capital*, I, chapter 14; this subject is also well treated in Braverman, 1974).

During this long period in which pre-capitalist methods of production were slowly transformed, the cost advantages of capitalist producers must have been pretty small, at least in comparison to later periods, and have to be set against high transport costs and high profit margins demanded by merchant middlemen. The process by which capitalist production undermines pre-capitalist modes of production by undercutting their prices therefore went on very slowly. The mechanisms of primitive accumulation were still going on, and were still the dominant factor in the growth of capitalism.

The situation is transformed by the rise of *modern industry*. The distinguishing feature of modern industry, or *machinofacture* (terms differ in different translations), is that the tools are taken out of the worker's hands and moved and regulated directly by a machine. Since mechanisms are not limited by the physiology of the human body, it now becomes possible for productivity to rise dramatically. A machine minder or operative can supervise machines which move much faster than a human worker and which can carry out many operations simultaneously.

This makes possible genuine mass production and an enormous cheapening of the prices of commodities. The dominance of merchant capital, dependent on monopolistic restrictions in trade, has to be swept aside, and the process of destroying pre-capitalist production can go on very rapidly, since capitalist production now has a decisive cost advantage. It is thus the emergence of modern industry that is the real turning point in the history of capitalism and of capitalist expansion throughout the world.

Modern industry does not, however, come into being simultaneously in all branches of production. When one branch of industry is revolutionised, it places greatly increased demands on branches connected with it, and thus creates strong pressures for further innovations. As Marx argues:

A radical change in the mode of production in one sphere of industry involves a similar change in other spheres. . . . Thus spinning by machinery made weaving by machinery a necessity. . . . The revolution in the modes of production of industry and agriculture made necessary a revolution in the general conditions of the social process of production, i.e., in the means of communication and transport. . . . Modern industry had therefore itself to take in hand the machine, its characteristic instrument of production, and to construct machines by machines. (*Capital*, I, chapter 15, pp. 383–4)

This did not, however, all happen immediately. 'It was only in the decade preceding 1866, that the construction of railways and ocean steamers on a stupendous scale called into existence the cyclopean machines now employed in the construction of prime movers' (p. 384). So Marx is saying that the process was hardly complete in his own time, the second half of the nineteenth century, although it had started in the late eighteenth century. In fact, some branches of production are still not fully industrialised even now. The transition to modern industry, generating these great disproportions between different industries, lasted for a whole historical epoch, broadly, the whole nineteenth century.

Pre-industrial methods of production persist alongside modern industry for a long time, and, to a certain extent, persist because of it. Where mechanisation makes masses of workers redundant, it forces down wages, and large numbers of workers may be employed in out-work, and in manufacturing processes, at very low wages and under very bad conditions.

This unevenness in the introduction of modern industrial methods is particularly important because without it it is difficult to see any basis for large-scale trade between industrial and non-industrial areas. Specifically, since cotton textiles were the first major product to be produced by industrial methods, and since England was the centre of this industrial revolution, England came to have a pressing need both for extended markets for cotton goods and for sources of supply of raw cotton. The consequences of this for India will be discussed in the next section.

Modern industry is the highest stage of capitalist development that Marx discussed, since it was the highest stage reached in his time. He discussed the forces of concentration and centralisation of capital, and foresaw the development of monopoly as an inevitable consequence of the competitive process, but it was left to his successors to designate *monopoly capital* (or *finance capital*) as a stage beyond modern industry.

Capitalism, then, after a long, slow start in which it met the external world primarily through the mediation of merchant capital, came to life with the rise of modern industry, sweeping aside merchant capital and imposing a whole series of massive transformations on the world economy. At the same time, however, huge parts of the world remained at this time in a pre-capitalist stage of development and resistant, because of their internal structure, to the impact of market forces. This is the context in which Marx's writings on colonialism must be set.

V Marx on colonialism

Marx did not discuss colonialism in general terms; his views must be deduced from scattered references in his major writings and, especially, from articles that he wrote about special cases, notably about Ireland, about the British empire in India and (much more superficially) about western, particularly British, dealings with China.

Marx wrote a considerable amount about Ireland (Marx and Engels, 1971, is a convenient collection), mainly in the form of speeches, passing references in correspondence and the like. Marx argued that Ireland's poverty and misery, as compared to England's status as the leading capitalist centre, were not caused primarily by any internal difference in the prior mode of production, but by external (English) oppression and exploitation. The expulsion of the peasantry and the creation of capitalist farms under the aegis (and to the benefit) of the (English) landed aristocracy followed essentially the same course as in England (primitive accumulation), though it was carried out with even greater brutality, but: 'every time Ireland was about to develop industrially, she was crushed and reconverted into a purely agricultural land. . . . The people had now before them the choice between the occupation of land *at any rent*, or starvation' (Marx and Engels, 1971, p. 132).

The main cause of industrial failure in Ireland was the absence of protective tariffs; Irish industry could not survive English competition. In this, Ireland's fate does not seem very different from that of various country districts of England, except in the absence of political constraints on exploitation. Just like workers from rural areas of England, the Irish were forced to migrate to seek work in the industrial cities of England. The difference was in the existence of a revolutionary (though not socialist) nationalist movement. Marx was especially concerned to see a nationalist revolution against the aristocracy in Ireland, since this would undermine their hold in England, reduce divisions between Irish and English workers in England, and thus advance the socialist revolution in England, which 'being the metropolis of capital . . . is for the present the most important country for the workers revolution, and moreover the *only* country in which the material conditions for this revolution have developed up to a certain degree of maturity.'

Neither Marx nor Engels thought that revolution in Ireland could be socialist. Engels, after Marx's death, argued that the Irish wanted land, to become independent peasants and 'after that, mortgages will appear on the scene and they will be ruined once more'. They should, however, be encouraged to 'pass from semi-feudal conditions to capitalist conditions' (p. 343). This view of the regressive effect of British rule in Ireland contrasts with Marx's view of its effects in India.

The articles about India and China (collected in Marx and Engels, no date, b, and with a useful introduction by S. Avinieri in Marx, 1969) were written for the *New York Daily Tribune*. The main series was published during 1853, and includes both commentary on issues of current interest and a number of articles in which Marx sets out his considered view on India. It is these few 'set piece' articles that are the main source. In 1853, five years after the writing of the *Communist Manifesto*, Marx had arrived substantially at his mature position, but the economic analysis which culminated in *Capital* was not yet worked out in detail. Where he does return to the same topics in *Capital*, however, there is little sign of any change in his thinking.

How much did Marx know about India? It is obvious, both from the articles and from the 'Notes on Indian History' which he compiled, that he had read virtually everything available to him on India and was exceedingly well informed on the political and military history of the sub-continent. It is, however, important to note that there was much that he did not know, probably because no one at that time (or perhaps since) knew it. Thus, in an article of 7 June 1858 (Marx, 1969, p. 313) he discusses debates then going on in England about the real nature of land tenure in India, without firmly coming down in favour of any one interpretation, and in an article of 23 July 1858 (Marx, 1969, p. 330) he discusses contemporary debates about the burden of taxation in India without being able decisively to settle the question of whether or not Indian cultivators are 'overtaxed', in the sense that taxation threatens the resources needed for reproduction. These two issues – land tenure or the relations of production, and the extent of exploitation and the size of the potential surplus product – should presumably be crucial to a Marxist analysis of Indian society, but the information was simply not available.

Starting with the historical background of British rule in India, Marx traces the origins of the East India Company to the period after 1688 when

> the old landed aristocracy [had] been defeated and the bourgeoisie [was] not able to take its place except under the banner of moneyocracy or the haute finance. The East India Company excluded the common people from the commerce with India. . . . [It was] the era of monopolies . . . authorised and nationalised by the sanction of Parliament. (Marx, 1969, p. 99)

The position of the East India Company rested essentially on corruption.

The East India Company had, from an early date, two objects: to develop trade, and also to 'make territorial revenue one of their sources of emolument'. As the company's territories expanded from the middle of the eighteenth century to the middle of the nineteenth, the time when Marx was writing, so it came more and more under the control of the British state, creating a peculiar hybrid of public and private power characteristic of the oligarchic British state of this transitional epoch.

The whole character of the British relationship with India was transformed in the early nineteenth century by the rise of industrial capital. Before then, Indian textiles were among products exported to Britain, with a drain of precious metals to India to pay for them. In 1813 trade with India was thrown open to competition, and the balance of trade soon turned the other way, India being flooded with British textiles.

By the mid-nineteenth century, the coalition of interests that lay behind the original British drive into India was breaking up.

Till then the interests of the moneyocracy which had converted

India into its landed estates, of the oligarchy who had conquered it
by their armies, and of the millocracy who had inundated it with
their fabrics had gone hand in hand. But the more the industrial
interest became dependent on the Indian market, the more it felt
the necessity of creating fresh productive powers in India, after
having ruined her native industry. You cannot continue to
inundate a country with your manufactures, unless you enable it to
give some produce in return. . . . The manufacturers, conscious of
their ascendancy in England, ask now for the annihilation of these
antagonistic powers in India, for the destruction of the whole
ancient fabric of Indian Government, and for the final eclipse of the
East India Company. (Marx, 1969, p. 107)

Here is the key to Marx's arguments. While merchant capital and its
allies exploit and destroy without transforming, industrial capital
destroys but at the same time transforms, through the process described
above by which capitalist industry draws new areas into its division of
labour.

What were British motives in India? Who were the beneficiaries of
empire? Once it became a territorial power, the East India Company
ceased to be profitable, the proceeds of taxation being eaten up by the
administrative and military costs of occupation. It was the need for
financial support that was a vital lever in driving the East India Company
into the hands of the British government.

Private citizens, however, principally the employees of the Company,
did very well, with inflated salaries and many opportunities to add to
these by private corruption, looting and perquisites of one sort or
another. This is characteristic of the rise of capitalism, a period in which
the state and the privileges it could grant were a major source of support
to the 'moneyocracy' and the 'oligarchy'.

The other principal beneficiaries were the industrial bourgeoisie.
Their interest was in markets, according to Marx. In this there is a
contrast with the arguments of certain later writers (Lenin, for example),
writing about a later period when conditions had changed, who stressed
the interest of monopoly capital in protected markets to monopolise and
the interest of financial capital in outlets for investment.

I have already discussed the ambiguities in Marx's discussion of the
need for markets. Here he is clear: it is not markets in general that are
needed, but markets for cotton textiles. 'At the same rate at which the
cotton manufactures became of vital interest for the whole social frame of

Great Britain, East India became of vital interest for the British cotton manufacture' (Marx, 1969, p. 107). This links up with the statement quoted above: 'You cannot continue to inundate a country with your manufactures unless you enable it to give you some produce in return.'

This leads to a general point: Marx presented a theory of capitalism in the abstract, but he knew that the real world was far from reducible to the play of pure economic abstractions. Marx does not argue that capitalism in Britain had to have colonies, but that once history had taken that turn, there was no going back. India became necessary, not to capitalism in general, but to capitalism as it had in fact developed, with a particular pattern of trade. England had a trade surplus with India (as a result of cotton exports), which India financed from its surplus with China (the opium trade), while China in turn exported tea and other products both to England and to Australia and the USA, which had surpluses in trade with England, closing the circle. Marx analyses the way in which the opium trade was a lynchpin of this pattern of trade, and therefore had to be protected and expanded (by force), while at the same time the effects of the opium trade in China actually diminished China's capacity to import other goods from the west. The creative tension between theory and historical specificity in Marx's writings is one mark of his greatness.

There is no suggestion in these writings that the workers in England benefit from the colonies, except in so far as the cotton industry in England expands, and thus employs more, at the expense of Indian textile production. They are no more secure in their jobs, nor are they better paid as a result:

> As to the working classes, it is still a much debated question whether their condition has been ameliorated at all as a result of the so-called public wealth. . . . But perhaps also, in speaking of amelioration, the economists may have wished to refer to the millions of workers condemned to perish, in the East Indies, in order to procure for the million and a half of workpeople employed in England in the same industry, three years of prosperity out of ten. (Marx, *Poverty of Philosophy*, 1847, cited in Marx, 1969. p. 35)

The quotations from Engels (not Marx) which Lenin uses to link the idea of a labour aristocracy to the possession of colonies (Lenin, 1950, p. 545) mostly date from later, and are all very ambiguous, referring to the bourgeois ideas of sections of the English proletariat rather than to any material benefit enjoyed by them. I will discuss this further in discussing Lenin (chapter 5).

Marx does not discuss, in any general way, why the promotion of trade should involve military conquest and direct administration of pre-capitalist areas. Two motives emerge from the particular cases he discusses: firstly, to exclude other nations and to ensure unimpeded entry of the conquering power's own goods and, secondly, because Asiatic society is very resistant to penetration by trade alone, so that the direct use of state power is called for. Marx also, however, stresses the inheritance both of colonial territory and of vested interests (such as the large and wealthy stratum of employees of the East India Company) from earlier stages of development. He also has a rather disturbing tendency to ascribe plans for expansion to the personal ambitions and ill will of particular individuals whom he dislikes; he had a special hatred for Palmerston. How far this latter emphasis is a product of the journalistic and propagandistic character of his writings on the subject is not clear.

What, then, was the effect of British rule in India? Marx sets out his views in a famous pair of articles: 'British rule in India', and 'The future results of British rule in India' (Marx, 1969, pp. 88 ff. and 132 ff.).

Asiatic society, according to Marx, is based on a village economy, characterised by a union, within the village, of agriculture and handicrafts, a traditional, hereditary division of labour and an absence of private property in land. The first two characteristics are reminiscent of the feudal structure from which capitalism emerged. Feudalism was broken up primarily by the expulsion of the peasants from the land, based on the conversion of feudal into bourgeois property in land. In the absence of private landed property, this form of transformation was blocked in India.

In the Asiatic mode of production, surplus was not creamed off by individual landlords, but by the state, as the highest representative of communal landownership, in the form of taxation. Marx quotes earlier writers as saying that the village structure stands unaltered as states and empires come and go above it. The East India Company, in occupying India, had, in the first instance, simply replaced these previous states.

Marx argues that it was the combination of a need for large-scale public works (irrigation works, etc.) for climatic and geographical reasons, together with a 'low level of civilisation', which called into existence 'the interference of the centralising power of government'. It is not purely the technical requirements which created Asiatic despotism: Flanders and

Italy, in Europe, also needed large-scale works but here, in a different social context, private enterprise was driven to voluntary association.

In a striking (and much quoted) phrase, Marx says:

> There have been in Asia, generally, from immemorial times, but three departments of Government: that of Finance, or the plunder of the interior; that of War, or the plunder of the exterior; and, finally, the department of Public Works. . . . Now the British in East India accepted from their predecessors the department of finance and of war, but they have neglected entirely that of public works. (Marx, 1969, p. 90)

(We can note, as a matter of interest, that both the argument and the phrases that embody it come from a letter by Engels to Marx, *ibid.*, pp. 451–2.) However, Marx admits immediately that 'in Asiatic empires we are quite accustomed to see agriculture deteriorating under one government and reviving again under some other government.' It seems, in fact, that the neglect of public works pre-dated the British conquest, being a result of the breakup of the Moghul empire, and that public works revived at around the time that Marx was writing, for the reasons already described (the interest of industrial capital in expanding markets).

The real devastation that British penetration into India brought with it was the destruction of the Indian handicraft textile production by competition from the mechanised textile production of Lancashire.

Marx discusses, with special reference to China, the reasons why Asiatic production is so resistant to capitalist competition (Marx, 1969, pp. 393 ff.). The production of cloth is integrated with farm work and the time when agricultural work is slack can be used for handicrafts, so that the costs of actually producing the cloth are almost non-existent. The producers control their own means of subsistence, and thus cannot be starved out by undercutting.

It was only with the direct assistance of state power, then, that the destruction of Indian textiles could occur, and even so it proceeded fairly slowly. In China, where direct European control was absent, the Lancashire textiles made even less impact: this, according to Marx, was a major reason behind British aggressiveness towards China. The exact mechanisms by which British textiles conquered the Indian market are left, however, rather unclear in Marx's writings.

Between the neglect of public works and the destruction of the textile industry, British rule produced unprecedented misery in India. It did, however, have its progressive side as well. English industrial capitalists, according to Marx, had an interest in the development of the Indian economy. This, above all, meant the building of railways, and Marx expected this to lead to further industrial development to produce loco-motives, etc., as well as breaking down the isolation of Indian rural life.

Marx also gives an impressive list of the modernising and integrating factors produced by British rule:

> [Political] unity, imposed by the British sword, will now be strengthened and perpetuated by the electric telegraph. The native army, organised and trained by the British drill-sergeant was the *sine qua non* of Indian self-emancipation. . . . The free press is a new and powerful agent of reconstruction. . . . private property in land – the great desideratum of Asiatic society. From the Indian natives . . . a fresh class is springing up, endowed with the require-ments for government, and imbued with European science. (Marx, 1969, p. 133)

In short, British rule was destroying the static Asiatic society and creating the pre-conditions both for industrial capitalism and for the creation of a modern Indian nation state.

This would not happen automatically or painlessly, however:

> All the English bourgeoisie may be forced to do will neither emancipate nor materially mend the social condition of the mass of the people, depending not only on the development of the productive powers, but on their appropriation by the people. But what they will not fail to do is to lay down the material premises for both. Has the bourgeoisie ever done more? Has it ever effected a progress without dragging individuals and peoples through blood and dirt, through misery and degradation?
> The Indians will not reap the fruits of the new elements of society scattered among them by the British bourgeoisie till in Great Britain itself the now ruling classes shall have been supplanted by the industrial proletariat, or till the Hindoos themselves shall have grown strong enough to throw off the English yoke altogether, (p. 137)

Marx's argument, then, can be summarised: British rule in India (a) causes massive misery, (b) creates the preconditions for massive advance and (c) must be overthrown before the benefits can be enjoyed. This argument has frequently been regarded as surprising and paradoxical. I cannot see why it should seem so to a Marxist; if we replace the words 'British rule' with 'capitalism' we have exactly the argument of the *Communist Manifesto*. Even the tone, the style is the same: the deliberate juxtaposition of the most exalted praise for material achievements and the shocking images used to bring home the concomitant human misery. This article was, after all, written only five years after the *Manifesto*.

There are, I think, two reasons why Marx's arguments have been regarded as an embarrassing lapse on his part. Firstly, Marxists have often (rightly) aligned themselves with broadly based movements of national liberation, and have wanted, for propagandist reasons, to ascribe all social evils to the foreign oppressors and to see the oppressed nation as inherently progressive and morally superior. Whether it is wise to cover up the evils of the past and of the indigenous social structure is another matter; Marx did not think so.

Secondly, it has seemed that Marx was wrong in his predictions. India did not, under British rule, develop into a major industrial country. The assessment here must depend on what time scale you think Marx expected for the developments he predicted – there is no clear indication in his articles. Other passages make it clear that the village organisation remains and is very resistant to change. The factors that Marx listed making Indian independence a future possibility – unity, the native army, the free press, an educated middle class – are surely exactly the factors that have given the independent Indian state of the years after 1948 the character that it has. I will not pursue these arguments here, since the reasons for the slowness of development in the Third World since Marx's time will be discussed in later chapters.

Is Marx's analysis of India inconsistent with his opinions on Ireland? Since Marx's writings on Ireland generally date from later (though he was writing in support of Irish nationalism as early as 1848), is there evidence of a change in Marx's views on colonialism? I think not. Marx wrote with detachment about the Indian revolt (mutiny) of 1857, expressing no support for the rebels and cataloguing the atrocities of both sides. The reason is clear: he regarded Indian independence at that date as unattainable since its material and social foundations did not yet exist. This is even clearer in his description of the Taiping rebels in China:

> It seems that their vocation is nothing else than to set against the conservative disintegration [of China] its destruction, in grotesque horrifying form, without any seeds for a renaissance. . . . Only in

China was such a sort of devil possible. It is the consequence of a fossil form of life. (Marx, 1969, pp. 442, 444)

In Ireland, by contrast, a modern democratic nationalist movement existed, since Ireland had a different mode of production and was at a different stage of development. Marx's political analysis was always based on analysis of particular situations.

VI Summary

Marx defined capitalism in terms of the relation between a class of free wage labourers and a class of capitalists. Competition between many capitals (distinct units of capital) compels accumulation and technical progress. Capitalism does not need a subordinated hinterland or periphery, though it will use it and profit from it if it exists. Up to the industrial revolution, capitalism's external relations were mediated through merchant capital, and did not necessarily transform other societies drawn into the world market. Once industrial capital had taken charge, capitalist conquest could play a progressive (though brutal) role initiating capitalist industrialisation. The origin and rapid development of capitalism in Europe and its slow penetration in Asia were the result of differences in the preceding modes of production in these areas; European domination was the result and not the primary cause of this difference.

3 · Rosa Luxemburg

After Marx's death in 1883, there was something of a lacuna in the development of Marxist thought up to about 1900. The period between 1900 and about 1920, on the other hand, saw an explosion of Marxist writing and, in particular, the creation of what I shall call the 'classical' Marxist theory of imperialism by Hilferding, Bukharin and Lenin. The development of that theory will be pursued at length in subsequent chapters, but I will deal first with the work of Rosa Luxemburg who stands apart from these writers, and much closer to Marx, in her preoccupations.

Her main work was *The Accumulation of Capital* (Luxemburg, 1951, cited below as *Accumulation*), first published in 1913. This work was heavily criticised, and in 1915 she wrote a reply to these criticisms, the *Anti-Critique* (Luxemburg, 1972, cited below as *Anti-Critique*), eventually published in 1921. A number of her arguments emerge much more clearly in the *Anti-Critique* than in the original presentation, so I will use it extensively. (Readers of *The Accumulation of Capital* may find it helpful to regard sections one and two of that book as a sort of enormously extended prologue, with the book itself starting on page 329 of the edition that I have cited.) A particularly thorough, though in parts sharply polemical, critique of both of these works was subsequently published by Bukharin (1972b) under the title of *Imperialism and Accumulation of Capital*. Some of the arguments put here derive from Bukharin.

Rosa Luxemburg really put forward two arguments, which I will consider separately. Firstly, she thought that she had detected a logical flaw in Marx's analysis of expanded reproduction which made it impossible to realise (i.e. to sell in exchange for money) goods corresponding to that part of surplus value which was destined to be reinvested as new capital, without having 'outside' (i.e. non-capitalist) buyers. For this reason, she argued, capitalism cannot exist in a pure form, but only in conjunction with non-capitalist systems. I shall argue that she was simply wrong on this point.

Secondly, she argued that capitalism had, as a matter of fact, grown up in a world where it is surrounded by pre-capitalist economic formations, and that competitive pressures drive capitalist firms and capitalist states to trade with these 'outside' economies and ultimately to break them up. In this she followed the same line of argument as Marx. I shall argue that she was substantially right in this part of her argument, though sometimes shaky in detail. The *Accumulation* contains a fair amount of historical material about the impact of capitalism on pre-capitalist societies; this remains relevant despite the failure of her first (and principal) argument, since its inclusion is justified by the second argument.

Rosa Luxemburg insists on an important conceptual point. When she draws a distinction between 'inside' and 'outside' from the point of view of capitalism (e.g. 'outside buyers') she means inside (or outside) of capitalist relations of production. The world is divided into nation states, colonies, etc., but it is also divided into a capitalist sector and a non-capitalist sector, and it is this latter division that is the relevant one for her purposes. This is a distinction that Marx also drew, but it is to Rosa Luxemburg's credit that she insists on it and maintains it consistently throughout her work.

The picture that she presents is not only of a capitalism that exists alongside other modes of production, but also of a capitalism remorselessly expanding into its non-capitalist environment, ultimately swallowing it all up. Since she argues that capitalism needs this non-capitalist environment to survive, it follows that capitalism's triumph, the conquest of all pre-capitalist territory, must also be the signal for its collapse:

> Capitalism is the first mode of economy with the weapon of propaganda, a mode which tends to engulf the whole globe and to stamp out all other economies, tolerating no rival at its side. Yet at the same time it is also the first mode of economy which is unable to exist by itself, which needs other economic systems as a medium and soil. Although it strives to become universal and, indeed, on account of this tendency, it must break down – because it is immanently incapable of becoming a universal form of production. (*Accumulation*, p. 467)

I The realisation of surplus value

According to Marx, and Luxemburg, surplus value originates in production, where the value produced by a worker exceeds the value of his labour power. The value created, however, is embodied in some commodity, and this must be sold to realise the value in money terms before the capitalist can buy fresh means of production and labour power to continue the circuit of capital.

Marx analyses the realisation of the product and the reproduction of the system as a whole in the context of a purely capitalist economy, containing only workers, capitalists, and non-productive hangers on (priests, prostitutes, etc.) who derive their incomes from the capitalists. Rosa Luxemburg argues that expanded reproduction is impossible in this context.

I have already outlined Marx's analysis of reproduction, but I will restate it here in order to see Rosa Luxemburg's objections. If reproduction is to continue smoothly, then the entire product at the end of a period of production must be realised, i.e. sold to someone. This, in turn, entails two conditions: that the total value of demand, of spending, must equal the value of the product and that the particular goods which make up the total product must match up with the wants of the purchasers. It is the first of these two conditions that is Luxemburg's main concern.

How does Marx deal with it? The product is in the hands of the capitalists. Where does the demand come from? Some comes from capitalists themselves; they must replace used up means of production, and also buy extra means of production in the case of expanded reproduction. They also buy goods for their own consumption. Another part of the total demand comes from workers who spend their wages on consumption goods. Since wages are paid out by capitalists, we can think of workers' demand for goods as being an indirect form of spending by capitalists. Finally we have the hangers on. Their spending again derives from a redivision of capitalists' incomes, so this again we can think of as indirect spending by capitalists.

We come then to the position that all the goods belong to capitalists and they are bought, directly or indirectly, out of the spending of capitalists. It seems strange, at first sight, that capitalists should buy their own products, and it is probably this apparent difficulty that lies behind Rosa Luxemburg's unwillingness to accept the argument. It is not, however, a problem at all when we realise that part of the definition of capitalism is that it consists of many capitals which exchange their products on the market. Money is purely an intermediary in the redistribution of products from their sector of origin to the sector where they are to be used. Marx presents this exchange in the simplified form of an exchange between just two 'departments' of social production.

The condition, then, for surplus value to be realised is that it should be spent. Capitalists get surplus value by paying less to workers than the value created, but they must (collectively) spend the surplus (on their own consumption or on buying extra means of production or on advancing wages to extra workers) in order to realise it. This will not necessarily happen: if the prospects for profits are poor, then capitalists may hold back from investment and thus make the situation worse.

How does Rosa Luxemburg approach the problem? The argument is not easy to pick out in the *Accumulation* (though it emerges fairly clearly in chapter 25) but in the *Anti-Critique* the problem is set out very clearly, and we can best understand what the problem is by extracting a series of quotations from the latter.

> Let us imagine that all the goods produced in capitalist society
> were stored up in a big pile at some place, to be used by society as
> a whole. We will then see how this mass of goods is naturally
> divided into several big portions of different kinds and destinations.
> (*Anti-Critique*, p. 51)

Replacement of means of production, workers' consumption and capitalists' consumption account for parts of this 'pile', and pose no serious problems of analysis – they are exchanged in the fashion described in Marx's analysis of simple reproduction. But in addition there must be

> a portion of commodities which contains that invaluable part of
> surplus value that forms capital's real purpose of existence: the
> profit designed for capitalisation and accumulation. What sort of
> commodities are they, and who needs them? (p. 55)

As Rosa Luxemburg herself says, 'Here we have come to the nucleus of the problem of accumulation, and we must investigate all attempts at a solution.' The buyers cannot be workers (their spending is accounted for) nor intermediate strata ('like civil servants, military, clerics, academics and artists'), since their income is derived either from diverted profit or from taxes on wages and their spending should, therefore, be included among the forms of consumption already considered, nor can the buyers be capitalists *qua* consumers (since this spending is at the expense of accumulation, and cannot bring accumulation about).

This is the crux: 'Perhaps the capitalists are mutual customers for the remainder of the commodities – not to use them carelessly, but to use them for the extension of production, for accumulation' (pp. 56–7). Here she is in line with Marx, the orthodox Marxist tradition, and also with modern post-Keynesian growth and cycle theories, but she rejects this possibility:

> All right, but such a solution only pushes the problem from this moment to the next . . . the increased production throws an even bigger amount of commodities onto the market the following year . . . [will] this growing amount of goods again be exchanged among the capitalists to extend production again, and so forth, year after year? Then we have the roundabout that revolves around itself in empty space. That is not capitalist accumulation i.e. the amassing of money capital, but its contrary: producing commodities for the sake of it; from the standpoint of capital an utter absurdity. (p. 57)

From this she draws the conclusion that there must be buyers outside capitalist relations of production.

What are we to make of this argument? Firstly, there is an implicit appeal to a teleological interpretation of capitalism which runs right through Rosa Luxemburg's treatment of accumulation. Production must have a purpose. We cannot have production for its own sake. This line of argument is surely misconceived. The essence of capitalism is that it is an anarchic (or, if you prefer, a decentralised) system. As a system it does not have, nor does it need, a purpose. Individual capitalists, workers' organisations of various sorts can have their own purposes (strategies, interests), but the system as a whole cannot. Individual capitalists accumulate (under favourable conditions) because they are forced to by the competitive struggle, something that she understands well enough in other contexts.

Secondly, she implies that if the surplus product is exchanged among capitalists for accumulation, then there is a continuous increase in the production of means of production somehow disconnected from consumption. This is incorrect; if productivity, the real wage rate and the proportion of surplus value accumulated all remain constant, then both workers' and capitalists' consumption will expand in line with total output. As capital accumulates, more workers will be employed and so there will be more spending on wage goods. At the same time, the amount of profit (surplus value) expands and, if a constant proportion is spent by the capitalists on consumption (or passed on to servants, charities, etc., to spend), then capitalists' spending will expand in line with accumulation. The whole system expands together. If these factors change, then the ratio of consumption to investment must change, but it does so in a determinate fashion. The rates of expansion of departments 1 and 2 (means of production and consumer goods) are not independent.

Thirdly, what of the need to accumulate money capital? Accumulation by capitalists must be clearly distinguished from hoarding by misers. Capitalists only accumulate money capital temporarily, in order to set it in motion as a functioning, profit-making capital. (This is what distinguishes money capital from idle hoards of money.) The conversion of surplus value into money is an essential intermediate stage in converting it into additional capital, but it is only a temporary stage, and there is no reason why all capitalists should seek to pass through this stage simultaneously. Provided some capitalists have additional funds (I will return to this condition), they can buy additional means of production (realising the surplus value of firms in department 1) and advance additional wages to new employees, which will be spent on the products of consumer goods industries, thus providing a further group of capitalists with money capital to spend on new investment and so on.

This leaves only the problem of where the initial money capital (which corresponds to the Keynesian finance demand for money) came from. Marx answers: from gold producers. Rosa Luxemburg complains that this explains the genesis of the money material for circulation, but not of money capital.

> Notice that we do not ask here, as Marx often does in the second volume of *Capital*: where does the money for the circulation of surplus value come from? to answer finally: from the gold miner. We ask rather: how does new money capital come into the pockets of the capitalists, since (apart from the workers) they are the only ones who can consume each other's commodities? (*Anti-Critique*, p. 72)

It is difficult to see what this criticism of Marx's solution amounts to. The gold producer exchanges his product for that of other capitalists, who have thereby realised their surplus value and acquired additional money capital, which is passed on when they spend it. In a modern monetary framework, of course, the additional money originates in part from the state and in part from the banking system through the bank multiplier. One suspects that Rosa Luxemburg would be even more suspicious of this as an answer.

Rosa Luxemburg's difficulty seems to arise from a confusion of levels of abstraction akin to her search for a 'purpose' of production. She insists that the problem of realisation must be examined on the level of the aggregate social capital, but she then treats the aggregate capital as though it were an individual capital among many which has to sell its products to others to accumulate money with which to buy commodities. She seems unwilling to recognise the difference between a system and a component element within a system.

Another question that she raises is: if surplus value can be realised within the system why should crises occur in which commodities cannot be sold? The answer is surely obvious: what has been shown is that it is possible for surplus value to be realised in this way, not that it necessarily will be. If new investment is expected to be profitable, it will be undertaken. If not, then investment will not take place, and the process breaks down. Again, she overlooks the anarchy of capitalist production; individual capitalists do not necessarily act in the interests of the system.

Joan Robinson, in her introduction to the *Accumulation*, suggests an interpretation of Rosa Luxemburg's arguments in terms of the possibility of deficient aggregate demand. Large parts of Rosa Luxemburg's writings can be interpreted in this way, but it is clear that her central theoretical emphasis is not on the possibility that capitalists might not choose to buy each other's products and thus enable the realisation of surplus value, but on the absurdity (in her eyes) of supposing that they could ever do so.

Fourthly, and lastly, we can ask what use non-capitalist buyers would be in solving what I have already argued is a non-problem. Once capitalists have converted surplus value into money capital, they must exchange the money for the elements of productive capital by buying additional means of production and employing additional workers who will in turn spend their wages on means of subsistence. Where are they to obtain these commodities from? If, following Rosa Luxemburg, we say that they cannot obtain these commodities by exchange within the system, then they must be obtained from non-capitalist sources. Either there must be pre-capitalist sellers of, for example, blast furnaces, machine tools, iron ore, computers, etc., or, following Bukharin's ironic suggestion, the capitalists must first sell these goods to non-capitalist buyers and then buy them back again. All this is clearly absurd.

In saying this, I do not deny that capitalism in fact trades with non-capitalist sections of the world economy. What Rosa Luxemburg argues is that it is specifically that part of the surplus which is destined to be reinvested that has to be exchanged with pre-capitalist producers. Trade outside the capitalist world is easily incorporated into the analysis (above) of exchange as a redistribution of the product between different branches of the economy. Where there is external trade, some part of the product is exported and goods equivalent in value take its place by being imported. So, for example, Britain in the nineteenth century produced more cotton textiles than were consumed domestically, but did not produce raw cotton. The one was exchanged for the other. Trade thus (abstracting from any inequality of exchange) alters the commodity mix of the 'pile' of products (using Luxemburg's metaphor) but not its value.

There are, however, other points arising from Rosa Luxemburg's work. In *The Accumulation of Capital*, she argues that Marx's schema of expanded reproduction cannot incorporate an increasing organic composition of capital. She deduces that there will be a shortage of means of production, and hence that non-capitalist suppliers of means of production are needed. Against this we can argue first that, as has been suggested above, there is no reason to believe that pre-capitalist systems could provide appropriate means of production for a modern industrial system, and second (and more substantively) that the difficulty arises only because Marx had picked figures specifically to illustrate the case of a constant organic composition of capital. Critics of Rosa Luxemburg immediately produced examples in which this difficulty did not arise, and she effectively conceded their point in the *Anti-Critique* (p. 48) in arguing the irrelevance of numerical or mathematical examples of the sort which she herself had relied on in the earlier work.

Rosa Luxemburg, along with Marx himself, gets into some difficulties in constructing numerical schemas of expanded reproduction by insisting that the surplus value of department 1 must be reinvested within that department, and similarly for department 2. She has a long and vitriolic attack (in the *Anti-Critique*) on Bauer for assuming a transfer of capital (which she interprets as a 'gift') from one department to another. It is, however, clear that the equalisation of profit rates requires free mobility of capital between sectors. I would argue, incidentally, that the analysis of transactions between sectors would be much more appropriately conducted in terms of prices of production than in labour value terms, since goods are actually exchanged at market prices.

She does raise some real problems about the commodity mix of output. Not only does the value of the product have to be matched by a corresponding value of spending, but the composition of output – the proportion of means of production, means of subsistence and so on – has to be right. So long as the proportions are right to start with and the system expands steadily then one can show that the proportions will remain right, even, as noted above, with an increasing organic composition of capital. This does not, of course, solve the problem in practice. Rosa Luxemburg is quite right to stress that capitalist production does not expand evenly and predictably, while it is also true that in some circumstances relatively small initial disproportions can grow into major ones so long as we insist on all of the product being used (see Morishima, 1973, chapter 10, for an example). Here again we step outside the orderly world of the schemas of reproduction. I shall touch on some of these issues in the next section, but will comment here, firstly, that capitalist firms normally carry stocks and retain some spare capacity, thus providing an elasticity that the schemas do not allow for, secondly, that in the real world there are recurrent crises which offer the opportunity of restructuring production, and, thirdly, that trade with non-capitalist sectors may sometimes help (if there is, say, a shortage of raw cotton) and sometimes not (if the shortage is, say, of blast furnaces).

II The process of capitalist expansion

If Rosa Luxemburg was wrong in arguing that capitalism needs a non-capitalist environment in which to grow, she was surely right to stress that it not only originated in such an environment, but remained surrounded by it up to her time (and even up to the present day):

> Capitalism arises and develops historically amidst a non-capitalist society. In Western Europe it is found at first in a feudal environment from which it in fact sprang . . . and later, after having swallowed up the feudal system, it exists mainly in an environment of peasants and artisans. . . . European capitalism is further surrounded by vast territories of non-European civilisation ranging over all levels of development. . . . This is the setting for the accumulation of capital. (*Accumulation*, p. 368)

These two sections of the world economy, capitalist and non-capitalist, do not live side by side in a state of peaceful co-existence. Rosa Luxemburg sees non-capitalist modes of production as essentially static: the equilibrium is not disturbed from that side. Capitalism, however, is driven into constant expansion:

Moreover, capitalist production, by its very nature, cannot be restricted to such means of production as are produced by capitalist methods. Cheap elements of constant capital are essential to the individual capitalist who strives to increase his rate of profit. . . . From the very beginning, the forms and laws of capitalist production aim to comprise the entire globe as a store of productive forces. Capital, impelled to appropriate productive forces for purposes of exploitation, ransacks the whole world, it procures its means of production from all corners of the earth, seizing them, if necessary by force, from all levels of civilisation and from all forms of society. (p. 358)

As well as seizing means of production wherever they are to be found, capital is also always on the lookout for labour power, and the geographical spread of capitalism has its implications for the sources of labour power, too.

Since capitalist production can develop fully only with complete access to all territories and climes, . . . it must be able to mobilise world labour power without restriction. This labour power, however, is in most cases rigidly bound by the traditional pre-capitalist organisation of production. It must first be 'set free' in order to be enrolled in the active army of capital. (p. 362)

Unfortunately, in the *Anti-Critique*, she rather went back on this line of argument (which is surely a good one, at least in terms of explaining the historical facts) when, attacking Bauer, she vigorously rejected his explanation of imperialism as a search for labour power, on the grounds that capitalism necessarily produces a massive and growing reserve army of labour in its homelands.

The arguments set out above are not, of course, wholly new; they are essentially the same as those of Marx which have already been discussed. In his earlier works Marx stressed the world-wide expansion of capitalism and this remained a constant theme in his writings, but it was to some degree pushed into the background in *Capital* by the theoretical task of analysing a pure capitalist mode of production. Rosa Luxemburg's importance is in bringing this aspect of Marx's thinking back into the limelight. She is surely right to argue that, in the real history of capitalism, the expansion of capitalist relations of production is one of the most important, perhaps the most important, process at work.

She then develops another line of argument. Capital can do things in the colonies that it could not get away with at home, and this gives it an elasticity and capacity to respond to events that it would not otherwise possess. Her example is the creation of 'immense' cotton plantations in Egypt during the 'cotton famine' caused by the American civil war:

> Only capital with its technical resources can effect such miraculous change in so short a time – but only on the pre-capitalist soil of more primitive social conditions can it develop the ascendancy necessary to achieve such miracles. (*Accumulation*, p. 358)

Here there is clearly some conception of the political and ideological conditions necessary for accumulation, but these are not spelt out in any systematic way.

Overall, Luxemburg's analysis is not really very sophisticated in the concepts used. In particular she deals, as many Marxists have done, in a single and undifferentiated concept of 'capital', without any clear specification of the stages of development which capitalism goes through, of the possible divergent interests of particular individual capitals or sectors or of the political mechanisms by which the interests of 'capital' are translated into policies of particular national states. In this her work represents a step backwards from Marx, who was very careful about these distinctions.

As Rey has noted, in her description of the pre-capitalist societies into which capitalism expands, there is a similar lack of distinctions, and a lack of analysis of the internal workings of these societies.

Pre-capitalist societies, for Rosa Luxemburg, are essentially covered by the category of 'natural economies'. A natural economy, in this context, means a system of local self-sufficiency, of production for direct use, rather than for commodity exchange. I have already discussed Marx's analysis of the resistance of such forms of economy to penetration by commodity trade. Rosa Luxemburg puts forward similar arguments:

> In all social organisations where natural economy prevails, . . . economic organisation is essentially in response to the internal demand; and therefore there is no demand, or very little for foreign goods, and also, as a rule, no surplus production, or at least no urgent need to dispose of surplus products. What is more important, however, is that, in any natural economy, production only goes on because both means of production and labour power are bound in one form or another. . . . A natural economy thus confronts the requirements of capitalism at every turn with rigid barriers. Capitalism must therefore always and everywhere fight a

battle of annihilation against every historical form of natural
economy. (*Accumulation*, pp. 368–9)

In this passage, and elsewhere, there is a direct identification of natural
economy with pre-capitalist organisation, with only simple commodity
production as an intermediate stage. Everything is subordinated to her
vision of a world divided between the ever-expanding domain of capital
and the surrounding 'medium and soil' of static, closed natural
economies, with a fringe of pre-capitalist societies in the process of
dissolution marking the boundaries. This is surely too simple. As she
recognises herself, capitalism in its expansion incorporates other forms of
organisation into its own world economy (slavery, bondage of various
forms), while at the same time, pre-capitalist forms of organisation (the
feudal *corvée* farm, to quote her own example) have, at various stages,
traded their surplus product on a large scale: a point she recognises
herself (p. 357). I shall discuss these issues in later chapters (see chapter
11), simply noting here that Luxemburg's own grasp of the real
historical process comes into a certain conflict with her attempts to
reduce it to the results of a single driving force, the accumulation of
capital.

How is the 'struggle against natural economy' carried out?
Luxemburg lists four ends pursued by capital:

(1) To gain immediate possession of important sources of
productive forces such as land, game in primeval forests, minerals,
precious stones and ores, products of exotic flora such as rubber,
etc.
(2) To 'liberate' labour power and to coerce it into service.
(3) To introduce a commodity economy.
(4) To separate trade and agriculture. (*Accumulation*, p. 369)

These fall into two groups. The first two together represent ways in
which a natural economy can be forced directly into capitalist production
(cf. Marx on primitive accumulation). The second two represent a more
indirect route in which simple commodity production is installed and
then undermined either directly, by means (1) and (2), or by competition
with the cheap products of capitalist industry.

Throughout, her emphasis is on the use of force, state power and
fraud. In this she follows Marx's treatment of primitive accumulation.
She says:

At the time of primitive accumulation, i.e. at the end of the

Middle ages . . . right into the nineteenth century . . .
dispossessing the peasant was the most striking weapon. Yet capital
in power performs the same task even today, and on an even more
important scale – by modern colonial policy . . . Accumulation can
no more wait for and be content with, a natural internal
disintegration of non-capitalist formations . . . than it can wait for
the natural increase of the working population. Force is the only
solution open to capital: the accumulation of capital, seen as an
historical process, employs force as a permanent weapon, not only
at its genesis, but further on down to the present day.
(*Accumulation*, pp. 369–71)

Her development of these themes is by means of examples; I will
survey them very briefly. Her discussion of India is rather disappointing
in its vagueness on critical points, but the story seems to be that the
British first set out to transform land into private property, and then to
ruin the producers by overtaxation, neglect of public works, etc., so as to
force them into debt and take over their lands. This is a process which
recurs in other cases, and seems to be a major route, in her view, by
which pre-capitalist formations are undermined. She seems, incidentally,
to have been unaware of Marx's writings on India, which present a
rather more complex picture in which British industrial capital wishes
simultaneously to break up the Indian village community and to promote
the prosperity of India in order to enlarge the market for British
products.

Her chapter on 'the introduction of commodity economy' is distinctly
disappointing; the only real example is the introduction by force of the
opium trade into China. This must be rather a special case, since it was
the addictive nature of the commodity, not force, that ensured it a
market, while the force was directed at the Chinese state, and not at the
'natural economy' of the Chinese villagers.

She then goes on to discuss the separation of industry from agriculture
under the title of 'the struggle against peasant economy', giving a very
interesting description of the evolution of American agriculture from the
self-sufficient peasant agriculture of the pioneer settlers on the frontier.
She describes the process thus: 'It is a recurrent phenomenon in the
development of capitalist production that one branch of industry after the
other is singled out, isolated from agriculture, and concentrated in
factories for mass production' (*Accumulation*, p. 395). The analysis of
this process turns out, however, to be rather difficult to fit in to her

general framework. The problem is that if a peasant household chooses to remain self-sufficient, producing the goods it consumes itself, there are really only two options: either they must be left alone, or they must be expelled altogether. Direct legal compulsion to produce only a limited range of cash crops, though it has been used in some colonies, was not of significance in the American case.

What, in fact, brings about the separation of agriculture from industry while still leaving behind an agricultural peasant class is the availability of cheap industrial products which induce the peasant to specialise, rather than forcing this specialisation. She is generally reluctant to admit to the material superiority of capitalist methods of production, in which she stands in contrast to Marx who always stressed the dual character of capitalism, at once brutal and progressive. Luxemburg does, of course, describe the cheapness of the products of capitalist industry, the massive scale of its works, the enormous transformations that it has made, but always in such a way as to stress the brutality behind it rather than the technical achievements, where Marx always stressed both. This characteristic of her thought reflects the general opinion among Marxists at the time that capitalism was coming to an end and that it had ceased to be a progressive force and had become, rather, a fetter on the development of the forces of production. The enormous development of production in the sixty-five years since then suggests that this was an over-simple view.

The other main means she discusses is the use of money taxes to force peasants to sell products. This is certainly an important method, but it forces the peasant to sell, not buy (it is the recipients of tax revenue who do the buying), and it does not, therefore, explain how markets are created among the peasantry, or how they are forced to specialise.

At the same time she describes how overtaxation, indebtedness, foreclosure of mortgages and so on were used to separate the American peasant from the land. This process leads, of course, to capitalist agriculture rather than to the separation of industry from a peasant agriculture.

Rosa Luxemburg's analysis focuses on the distinction between capitalist and non-capitalist modes of production and not on differences or conflicts between nation states. This focus is what gives the analysis its distinctive character and constitutes a large part of its importance. To deal with the developments of her own time (the run-up to the First World War), she clearly has to link her work to the system of national states. I will not spend long on this aspect of her writing, since there is less of interest in it, and much of it depends on the arguments about realisation of surplus value that I have already dismissed as false.

The main ways in which the state intervenes, apart from those described already, are through organising international loans, through imposing protective tariffs and through armaments expenditure. Her basic argument is that since non-capitalist markets are necessary to the existence of capitalism, and since they are becoming scarce relative to the massive volume of surplus value to be realised, there is a struggle between capitalist states to establish spheres of interest and to bind them with protective tariffs to the 'mother country', in order to ensure a sufficiency of markets for the capitalists of the state concerned. This argument loses most of its force if, as I have argued, the need for external markets is illusory. Her second line of argument remains; the struggle for cheap raw materials, labour, etc., can explain inter-imperialist rivalry. This is, in fact, a component of the arguments of Bukharin and Lenin (chapter 5). Her analysis remains weak, however, because the connections between competing capitals and competing states are not spelled out; this was the question Bukharin focused on.

International loans, she argues, serve as a way of reducing backward, but nominally independent, states (her example is Turkey) to servitude, though they can also serve to finance the initial development of young capitalist states. More important, she argues, is their function in financing the infrastructure (particularly railways and other means of transport) which is needed to incorporate new areas into the capitalist sphere, and simultaneously in providing a method by which capital originating in the old centres of capitalism can participate in the exploitation of new areas. She gives the example of German loans to Turkey, in which tax revenue originating in pre-capitalist agriculture is paid over as interest to German capitalists who have made loans to finance railway construction. This emphasis on the interlinking of capitalist and non-capitalist forms of exploitation is a valuable contribution.

III Summary

Rosa Luxemburg's work remains of seminal importance, despite its analytical failings. At a time when there was a danger that Marxist thought would focus on the advanced sectors of industry in the advanced countries, she forced Marxists to pay attention to the masses of people who were in the process of being incorporated into the capitalist mode of production, or who still remained outside it. These were, and still are, the majority of the world's population. In this, her work runs parallel to that of Lenin (in *The Development of Capitalism in Russia* and, above all, in his political practice; not in his *Imperialism*), who was in many other respects her opponent.

Her real contribution, then, is to insist that the mechanisms of primitive accumulation, with the concomitant use of force, fraud and state power, are not simply a regrettable aspect of capitalism's past, but persist throughout the history of capitalism at the margin where capitalist and pre-capitalist economic systems meet. This margin is not geographic but social, it exists within countries rather than between them, and if the capitalist form of organisation has triumphed completely in a few places (England, for example), the unequal struggle still goes on in vast areas of the world.

Part II

Classical Marxist theories of imperialism and inter-imperialist rivalry

4 · Hilferding

I The concept of imperialism

Between 1900 and 1920, the term *imperialism* was introduced into Marxist theory, and a systematic concept and theory of imperialism emerged. Three writers, Rudolf Hilferding, Nicolai Bukharin and Vladimir Ilych Lenin, are primarily responsible for this. I shall call their theories the 'classical Marxist theories of imperialism', since I use the term 'classical Marxist' to denote the Marxist writers from Marx himself down to Lenin and Trotsky, and Marx, as we have seen, did not use the term imperialism.

The contributions of these three writers are not easy to separate. Hilferding came first, and his massive *Finance Capital* contains almost every major point made by the others. One could, therefore, argue that he deserves the real credit. He did not, however, put these arguments together into a definite concept of imperialism. Bukharin, in my view, deserves the credit for this. In his *Imperialism and World Economy* he transformed Hilferding's picture of developments inside the advanced capitalist countries into a coherent theory of the transformation of the world economy. I shall argue that Lenin's contribution, in his *Imperialism, the Highest Stage of Capitalism*, was primarily to popularise the theories of Hilferding and Bukharin.

The judgments I have made about the contributions of these writers are based solely on their published work. The period before the First World War was one of unprecedented creative ferment in Marxist circles, both in Vienna and Berlin, where Hilferding worked, and among Russian *émigrés*. Ideas were in the air, especially about imperialism, and their original sources may be hard to trace. Bukharin and Lenin, especially, worked almost simultaneously, and were very close to each other politically and intellectually. To sort out the real author of some of their ideas would be a research project in itself.

It is easy to misunderstand the classical Marxist theories of imperialism, since the very word 'imperialism' has expanded and altered its meaning since then. Today, the term imperialism is generally taken to refer to the dominance of more developed over less developed countries. For the classical Marxists it meant, primarily, rivalry between advanced capitalist countries, rivalry expressed in conflict over territory, taking political and military as well as economic forms, and tending, ultimately, to inter-imperialist war.

The dominance of the stronger countries over the weaker is certainly implicit in this conception, but the focus is on the struggle for dominance, a struggle between the strongest in which the less developed countries figure mainly as passive battlegrounds and not as active participants.

The classical Marxists have often been accused of Eurocentrism, and the charge is, to a fair extent, justified. Their concentration on the most advanced countries reflected the political realities of the times. Hilferding wrote during the build up to the First World War, Bukharin and Lenin after the war had started. It was of central importance for the socialist movement to hammer out a policy towards the war. All three regarded socialist revolution in the advanced countries as the necessary route towards socialism and the precondition for advance in less developed areas.

All three of the writers named saw themselves as up-dating Marx to take account of a development that had taken place since Marx's time (though Marx had predicted it), the rise of *monopoly*. In this they differ from Rosa Luxemburg, who did not draw any important distinctions between different stages in the development of capitalism, and who saw herself as correcting what she thought was a mistake by Marx.

There is another point of terminology that should be emphasised here to avoid misunderstanding. The term 'monopoly' in bourgeois economics is used to mean a single seller who has no rival within a given market. In the Marxist tradition, however, 'monopoly' refers to any major departure from free competition. Where there are relatively few producers, then, we can speak of a growth of monopoly, and this does not exclude very fierce competition. Competition, in this case, does not take the form of price competition in a relatively impersonal market, as it does for competitive capitalism, but is instead a direct rivalry which can take a great variety of forms.

II Monopoly capital

Hilferding's major work is *Finance Capital** (Hilferding, 1970, cited below as *FC*), largely written around 1905 in Vienna, but not completed and published until 1910, by which time he was living arid working in Germany. It is mainly concerned with the internal development of advanced capitalist countries. I will have to examine this aspect of his work, since it is basic to his treatment of imperialism as well as to much work by subsequent writers. At the same time, I cannot give it the full discussion it deserves, since it falls rather outside the scope of this book.

He starts from an interesting, but rather eccentric, treatment of the theory of money, a topic which I will pass over entirely here, only remarking that the obscurity of this first part of the book may well be one reason why the work as a whole has been treated with a kind of respectful neglect.

The next major topic in his argument is the rise of the joint stock company as a new form of organisation for the capitalist firm. A joint stock company is, in effect, a kind of coalition of capitalists who share in the profits and in the control of the firm in proportion to their holding of 'shares' in the firm. Hilferding's treatment of the joint stock company, although it has some points in common with Marx's very fragmentary comments on the subject (*Capital*, III, chapter 27, pp. 427 ff.), is really the first serious treatment of this very important topic in the Marxist tradition.

Hilferding emphasises that the formation of joint stock companies represents a modification of the function of the capitalist. The previous form of organisation, the individual enterprise, was limited in size by its owner's wealth, and could only grow in so far as the individual capitalist saved his profits and ploughed them back. The joint stock company can assemble capital from many small shareholders. This permits an enormous acceleration in the *centralisation* of capital, the amalgamation of many capitals into one. At the same time, personal wealth ownership may be concentrated into fewer hands by the opportunities for swindling and speculation in shares, and the manipulations which holders of controlling blocks of shares can carry out. In any case, what Hilferding really stresses is the opportunity for owners of large blocks of capital to use the joint stock form of organisation to gain control of the capital of

---

*Page references are to the French translation throughout, but quotations are translated from the original. I would like to thank Karen Snodin for help with translations.

many small shareholders. Whatever its effects on the concentration of personal wealth, the rise of the joint stock company represents a massive concentration of economic power as well as a concentration of production. This was a fairly common theme among left-wing writers of the time; it was, after all, the time when magnates like Rockefeller and Carnegie were demonstrating the full possibilities of these financial manipulations in practical terms.

All of this has to be set in the context of the process of concentration and centralisation of capital, in which small capitals are driven out by larger capitals, generating a tendency to monopoly. This is, of course, central to Marx's work and to virtually all subsequent Marxist thought. The development of the joint stock company simply accelerated a process already at work. These developments were very visible in the main capitalist countries at the time, and especially in Germany and Central Europe. Hilferding discusses the different forms which the centralisation of capital can take in considerable detail.

The rise of monopoly in one sector has consequences for other sectors which deal with it, creating 'relations of mutual dependence and dominance'. In a competitive system where each firm has many potential suppliers and customers, it can be relatively indifferent to the policies of any single firm. Where the firm has only a few customers or suppliers it cannot be indifferent; a relation of mutual dependence grows up. As long as the firms that deal with each other are independent, there will be a struggle for dominance, since there are direct conflicts of interest between them (over the price at which they trade, for example). Hilferding asserts that: 'In the relations of mutual dependence between capitalist enterprises, it is financial strength which determines which enterprises will become dependent on others' (*FC*, p. 315).

In particular, where a relatively competitive industry deals with a monopoly or cartel, it will fall under the control of the monopoly and the competitive firms will be reduced to the status of mere agents, unless they react by forming their own cartel or amalgamating in self-defence. In either case the monopolised sector of the economy will be effectively expanded. Monopoly is thus, in a sense, contagious; beyond a certain stage it tends to spread very rapidly.

It was this process of rapid spread of monopoly, and, accompanying it, the tight linking together of different sectors of the economy by direct relations of interdependence and dominance (in place of impersonal market links), which Hilferding regarded as the fundamental force behind the transformation of capitalism which was going on at the time.

III Finance capital

For Hilferding, the central actors in the growth of monopoly were the banks. I have omitted all mention of banks from the previous section in order to show that the main lines of Hilferding's account of the transition to the monopoly stage of capitalism do not depend on his theory of the role of the banks. This theory is dubious because it was based on the German case, where the banks did play a central role, whereas in other countries essentially the same results came about in rather different ways.

The main function of banks is to centralise money capital, gathering together idle funds (capitalists' reserves, depreciation funds, etc., as well as the savings of other social strata). On the principle of 'pooled reserves' most of the money can then be re-lent for productive (profitable) use, with only a relatively small portion held in cash as reserves. In Germany, banks carried out a wide range of other functions, acting on behalf of their customers in the buying and selling of shares, for example, so that they effectively controlled all the sources of money capital and thus, as a group, had enormous potential power. As long as banking was relatively competitive this made little difference; if one bank refused a loan there were others to turn to. However, the banks were in the forefront of the tendency towards monopoly, and in Germany the number of major banks fell to nine and then to six. (See Bukharin, 1972a, p. 71; Lenin, 1950, pp. 210 ff. Hilferding only gives factual detail in passing: e.g. *FC*, p. 181n.)

Given a rapid development of monopoly in banks together with the concentration in the banking system of control over all major sources of finance, it is easy to see how banks came to play a dominant role in the tightly interconnected, hierarchical capitalist system that Hilferding described.

The banks, in turn, have a strong interest in promoting cartelisation among their clients, since this reduces the risk that the firms to whom they have lent money will go bankrupt. They also have a strong interest in promoting mergers so that the centralisation of capital can go ahead, with the weaker firms absorbed by the stronger (safeguarding the bank's money) rather than being driven to the wall by competition.

This is the context of Hilferding's concept of *finance capital*, undoubtedly his best-known contribution to the vocabulary of Marxism. Marx analysed the division of capital into three fractions: *industrial capital* (productive enterprises, including capitalist agricultural enterprises), *financial capital* (banks and similar capitalist enterprises dealing in money capital), and *commercial capital* (merchant's capital; buying and selling goods rather than producing them). Hilferding argues that the separation of industrial and financial capital, which was characteristic of the era of competitive capitalism, disappears in the epoch of monopoly capitalism. *Finance capital is the product of the fusion of industrial and financial capital.* It is therefore vital not to confuse finance capital with financial capital.

He argues that as bank deposits grow and opportunities for investment in commerce decline (because of the *krise* of monopolies which take direct control of buying and selling activities), the banks are effectively forced into investing directly in production.

> The dependence of industry on the banks is . . . the consequence of property relations. A growing fraction of the capital of industry does not belong to the industrial capitalists who use it. They only get the use of it through the bank, which stands to them in the relation of a proprietor. On the other hand, the bank has to fix an increasing proportion of its funds in industry, and thus becomes, to an increasing extent, an industrial capitalist. *I call bank capital, consequently capital in money form, which is in this way transformed in practice into industrial capital, finance capital.* (*FC*, pp. 317–18, emphasis added)

The concept of finance capital, as Hilferding presents it, is not entirely unambiguous. At a very simple level it is a label for that part of the total capital which comes into the hands of industrial capital via the banks or, more generally, via the financial system. Hilferding frequently uses it, however, to indicate a unit of control: that part of a (capitalist) economy which is under the control of the banks. Perhaps the way of looking at it which best covers the way Hilferding and his successors have used the term, is to understand 'finance capital' as that fraction of capital in which the functions of financial capital and industrial capital are effectively united, in which the assembly of funds from a variety of sources is carried out by the same enterprise as that which effectively controls the productive use of these funds.

If this generalisation of the concept is accepted, it opens the way to regarding the large multi-national companies of today as part of finance capital. These companies are certainly not under the control of banks, but their head offices do perform many of the functions of financial capital in raising money from many sources (including small shareholders, by means of share issues), and also channel flows of capital from one subsidiary enterprise to another. Hilferding recognises the analogy between joint stock companies and banks, in that both can assemble a large capital from many sources (*FC*, p. 183).

If we are to speak of an epoch dominated by finance capital it is essential to widen the concept and free it of its association with the dominance of banks, since this was not characteristic of all advanced capitalist countries. Hilferding recognises that the role of the banks was rather different in England, where banks only gave credit for circulation and did not finance long-term capital investments. The result was a low interest rate on bank deposits, with the public buying shares via the stock exchange. Industry was therefore less dependent on the banks (see *FC*, p. 317).

He explains the greater dominance of the banking system in Germany, probably correctly, by the later and more rapid development of capitalism in Germany. In England, wealth became concentrated into the hands of industrial capitalists over a long period of time. German industrialists, to catch up, had to draw on the savings of other classes through the banks and through the formation of joint stock companies (*FC*, p. 414). This explanation should, perhaps, be taken a step further: the slower pace of development in England, together with the development of parts of the financial structure during the period of the dominance of merchant's capital, led to the emergence of a more varied financial system in which the various financial functions, united in the banks in Germany, were carried out by different parts of financial capital (stockbrokers, merchant banks, clearing banks, etc.).

There is no doubt that the whole process of concentration and centralisation was somewhat retarded in Britain. This has substantial implications (since Britain, the least monopolised of the great powers, had the largest empire), but the explanation is probably fairly simple: it is the competitive struggle that enforces the centralisation of capital. Given Britain's relative lead in industry, the pressure of competition, eliminating the weakest firms, was felt less than in slightly less developed countries.

This section is best summed up in Hilferding's words:

> Finance capital marks the unification of capital. The previously
> distinct spheres of industrial capital, commercial capital and bank
> capital are henceforth under the control of high finance, in which
> the magnates of industry and the banks are closely associated. This

association, which is founded on the suppression of competition between capitalists by the great monopolistic combines, has, of course, the effect of changing the relations between the capitalist class and the state. (*FC*, p. 407)

IV Protectionism and economic territory

Protective tariffs, that is taxes on goods imported into a territory, placing them at a disadvantage relative to domestically produced goods, play a crucial role in Hilferding's arguments. This may seem surprising, since tariffs are often, today, regarded as rather trivial and boring things best left for specialists to debate. It is necessary to remind ourselves that the triumph of industrial capital in England was marked by the abolition of the Corn Laws, a form of protection for agriculture, and that protectionism versus free trade was the major issue of economic policy in all the advanced capitalist countries at the time Hilferding was writing. 'With developed capitalist production, there is no doubt that free trade would unify the entire world market, guaranteeing the maximum possible productivity of labour and the most rational international division of labour' (*FC*, p. 421). It is interesting to note, in passing, Hilferding's almost naive faith in the efficiency of free trade; it corresponds to a typical classical Marxist belief in the efficiency of capitalism in developing the forces of production. It would not be shared by many contemporary Marxists.

Hilferding, like Luxemburg, stresses the pressure in a capitalist system to make the maximum possible use of the different natural conditions and resources to be found in different parts of the world, and the importance of large-scale operations in reducing costs. Capitalists must always seek, therefore, to maximise the territory open to them for their operations.

The importance of tariffs is that they define a distinct national territory. With free trade the advantages of operating in a large, rather than small, national territory would be minimal (knowledge of national customs and tastes, etc.), but once protective tariffs are established to diminish the scope for the international division of labour, the size of the national territory is much more important. Small countries (he cites Belgium) are generally in favour of free trade.

Why then should tariffs be imposed? Limitations on trade are important in the earliest stages of capitalism, when they are part of the whole apparatus of state intervention sought by monopolistic commercial capital. In the epoch dominated by competitive industrial capital, 'infant industries' seek tariffs to enable themselves to get started protected from foreign competition. England, as the first industrial nation, had no need of tariffs for this reason, and was therefore the protagonist of free trade, but as other countries (the USA, Germany, etc.) followed in industrial development, they felt the need for infant industry tariffs.

Hilferding argues that, if successful, these infant industry tariffs are self-liquidating in competitive capitalism since, if the industry develops to the stage of exporting, the exported goods will have to be sold at the world market price and competition will ensure that the price on the home market matches the export price. If the home market price were above the export price, firms would switch their production to the more profitable home market until the differential was eliminated. Once home and foreign prices are equalised, the tariff is ineffective.

The rise of monopoly transforms the role of tariffs. Hilferding's arguments rely critically on the idea that it is much easier to monopolise a national market for a particular product than it is to monopolise the world market. He argues this mainly on the grounds that a much higher degree of concentration of capital than that yet achieved would be needed for cartelisation to be possible on a world scale, as well as that 'the solidity of cartels would be smaller in this case' and that there would be resistance to foreign based cartels. These are not very strong arguments, at least as Hilferding puts them (*FC*, p. 423), and it seems that he does not realise how crucial they are to his whole argument.

He tends to take it for granted that cartels must form on a national basis, perhaps because the whole focus of his work is on a single national economy. It was Bukharin, for whom the subject of study was the *world* economy, who really saw that this was a problem. Both Bukharin and Lenin devoted more attention to the possibility of cartelisation on a world scale because they wished to refute Kautsky's theory of 'ultra-imperialism', a topic I will take up in the next chapter.

Given the impossibility of monopolising the world market, tariff protection is necessary for trusts or cartels formed on a national basis to get any advantage from their monopoly position. Without protection, imports would pour in and undercut the monopoly as soon as the price was pushed above the price level in the world market. (In practice, transport costs would give some small margin of protection without tariffs, but Hilferding generally assumes that these are pretty small.)

The extent to which a national monopoly can raise the price above the world market price is directly determined by the tariff, up to the monopoly price level which they would set if the market were completely isolated. Thus monopolies and finance capital have a direct interest in increasing the level of protection. The late nineteenth and early twentieth centuries, the period of the rise of monopoly, also saw protectionism become much more widespread, after a period in the mid-nineteenth century when the tendency was, rather hesitantly, towards free trade.

It should be pointed out here that this analysis of tariffs was not original to Hilferding. It was hinted at by Engels, and was widely discussed in the economic literature of Hilferding's time. Hilferding's contribution is to place it in a Marxist analysis of the rise of finance capital. (See the references in Bukharin, 1972a, p. 75, n.2.)

Hilferding's argument that monopolies seek tariff protection only applies to particular sectors. If a tariff is imposed on all goods, and if their prices rise correspondingly (prices of imported goods rise because the tariff is actually paid, home market prices of exported goods rise because of the scope for monopoly price fixing created by the tariff) then wages will, in a Marxist framework, have to rise in money terms to keep the real wage (together with the value of labour power) the same. Monopoly profits, in Hilferding's framework, are a redivision of surplus value, increasing the profit of the monopolies at the expense of remaining competitive sectors.

Hilferding is not very consistent on this point. He talks of the price increases resulting from cartelisation and protection as 'a tribute imposed on consumers as a whole' and not 'a deduction from the profit of other non-cartelised industries' (*FC*, p. 417). He also argues that heavy industry is not very concerned about increases in the cost of living because labour costs are relatively unimportant given the high organic composition of capital (p. 418). This will not really do, since wage increases will affect the price of the means of production used by heavy industry as well as their direct labour costs. He does, on the other hand, consider the possibility that protectionism may reduce the overall rate of profit through the reduction in efficiency which follows from a reduction in the international division of labour. The fact is that Hilferding does not have a complete theory of wages, or of prices and profits, in an economy where both monopoly and external prices modified by tariffs are affecting price levels. This cannot really be held against him, since I know of no one else who has such a theory.

We have seen that tariffs on exported (or potentially exported) goods are ineffective in a competitive industry. For a monopolised industry, however, they are not ineffective, because a monopoly can sell at different prices in different markets. Where there are many firms, they will each divert supplies into the high price market because each reckons its own effect on the price to be negligible. A monopoly, on the other hand, can act deliberately to hold up the price on the home market. Prices are no longer determined by impersonal market forces, but are, within limits, under the deliberate control of monopoly organisations.

To push up the price in the home market, the monopoly (cartel, trust or whatever) must restrict the amount sold, since at a higher price consumers will buy less. The surplus can be sold on the world market at whatever price it will fetch, provided that the price is enough to cover costs. Given that costs fall with increasing output, what is relevant is that the price should be enough to cover the extra cost of producing the extra output, and this will be lower than the average cost of producing the whole output. (See any standard economics textbook on average cost, marginal cost and discriminating monopoly.)

It may, therefore, pay a monopoly to sell in the world market at a price below the average cost of production, not just to get rid of a temporary surplus, but as a regular practice. An example may make this clear. Suppose that the cost of producing 100 units is $100, and of producing 200 units, $150. The average cost of 100 units is thus $1 per unit, and of 200 units is $0.75 per unit. Now consider the pattern of sales set out in the table.

home market :	sales 100 units,	price $1.50:	receipts $150
export market :	sales 100 units,	price $0.60:	receipts $ 60
total:	sales 200 units,		total receipts $210

Selling on the home market alone would bring a profit of $50 (revenue of $150, cost of $100). The export of 100 units has brought in extra revenue of $60 and increased costs by $50, increasing profit to $60 ($210—$150), despite the fact that the 100 exported units have been sold at below the average cost of producing all 200 units ($0.60 compared with average cost of $0.75).

Still using the same example, consider now an enterprise without a protected home market which has to sell all of its output at the world market price. If it too had an output of 200 units, then it would be operating at a loss: receipts of $120 and costs of $150; loss of $30. It is true that a sufficiently large enterprise might be able to overcome this disadvantage (say: output 600, cost $300), but it is clear that enterprises which have a protected home market and monopoly control over it are at an enormous advantage in the competitive struggle for survival in the world market.

Hilferding therefore argues that: 'the function of protectionism has been completely transformed. From a means of defence against the conquest of the home market by foreign industries, it has become a means of conquest of external markets by the national industry' (*FC*, p. 419). Possession of a protected home market becomes a necessity for survival, and the larger the home market, the larger the advantage gained by the national industry.

It may be asked: if all countries protect their markets, where is this 'world market' or 'external market' to be found? Hilferding does not give a clear answer to this. It seems that he assumed an incomplete development of protection, leaving large sections of the world unprotected, to constitute a world market. It could also be pointed out that if monopolies take full advantage of the tariff to raise their price, then foreign goods can still penetrate the protected home market. To continue the example given above, if the world market price is $0.60 and the tariff, per unit, $0.90, then a domestic monopolist can sell at $1.50, but a foreign supplier could also sell at $1.50, pay the $0.90 in customs duty and receive a net revenue of $0.60, just as if he had sold in an unprotected part of the world market. Each country's home territory is thus part of the world market for its competitors. (The figures given assume an unrealistically high level of protection, for the sake of clarity.)

> We have seen that protectionism assures a super-profit to the capitalist monopoly on its sales in the internal market. The larger the economic territory and the sales in the home market . . . the larger is the resulting profit of the cartel. The larger the profit, the larger the discount that can be given on exports and as a result the cartel's competitive position in the world market will be strengthened. (*FC*, p. 424)

It should be stressed, to avoid misunderstanding, that Hilferding does not argue that the advanced *country* exploits its *colonies* by monopolistic pricing. He argues that monopolies exploit all consumers within the territory that they control, whether these consumers live in the metropolitan areas or in the colonies. The relation of exploitation is a *class* relation, and not a national one, and protectionism, by supporting monopoly, serves the interests of a ruling class, and specifically of a section of that class, finance capital.

It is thus protectionism that divides the world into distinct national economic territories, and it is the rise of monopoly which impels protectionism to new heights.

We have already got a basis for a theory of imperialism (though Hilferding adduces further arguments, which I will discuss in the next section). To quote him:

> Finance capital thus pursues three objectives: firstly, to create the largest possible economic territory, which, secondly, should be protected by high tariff barriers against foreign competition and which is, thirdly, reserved for the national monopoly combines. (*FC*, p. 440)

V Capital export

The international movement of capital arose on a really large scale around the 1870s, and reached a peak in the years immediately before the First World War. It was never again to reach such levels, relative to the scale of total investment, but the Marxists of that time were not, of course, to know this. The export of capital was therefore an important topic in their writings. It had become almost a truism to say that 'the export of capital tends to replace the export of commodities'; somehow this had to be incorporated into the analysis.

It is clear that Hilferding regards the movement of capital from one geographical area or industrial sector to another as an entirely normal part of capitalism. Of course capital seeks out the cheapest locations for production, the most favourable natural conditions and the richest natural resources.

There are, however, distinctions which Hilferding does not draw but which are important to the arguments that he develops. Starting with his concept of a 'national economic territory' (which may be larger than the 'nation' narrowly defined, because it includes colonies, spheres of influence, etc.) we can distinguish three forms of capital export. Firstly, there is the movement of capital to underdeveloped parts of the economic territory. There is, according to Hilferding, a motive to expand territory in order to gain these fields for investment. Secondly, there is investment in 'unclaimed' or independent, but backward, parts of the world. This investment may serve as a means of incorporating the area concerned into the national territory (preferential treatment may be a condition of granting a loan), or it may create a motive for its subsequent incorporation in order to safeguard the investment. Thirdly, there is investment within the territory of another nation. This would tend to decrease the importance of the division of the world market into different territories, rather than creating a motive for territorial expansion.

What are the reasons for capital export? Hilferding regards the constant movement of capital in search of maximum returns as normal, but there are some additional arguments that apply specifically to capital export.

One is the desire to overcome other countries' protective tariffs by producing within their tariff walls, thus taking advantage of the tariffs that are designed to shut you out. In the case where the tariffs are imposed by a weak state, this falls into my second category, and may be a prelude to the incorporation of the capital importing country into the sphere of influence of the capital exporter. Where the capital importing country is a major power, however, it falls into my third category, and tends to undermine the effect of protective tariffs in reserving the 'national territory' for the national capital. Those countries strong enough to export capital on a large scale thus gain a competitive advantage (in terms of the world wide strength of 'their' capitalist firms, not in terms of exports or employment); one thinks immediately of America today. Hilferding here anticipates some of the concerns of more recent theorists (see chapter 12).

Hilferding does mention the 'falling rate of profit' (p. 426), but immediately, and rightly, qualifies the argument by pointing out that the price of internationally traded goods is not determined by conditions in the most advanced countries alone. This is a lesson that has not been learned by many subsequent theorists. Hilferding disposes of the point very quickly, but the argument that I would put to amplify his treatment is that both advanced and underdeveloped countries have to sell their goods on the world market at a single price. If it is true that the advanced countries have a higher organic composition of capital, then they will have adopted these 'capital intensive' methods of production because they are more profitable at the existing prices. Underdeveloped areas producing the same goods by less advanced methods must have higher costs and a lower rate of profit (unless they have other advantages, such as low wages, which are, in themselves, sufficient explanation for the movement of capital).

Hilferding does, however, regard differences in interest (and profit) rates as an important motor of capital exports. The highly developed financial systems of the advanced countries lead to lower interest rates and greater availability of (money) capital, hence they are the main centres for raising loans and floating new enterprises.

Underdeveloped countries also attract investment because wages are low, the low quality of labour being compensated by long working hours, and also because rent on land is low. These reasons need no discussion, since they are so obvious.

Hilferding also discusses the creation of markets for capital goods by the export of capital, but he treats these primarily as effects of capital export rather than causes of it. The export of capital stimulates the development of the capital goods industries, creates supplies of cheap goods and raises the rate of profit. It therefore generates a period of accelerated growth for capitalism.

What is the connection between the rise of finance capital and the growth of the importance of capital export? This is clearly a vital question for Hilferding, since he wishes to trace the main developments of capitalism in his time to the rise of finance capital. The answer seems to be mainly that it is institutional changes that make the difference: the adoption of the joint stock form of organisation and the connections be-tween banks and industrial firms. Most of the reasons for capital export have been there throughout the history of capitalism, but opportunities of profit have gone unused for lack of adequate organisational forms to take advantage of them. The joint stock form makes it possible for subsidiaries to be established abroad without the emigration of the capitalist himself. The link between the banks and industrial companies allows easy access to the necessary finance, often via a foreign subsidiary of the bank. The large size of a company is, by itself, enough to give it a great advantage in setting up a new installation from scratch in a new location.

The development of finance capital also alters the form of capital export. Countries in which finance capital had not developed far (Britain, France) exported capital by *portfolio investment*, the granting of loans and the purchase of shares in foreign enterprises. Where finance capital was more developed (Germany, USA), capital export tended to take the form of *direct investment* in productive enterprises controlled from the capital exporting country. This form ensures that the exporter of capital has far tighter control. The greater efficiency of finance capital compared with competitive capital in investment abroad is a competitive advantage which hastens the transformation of capital into finance capital.

I have already touched on some of the connections between the export of capital and the creation and expansion of a 'national economic territory'. Territorial expansion opens up new opportunities for investment, while the 'home' state may be called in by investors to create a political and juridical environment suitable for their activities. Trade can go on between various different social organisations, but capital investment requires the creation of capitalist relations of production. Where these are not already well established, colonial control may be a way of creating them. Hilferding's arguments here are similar to those of Marx and Luxemburg that have already been discussed.

The emphasis in Hilferding's book is on the most advanced countries, the centres of the rise of finance capital. He does, however, have something to say about the impact of these developments on the less developed areas which are incorporated, willingly or not, into the territories of the major powers.

The establishment of capitalist relations of production in new areas is carried through, where necessary, by force. Hilferding's comments could have been taken direct from Rosa Luxemburg (or vice versa); they do not differ on the methods of capitalist expansion, and there is, as we have seen, a fair measure of agreement on the reasons behind it. Hilferding writes:

> Violent methods are an integral part of colonial policy, which without them would lose its capitalist character, just as the existence of a landless proletariat is a necessary condition for capitalism. To carry out a colonial policy avoiding violence is as absurd as wishing to abolish the proletariat without abolishing capitalism. (*FC*, p. 431)

The export of capital is the primary driving force behind this violent breakup of pre-capitalist societies:

> The export of capital, particularly since it took the form of industrial capital and finance capital, has greatly accelerated the transformation of all preexisting social relations and the extension of capitalism over all the surface of the globe. Capitalist development does not take place separately in each country. The import of capital brings with it capitalist production and relations of exploitation and these always at the level reached in the most advanced countries. . . . Capitalism is imported today into new countries at its highest level, and consequently has revolutionary effects more quickly and with greater force. (*FC*, p. 435)

The import of capital could have favourable effects on the development of capitalism in less developed areas, especially in an earlier period when capital was imported to build railways and build up industries serving the local market. Even in this case, there are disadvantages of capital import in the drain of profit abroad, though a large enough territory may be able to 'naturalise' foreign capital (Hilferding's example is the absorption of French and Belgian capital in Germany). However, the export of capital is increasingly directed to the production of raw materials for export. This leads to economic and political dependence (*FC*, pp. 445–6). In all of this Hilferding strikingly anticipates the arguments of later writers. Characteristically, however, he turns away from these issues to discuss the way in which small countries become the battlefield for the struggles of the major powers, and hence gets back to the subject of the advanced countries, his main interest.

VI Classes, ideology and the state

The changes in capitalist society brought about by the rise of finance capital are not confined to the economic level alone, but represent a fundamental transformation in class structure, in the role of the state, and in the ideological sphere.

The starting point for discussing these changes must be the structure of capitalism before the rise of finance capital, in the epoch of competitive capitalism and the dominance of industrial capital. Capital in this period was divided into three distinct fractions: industrial, commercial and financial capital. The dominant ideology of industrial capital was liberalism, both economic liberalism or *laissez-faire*, and the more radical political liberalism in which the claim to independence of individual capitalists and commodity producers was translated into a doctrine of the rights of the individual citizen.

This ideology never became dominant in a pure form. Hilferding draws an interesting contrast between England, on the one hand, and continental Europe on the other. In England, the victory of capitalism was won at a very early stage, before liberalism had achieved its classical political form, and as a result English ideology was dominated by the narrowly economic doctrines of *laissez-faire*. Political liberalism never took root in its stronger forms. Free trade, on the other hand, perfectly expressed the interests of industrial capital in England at the time when England was the dominant industrial nation and had nothing to fear from international competition. This dominance of the ideology of competition proved difficult to shake off when it became outdated with the rise of finance capital in other nations.

In continental Europe, on the other hand, industrial capital needed protection and state assistance from the beginning, being weaker initially as a result of a later start. As a result, *laissez-faire* ideology never took so firm a hold, and the classical liberal hostility to the state was very much weakened. The protagonists of free trade, for a long time, were the agricultural interests, since northern Europe was a grain exporting region. The struggles in Germany, Italy and Austria to create modern nation states out of pre-capitalist political structures also generated support for the state. There were, therefore, considerable elements of statist ideology for finance capital to build on. Pre-capitalist ideologies were never wholly eliminated, and large elements of these could be incorporated into the ideology of finance capital.

The rise of finance capital constituted the unification of industrial and financial capital. Commercial capital was reduced to a totally subordinate status. The primary justification for the separate role of commercial capital was the need to amalgamate the products of many small firms in order to gain the economies of trading on a large scale. Once production was concentrated into large units, this justification vanished, especially in exchanges between one sector of production and another, where large firms prefer to deal directly with each other. Where commercial capital survived at all, then, it was reduced to the status simply of an agent for finance capital.

The integration of capital by finance capital is cemented, according to Hilferding, by a 'personal union'. By this he means that different sectors of capital are not only linked economically but their personnel become interchangeable. Representatives of banks sit on the boards of industrial firms, and industrialists sit on the boards of banks. Family and social ties also link the ruling class together.

Smaller capitalists in fact suffer from the rise of monopoly, but Hilferding is not optimistic that they will react against finance capital, and he gives a series of reasons why they should not do so. Dependent on the banks (for loans) and on the monopolies (for orders and for supplies), they are reduced to a subordinate position and integrated into the hierarchical structure. They may also become shareholders in the big firms.

The spread of share ownership is very important in integrating the non-producing classes generally: landlords, professionals, state employees and rentiers. Rural interests are also incorporated through the penetration of finance capital into the countryside in the form of establishments for processing agricultural products and the like.

All of these sections of the 'possessing classes' are united politically by the fact that they face a common enemy, the working class.

Hilferding, therefore, argued that the rise of finance capital led to the creation of a ruling class relatively unified in political affairs under the leadership of the 'magnates of finance capital', corresponding to the relatively unified and hierarchical economic structure. This change in the structure of the ruling class naturally involved a change in its relation to the state, a relation which became much more close and direct. Hilferding did not go as far in this direction as his successors, who tended to see the state as the more or less direct property of a handful of monopolies, but even so it is possible that he went too far. He was describing tendencies which had not, at that date, fully worked themselves out, and it is doubtful whether the various strata and fractions of the capitalist class and their political allies were ever as thoroughly integrated as he suggested.

Hilferding also described the growth of new strata of white collar workers called into existence by the enormous increase in the scale of enterprises and the consequent mushrooming of paperwork and administration. He foresaw their continued increase and fully realised their importance. Although he regarded them as potential allies for the working class, he recognised that they were, at the time, among the most deeply reactionary sections of the population and that their position could be at best ambivalent.

The political position of finance capital was thus very strong. Together with this, Hilferding stressed that finance capital needed the power of the state. In the first instance, tariff protection was needed to gain the benefits of monopoly. Given protection, we have seen the reasons why finance capital should press for territorial expansion, and this required a powerful state.

The ideology of finance capital thus makes a decisive break with classical liberalism, the ideology of industrial capital in an earlier epoch. Hilferding says:

> The demand for an expansionist policy overthrows the entire world
> view of the bourgeoisie. It ceases to be pacific and humanitarian.
> The old free-traders saw in free trade not only the most just
> economic policy, but also the basis for an era of peace. Finance

capital gave up this belief long ago. It does not believe in the harmony of capitalist interests, but knows that the competitive struggle becomes more and more a political struggle. The ideal of peace fades, and the idea of humanity is replaced by the ideal of the grandeur and power of the state. . . . The ideal is to insure for one's own nation the domination of the world. . . . Founded in economic needs, it finds its justification in this remarkable reversal of national consciousness. . . . Racial ideology is thus a rationalisation, disguised as science, of the ambitions of finance capital. (*FC*, pp. 452–4)

VII Imperialism and inter-imperialist rivalry

Hilferding does not generally use the term 'imperialism', tending instead to use phrases like 'modern protectionist policy', 'modern colonial policy' and 'the external policy of finance capital'. Where he does use it, it does not have any clear meaning in his theoretical framework; it is a generalised descriptive term for the militarist and expansionist tendencies in the capitalism of his time that he wanted to oppose, so we get phrases like: 'modern protectionist policy, which is inextricably bound up with imperialism' (*FC*, p. 491), 'capital cannot adopt any other policy than an imperialist one', and 'socialism must be put forward as the only response to imperialism' (both p. 492). All these references occur in the last chapter of the book. Imperialism was a word which was around at the time, and which Hilferding found useful to add punch to his peroration.

The use of words is not of essential importance. What is important is the absence of any clear concept corresponding to imperialism, an absence which is indicated by the variety of phrases which Hilferding uses to indicate different aspects of the phenomenon. The major elements of the idea are there, but they are never pulled together: the credit for that must go to Bukharin. The reason why Hilferding did not arrive at the concept of imperialism is fairly clear. His interest was in the internal developments in the major capitalist centres, in the rise of finance capital. That is the title of the book, it is his concept, and nobody can take it away from him.

Pulling together the scattered indications that Hilferding gave on the phenomena that came to be called 'imperialism', will show immediately how much Bukharin and Lenin took from him. The quotation given above (p. 91) is the heart of the matter (Lenin copied it out in his note-books with heavy underlinings and favourable comment). Finance capital has a direct interest in maximising the extent of the protected national economic territory. In addition there is the search for exclusive fields for capital export. Both point inexorably to a policy of expansion, one bound to bring about conflicts between capitalist powers.

Hilferding was rather cautious in discussing the inevitability of conflict. On the one hand, the further the process of monopolisation goes, and the more unequal the strength of the contending parties, the more violent the struggle for dominance becomes. The rise of German finance capital, controlling a relatively narrow territory, and the relative decline of Britain, with an enormous empire, in particular, together with other disproportions between economic strength and size of territory, created a set of circumstances which Hilferding summed up: 'A situation which tends to aggravate tension between Germany and Britain with her satellites, and cannot but tend to a solution by force' (*FC*, p. 448).

On the other hand, he argued, the low level of development of finance capital in Britain and France led to the export of capital in the form of loans, often to American and German enterprises, thus creating a 'certain solidarity' of the international interests of capital. He also cited the fear of socialism as a factor deterring capitalist states from going to war. He preferred to remain agnostic as to which of these tendencies would predominate, commenting that it all depended on the circum-stances of particular cases, just like the choice for particular firms between entering a cartel or trying to achieve dominance by under-cutting its rivals.

In the conflict between Kautsky and Lenin, discussed in the next chapter, Hilferding's position was characteristic of his politics: somewhere in between. It was, of course, relatively easy for Lenin to announce the inevitability of war when the war had actually broken out.

VIII Summary

Competition tends to create monopolies, and monopolies can exer-cise control over small firms that they deal with. There is therefore a tendency towards the formation of huge blocs of capital organised in a hierarchical way. Financial, industrial and commercial capital are linked together, as *finance capital*, in these financial groups, which Hilferding saw as dominated by banks. Since monopolies cannot yet control the world market, they need the protection of tariffs, and they then seek to extend their protected markets to the maximum possible extent, hence the support of finance capital for expansionist policies. By setting out these arguments, Hilferding became the real founder of the classical Marxist theory of imperialism.

5 · Bukharin and Lenin

In August 1914, on the outbreak of the First World War, the socialist parties of the Second International almost without exception abandoned their commitments to internationalism and supported their national governments. The Bolshevik wing of the Russian Social Democratic Party was almost the only organised party which held firm against this disintegration, though individuals and groups in other parties also stood firm.

In this desperate situation, exiled and condemned to inactivity, two of the leaders of the Bolsheviks wrote works on imperialism, setting out their analyses of the connections between war and the development of capitalism. These two works, both based on Hilferding's writings, are the foundations of the Marxist analysis of imperialism.

Bukharin's *Imperialism and World Economy* (Bukharin, 1972a, cited below as *IWE*) was written in 1915, though the manuscript was lost for a time, and it was only published after the success of the Russian revolution. Lenin wrote a laudatory preface to it, which was not rediscovered and published until 1927. In the meantime, Lenin himself had written on the same topic. His *Imperialism, the Highest Stage of Capitalism* (Lenin, 1950, cited below as *Imperialism*) was written in early 1916, in other words, shortly after the preface to Bukharin's book, dated December, 1915. Lenin's pamphlet had a slightly more successful passage through the hazards of underground revolutionary work in wartime and was published a few months earlier than Bukharin's. The dating of Lenin's preface, however, establishes as clearly as one can in such circumstances that Bukharin's work came before Lenin's. I will therefore start with Bukharin. We should, however, note that Bukharin acknowledges a 'debt of deep gratitude' to Lenin, though it is not clear for what; the context suggests that it may simply be for providing the introduction.

I make these points not to disparage Lenin – his reputation is safe on other grounds in any case – but to reclaim for Bukharin the credit that he deserves. Bukharin's subsequent career was erratic, and he ended by being disgraced and executed in the climactic Stalinist purge. This fate must largely account for his subsequent neglect.

Bukharin and Lenin use the term 'imperialism' in rather different ways. Bukharin defines it as follows:

> We speak of imperialism as of a *policy* of finance capital. However, one may also speak of imperialism as an *ideology*. In a similar way *liberalism* is on the one hand a policy of industrial capitalism (free trade, etc.) and on the other hand it denotes a whole ideology (personal liberty, etc.). (*IWE*, p. 110n.)

However, he insists, on the one hand, that a policy of conquest only counts as imperialism if it is the policy of finance capital, on the other hand he argues that this policy is inevitably followed by finance capital. Furthermore, looked at on a world scale, what matters is not the fact that any one particular state follows an imperialist policy but the rivalry between them; this comes out clearly in his chapter heading 'Imperialism as the reproduction of capitalist competition on a larger scale'. His argument moves, therefore, from imperialism as a *policy* and as an *ideology*, to imperialism as a *characteristic of the world economy* at a particular stage of development.

Lenin took this further: he treats imperialism as a *stage* in the development of capitalism. Policies which other writers had called imperialist are part of the characteristics of this stage, but so are other phenomena: the rise of monopoly, of finance capital, etc. All are subsumed under the heading of imperialism. (For an interesting discussion of Lenin's definition and the problems it poses, see Arrighi, 1978.)

This definition has caused some confusion, since many subsequent Marxists have wanted to talk more narrowly about imperialism as the domination of one country over another (yet a third definition), and this has become the most common use of the term. The words we use are, of course, not important in themselves. They only become important when they are a source of confusion. I will generally use the term imperialism in the sense intended by the writer that I am discussing at the time – to do otherwise would be intolerably clumsy – and I hope that this warning will avoid any misunderstandings.

I Bukharin

It is difficult to convey either the quality or the importance of Bukharin's writing on imperialism, since his originality was not essentially in producing new ideas, but in putting existing ideas together to make a coherent and novel whole. Much of his theory was taken from Hilferding, and in setting out Hilferding's views in the last chapter I have essentially picked out those elements in Hilferding's slightly chaotic writing that Bukharin subsequently welded into a coherent picture.

The essential difference between them is that where Hiferding sees *one* process at work, the concentration and centralisation of capital with all its ramifications, Bukharin sees *two*: the *internationalisation* and *nationalisation* of capital, the growth of international interdependence, of the world economy, and its division into national blocs. The contradiction between these two opposed tendencies drives the system into war and breakdown, just as, for Marx, the contradiction between social production and private appropriation is the ultimate contradiction of capitalism. The contradiction that Bukharin stresses is, in fact, a form of the same contradiction that Marx identified.

I shall quote extensively from Bukharin, because his theoretical statements are so concise that they frequently defy any shorter summary. The major part of what is, in any case, a short book, is taken up with the factual evidence which he adduces to support each step in his argument.

'Just as every individual enterprise is part of the ''national'' economy, so every one of these ''national economies'' is included in the system of world economy' (*IWE*, p. 17). The exchange of goods between countries, international trade, is simply a version of the social division of labour essentially the same as the exchange of goods between different enterprises. It establishes *social relation of production on a world scale*.

The international division of labour is based on two factors of changing importance: firstly on the different natural conditions in different areas of the world, and secondly on the different levels of development attained in different areas. 'Important as the natural differences in the conditions of production may be, they recede more and more into the background compared with differences that are the result of the uneven development of productive forces in the various countries' (*IWE*, p. 20). Bukharin cites Marx: 'The foundation of all highly developed divisions of labour that are brought about by the exchange of commodities is the cleavage between town and country. We may say that the whole economic history of society is summarised in the development of this cleavage' (Marx, *Capital*, I, p. 352 cited in the translation used in *IWE*, p. 2). He then continues:

> The cleavage between 'town and country' as well as the 'development of this cleavage', formerly confined to one country alone, are now being reproduced on a tremendously enlarged basis. Viewed from this standpoint, entire countries appear today as 'towns', namely, the industrial countries, whereas entire agrarian territories appear to be 'country'. (*IWE*, p. 21)

This international division of labour is growing, because of the great improvements in transport, continued unevenness of development, and the simple fact of general economic development. The factors that underlie it are not accidental and will not go away. The internationalisation of economic activity is a fundamental fact.

> The international division of labour, the difference in natural and social conditions, are an economic *prius* which cannot be destroyed, even by the World War. This being so, there exist definite value relations, and, as their consequence, conditions for the realisation of a maximum of profit in international transactions. Not economic self-sufficiency, but an intensification of international relations . . . such is the road of future evolution. (*IWE*, p. 148)

As well as world markets for goods, there emerges a world market for money capital. The export of capital establishes relations of production not only between different production units, but relations between the workers and capitalists of different countries. Capital export appears in Bukharin's argument as an integral part of the growth of the international division of labour and of the internationalisation of capital. He does, however, suggest in passing that the movement of capital will be from the more developed to the less developed countries, because there is 'overproduction' of capital in the former and the organic composition of capital is lower in the latter (pp. 45–6). This argument is doubly dubious; the theory of the falling rate of profit is now widely regarded as incorrect, and in any case its application to comparisons between countries in a partially integrated world system has yet to be worked out properly.

All of this follows Marx (and Rosa Luxemburg) in stressing the expansive nature of capitalist *social relations*, their tendency to break down international barriers and to establish a unified world market. This aspect of Marx's analysis of capitalism comes out most strongly in the *Manifesto*.

However, the process of concentration and centralisation of capital, the tendency towards monopoly, is also going on, and at a tremendous pace. At the stage where monopolistic control of markets becomes possible, the formation of cartels and trusts, what Bukharin calls the 'organisation process', proceeds very rapidly. There is no need to go into details: Bukharin follows Hilferding closely in the main lines of his argument.

What Bukharin does do, and it is crucial, is to ask the question *why should the 'organisation process' proceed on a national basis?* This is a question that is of great relevance today, when some theorists are proclaiming the irrelevance of the nation state in view of the internationalisation of capital. Bukharin answers:

> The organisation process . . . tends to overstep the 'national' boundaries. But it finds very substantial obstacles on this road. First, it is much easier to overcome competition on a 'national' scale than on a world scale . . .; second, the existing differences of economic structure and consequently of production costs make agreements disadvantageous for the advanced 'national' groups; third, the ties of unity with the state and its boundaries are in themselves an ever growing monopoly which guarantees additional profits. Among the factors of the latter category . . . [is] . . . the tariff policy. (*IWE*, p. 74)

The arguments about the role of tariffs in protecting national monopolies are essentially those that have already been discussed. In Bukharin's argument they have a new significance. Instead of being simply reasons for protectionism, they become reasons both for protectionism and for the formation of cartels on a national basis. Instead of the link-up between finance capital and the state being a conclusion of the argument (as it is in Hilferding), it becomes a step in the argument.

The essential point is that monopolies, in the first instance, take the form of cartels. These are rather fragile forms of organisation, because there is a constant temptation for any single firm to break with the cartel and try to increase its share of the market. Cartels can only hold together if their members remain satisfied with the way the market is divided and do not believe that they could improve their profits by breaking with the cartel and trying to win the ensuing competitive struggle.

A cartel is particularly liable to break up if the competitive strength of its members is very unequal, so that the strongest come to think that they have more to gain by breaking up the cartel than by staying in it, and if the relative strengths of the members change, so that a division of the market agreed at the outset becomes no longer appropriate.

Bukharin argues that both of these factors tending to break up cartels operate particularly strongly on an international level, because uneven development is particularly marked between different nations within the world economy.

Since cartelisation and the formation of monopolies promise both super-profits and a great competitive advantage in the world market, there is a tremendous incentive for capitalist enterprises to link together on a national basis. Bukharin thus has two processes: the *nationalisation* and the *internationalisation* of capital. 'Together with the internationalisation of economy and the internationalisation of capital, there is going on a process of ''national'' intertwining of capital, a process of ''nationalising'' capital, fraught with the greatest consequences' (*IWE*, p. 80). The result is the creation of national blocs of capital set in the context of a world economy:

> various spheres of the concentration and organisation process
> stimulate each other, creating a very strong tendency towards
> transforming the entire national economy *into one gigantic
> combined enterprise under the tutelage of the financial kings and
> the capitalist state, an enterprise which monopolises the national
> market*. . . . It follows that world capitalism, the world system of
> production, assumes in our times the following aspect: a few
> consolidated, organised economic bodies ('the great civilised
> powers') on the one hand, and a periphery of underdeveloped
> countries with a semi agrarian or agrarian system on the other.
> (*IWE*, pp. 73–4)

This is a striking description, and one that contains a great deal of truth, but it must still be qualified. Bukharin speaks only of a *tendency* towards the formation of a single 'gigantic combined enterprise' on a national basis. However, like many Marxists, he often treats a tendency as an established fact and ignores counter-tendencies.

Firstly, it is not true that competition was, then or later, completely suppressed within national boundaries. I am not concerned here with the remaining fringe of small businesses, though they should not be ignored, but with competition between different big businesses and groups of finance capital. The tendency since has in fact been, at least in some sectors, for these different big corporations to spread out from their national base and compete all over the world, rather than uniting to face foreign competition. Thus, to give an example, one of the major sources of competition in the world motor industry is competition between the two American multi-nationals, Ford and General Motors.

Secondly, Bukharin's treatment of the state is over-simple. He, with many of his contemporaries, seems to have regarded the 'relative autonomy' of the state (a modern phrase) as the product of the separation of the state from the capitalist class, while this in turn was the product of the division of the capitalist class into distinct fractions and into many competing capitals. With the unification of the capitalist class by finance capital, the separation broke down, and a direct identity between the magnates of capital and the state took its place.

This line of argument has influenced the orthodox communist parties ever since ('State Monopoly Capitalism'), and is still to be found today. It contains, no doubt, a grain of truth; big firms can have much more direct links with the apparatuses of the state than can a multitude of small firms. It has, however, been widely criticised, firstly, because the unification of the capitalist class was, as I have pointed out above, never complete; secondly, because support from the various strata of professionals, state employees, etc., has always been vital, and has generally been mobilised by the incorporation of these groups into political organisations, and finally, because of the need to contain and absorb working-class pressure rather than simply repressing it. For all of these reasons, the state has much more autonomy than Bukharin, or the other classical Marxists, admitted. It may represent the *interests* of finance capital; that is not the same thing as acting as their direct *agent*.

In a sense, Bukharin's vision of the world represents an abolition of the state as a body distinct from 'civil society'. It has often been argued that the state is needed to contain the centrifugal pressures of the anarchy of economic life. In Bukharin's vision, the anarchy of capitalist competition is entirely suppressed at the *national* level, only to re-emerge in an even more disruptive form at the *world* level. On a world scale, no state exists to suppress the threats to stability that competitive anarchy generates.

To complete the description of Bukharin's analysis of imperialism, one more point must be made. The tendency towards monopoly does not, in his view, represent a steady decline in competition. On the contrary, the tendency towards monopoly implies an intensification of competition, as the few remaining businesses slug it out for the prize of complete monopoly. Total monopoly, monopoly in the sense of bourgeois economics, might indeed end competition, but Bukharin did not expect this stage to be reached: capitalism would perish first. The concentration and centralisation of capital therefore produces, not an end to competition, but a change in its form. Previously competition took place primarily inside national boundaries, and competition in the world market was weak. Now that competition is largely eliminated within each state, it is whole countries that are absorbed by others, instead of small businesses by large. 'Imperialist annexation is only a case of the general capitalist tendency towards centralisation of capital, a case of its centralisation on that maximum scale which corresponds to the competition of state capitalist trusts' (*IWE*, pp. 119–20).

II Lenin

Lenin's pamphlet, *Imperialism, the Highest Stage of Capitalism*, is the most famous Marxist work on imperialism. It was, for me, a surprising discovery that it makes little or no contribution to the development of a theory of imperialism. Its theoretical content is slight and derives from Hilferding, Bukharin and Hobson.

This should not, perhaps, be a surprise. The work is a pamphlet (and Lenin describes it as such in his preface) not a substantial book, it is subtitled 'A Popular Outline', and Lenin says in the first paragraph that

> what has been said of imperialism during the last few years,
> especially in an enormous number of magazine and newspaper
> articles, and also in the resolutions, for example, of Chemnitz and
> Basle congresses which took place in the autumn of 1912, has
> scarcely gone beyond the ideas expounded or, more exactly,
> summed up by [Hilferding and Hobson]. (*Imperialism*, p. 442)

Lenin was, it seems, not claiming to be doing more than to gather together this material. This 'popular outline' is a kind of work that has an honourable and important part in Marxist literature: a factual survey of the current situation together with a summary of the results of theoretical analysis (though not the detailed theoretical argument itself), designed to provide a basis for *political* decisions.

To argue that the work contains no important theoretical innovations is not, therefore, a criticism of Lenin, but of the orthodox Marxist tradition which has turned the work into a sacred text. To treat any work as sacred is a thoroughly unscientific attitude; to treat a minor work (with the weaknesses which this one has) as sacred is also a serious lapse of judgment. Since *Imperialism* has been treated as a theoretical work, I shall have to criticise it as such.

Lenin's major purpose in writing the pamphlet was to counter the propaganda of Kautsky and other ex-Marxists (he includes Hilferding in this category) who were, in his view, leading the shattered remnants of the Second International in entirely the wrong direction. From this point of view, the most important sections of the work are those directed against Kautsky's theory of 'ultra-imperialism' and those describing the rise of a 'labour aristocracy' which was, Lenin argued, the material base for the support that Kautsky's revisionism had gained in the major imperialist countries. I will examine these parts of Lenin's argument in separate sections of this chapter.

Lenin's basic method, in this work, was to set out a series of trends or tendencies in the development of capitalism in the period in which he was writing, and to document each with factual evidence. The evidence was drawn, deliberately, from unimpeachably bourgeois sources, so as to condemn the bourgeoisie, so to speak, with their own words (or those of their apologists).

Lenin lists these tendencies in several places in slightly different forms. One such list reads:

(1) the concentration of production and capital has developed to such a high stage that it has created monopolies which play a decisive role in economic life;

(2) the merging of bank capital with industrial capital, and the creation, on the basis of this 'finance capital' of a financial oligarchy;

(3) the export of capital as distinguished from the export of commodities acquires exceptional importance;

(4) the formation of international monopolist capitalist combines which share the world among themselves; and

(5) the territorial division of the whole world among the biggest capitalist powers is completed. (*Imperialism*, p. 525)

The problem with this method is that each tendency is described separately, and their interconnections are only examined either in passing sentences or later in the work, in the polemical sections directed against Kautsky. From the point of view of constructing a *theory* of imperialism it is precisely the interconnections that are crucial; is it just a matter of historical chance that these developments occurred at the same time, or are there essential connections between them that make it inevitable that they should occur together? Lenin does say that the 'briefest possible definition of imperialism' is 'the monopoly stage of capitalism', implying that the rest flows from the development of monopoly, but he does not properly specify *why*.

To Lenin, this question was perhaps irrelevant, academic. These tendencies did in fact dominate the development of capitalism at the time, and the real problems were problems of political strategy in building a revolutionary party in these circumstances. To us the question is not academic, since the trends that Lenin described have not worked themselves out in the way that he expected. (In the list above, the first tendency, the growth of concentration, has gone much further, while the last, the territorial division of the world, has been substantially reversed, with decolonisation; I do not argue that decolonisation removes imperialist dominance, only that it blurs the *division* of the world between *rival* powers.) We can only deal with a changed situation either by denying Lenin's relevance altogether or by understanding the processes at work behind the observed tendencies.

The first two tendencies in the list, the rise of monopoly and of finance capital, pose few new problems since Lenin followed Hilferding very closely. He quotes a variety of sources to establish that production had become concentrated into fewer and fewer units, as Marx had predicted:

> Marx . . . by a theoretical and historical analysis of capitalism
> proved that free competition gives rise to the concentration of
> production which, in turn, at a certain stage of development, leads
> to monopoly. . . . For Europe, the time when the new capitalism
> *definitely* supersedes the old can be established with fair precision:
> it was the beginning of the twentieth century. (*Imperialism*,
> p. 448)

He differs in emphasis from Hilferding in arguing that although protective tariffs help in the formation of cartels, the same tendencies are emerging, 'though somewhat later', in free trade England.

He also describes the development of monopoly in banking, and the dominance of bank capital over industrial capital. Even more noticeably than Hilferding, he stresses the dominance of the banks, and hence of *rentiers*, of idle owners of money capital who play no active part in production at all. This foreshadows his discussion of 'parasitism'.

The only point worth commenting on is that Lenin shows a disturbing tendency to stress the role of financial swindles in the rise of finance capital (see *Imperialism*, pp. 480 ff.). While these swindles certainly happened, and played a part in events, it is surely better to follow the line that Marx took in dealing with the role of fraud and dishonesty in explaining surplus value: the functioning of the system was to be explained in terms of legitimate dealings; swindles were just an optional extra. I make this rather trivial point because too many Marxist writers have devoted their efforts to 'exposing' these shady deals and, while this makes entertaining reading, it tends to divert attention away from the workings of the system as a whole.

The section on the export of capital raises more problems. Why should the export of capital become especially important at this stage, and what is its significance? Lenin says:

> The possibility of exporting capital is created by the fact that a number of backward countries have already been drawn into world capitalist intercourse; main railways have either been or are being built there, the elementary conditions for industrial development have been created etc. The necessity of exporting capital arises from the fact that in a few countries capitalism has become 'over-ripe' and (owing to the backward stage of agriculture and the impoverished state of the masses) capital cannot find a field for 'profitable' investment. (*Imperialism*, p. 495)

What are we to make of this? The first half of the quotation gives no difficulty, though Lenin does not have anything to say on the creation of a proletariat in the backward countries, a topic which had concerned Marx, Luxemburg and Hilferding. In view of Lenin's discussion of the formation of a proletariat in Russia in his *Development of Capital in Russia*, however, we can assume that the omission is simply because the point was not relevant to Lenin's immediate purposes.

It is the second half of the quotation, the 'over-ripeness' of capitalism, that is generally quoted and that is very difficult to interpret.

Many commentators have taken this as a reference to the 'law' of the falling rate of profit. This interpretation cannot, however, be accepted, since 'the backward stage of agriculture and the impoverished state of the masses' are not factors that lead to a fall in the rate of profit at all. The backward stage of agriculture should reduce the average organic composition of capital and thus raise the rate of profit (unless, by a strict application of Marx's very dubious theory of absolute rent, we argue that the benefits of a low organic composition of capital are captured by landowners as rent). Backward agriculture might reduce the rate of profit by raising the value of subsistence goods and thus the value of labour power, but this should be offset by the 'impoverished state of the masses'.

If the reference to the poverty of the masses and the backwardness of agriculture is to mean anything (and Lenin repeats it: it is not a passing reference), it must surely represent an *underconsumptionist* analysis. Accumulation is held up by a lack of markets resulting from the low demand for consumer goods, which in turn is a result of the poverty of the masses. This is the argument put forward by Hobson, and Lenin thought very highly of Hobson and drew on his analysis extensively. On the other hand, Lenin's major economic work, *The Development of Capitalism in Russia*, is directed specifically *against* the Narodnik argument that capitalism in Russia was doomed to failure because of the lack of a 'home market' resulting from the poverty of the masses. The two works were separated by twenty years, and it is possible that Lenin had changed his mind in the interim, but one would require clearer evidence of a change of mind than these cryptic phrases provide.

Because of his influence on Lenin, Hobson deserves a brief mention here, although he falls outside the scope of a book on Marxist theories of imperialism since he was not a Marxist. Hobson held an underconsumptionist theory, arguing that the low level of wages and the high proportion of profits saved led to a chronic shortage of demand. He was aware that investment demand could fill the gap between productive capacity, on the one hand, and consumption spending on the other, but he argued that there would not be sufficient investment opportunities at home to sustain demand. This was, in part, due to the rise of monopoly, which leads to a restriction of output and hence of investment. This argument is essentially the same as that later put forward in a Marxist framework by Sweezy and Baran, which will be examined in due course (see chapter 6).

Hobson wrote several books on these themes, of which *Imperialism* (Hobson, 1938) is the most relevant. In this he argues that the economic driving force behind colonial expansion is the search for investment outlets to absorb the surplus saving. Hobson thought that this process could be reversed, without overthrowing capitalism itself, by raising wages and hence raising consumer demand and reducing the volume of saving and the pressure to find new investment outlets. It may have been this argument that Lenin was referring to when he said 'if capitalism could . . . raise the standard of living of the masses . . . there could be no talk of a superabundance of capital. . . . But if capitalism did these things it would not be capitalism' (*Imperialism*, p. 495). It is clear that Hobson advocated a liberal and not a Marxist solution to the problem. (For further discussion of Hobson, see Bleaney, 1976, chapter 8; and Kemp, 1967, chapter 3.)

There are, of course, other reasons for the export of capital to backward countries beside the 'overripeness' of capitalism, and Lenin mentions them briefly: 'In these backward countries profits are usually high, for capital is scarce, the price of land is relatively low, wages are low, raw materials are cheap' (*Imperialism*, p. 496). The strongest motive that Lenin advances is the desire to gain control of sources of raw materials, or at least to prevent others from gaining monopoly control of them. To bring these sources of primary products into use requires investment.

These reasons are perfectly adequate to explain the export of capital, but what they explain is the incentive to export capital and, in a capitalism still driven by competition (between monopolistic groups), the inevitability of capital export. They do not amount to a necessity in the sense that capitalism could not survive without capital export, a sense which might be implied by phrases like 'superabundance' of capital.

My conclusion is that the few remarks Lenin gives about the causes of capital export do not amount to an explanation or to a complete theory and cannot usefully be cited in support of any arguments about the importance of capital export to the more advanced capitalist countries. Michalet (1976) recognises the weaknesses in Lenin's treatment of capital export (and of other topics), and discusses them from a rather different angle from that presented here.

What of the effects of capital export? In the backward areas the effect is to *accelerate* development. Here again, Lenin is in the direct line of descent from Marx, and especially from the *Communist Manifesto*. He does not stress the obstacles which this development meets, nor does he stress its one-sided and limited effects, in the way that Hilferding, and more recent writers (for example, Baran) have done.

> The export of capital affects and greatly accelerates the development of capitalism in those countries to which it is exported. While, therefore, the export of capital may tend to a certain extent to arrest development in the capital exporting countries, it can do so only by expanding and deepening the

further development of capitalism throughout the world.
(*Imperialism*, p. 498)

The remark about the arresting of development in the capital
exporting countries, in the extract quoted above, is developed at greater
length in the discussion of 'parasitism and decay'. Here Lenin diverges
from the Marxist tradition, and recognises the fact by saying that 'the
Marxist Hilferding takes a step backwards compared with the non-
Marxist Hobson' (*Imperialism*, p. 536) in not recognising 'parasitism,
which is characteristic of imperialism'.

In saying that Lenin diverges from the Marxist tradition, I do not
imply that there is anything inherently un-Marxist in the argument.
Marx argued that a mode of production falls when it becomes a 'fetter on
the forces of production'. Lenin, essentially, judged that imperialism had
become such a fetter, a brake on development, at least in the most
advanced countries, although, as the quotation above shows he regarded
imperialism as a force for development in the world as a whole. 'On the
whole', he says, 'capitalism is growing far more rapidly than ever before;
but this growth is not only becoming more and more uneven in general,
its unevenness also manifests itself, in particular, in the decay of the
countries which are richest in capital (England)' (*Imperialism*, p. 564).

One basis for the decay of capitalism, is the decline in the pressure to
innovate and to reduce production costs once competition is eliminated.
There is a 'tendency to stagnation and decay, which is characteristic of
monopoly, and in certain branches of industry, in certain countries, for
certain periods of time, it gains the upper hand' (*Imperialism*, p. 537).
This argument is surprising, in that it implies that the growth of
monopoly reduces competitive pressures, where Lenin generally follows
the Hilferding–Bukharin line in seeing the transition to monopoly as a
period of greatly intensified competition. He seems to imply that price
competition has been completely supplanted by political-military forms
of rivalry. In any case, this treatment of monopoly as a force retarding
technological development foreshadows the arguments of Baran and
other recent writers.

More important to his argument is the effect of capital export on the
capital exporting countries:

> Further, imperialism is an immense accumulation of money capital
> in a few countries. . . . Hence the extraordinary growth of a class,
> or rather, of a social stratum of rentiers, i.e. people who live by
> clipping coupons, who take no part in any enterprise whatever,

whose profession is idleness. The export of capital, one of the most essential economic bases of imperialism, still more completely isolates the rentiers from production and sets the seal of parasitism on the whole country that lives by exploiting the labour of several overseas countries and colonies. (*Imperialism*, p. 537)

It is easy to see how the *capitalists* can be called parasitic, but how can one say that a whole *country* is parasitic? The only circumstances in which it would be reasonable to say this would be where a growing proportion of the workers were drawn into unproductive work, as servants, clerks in the offices of the financiers and so on, and it seems that this is what Lenin has in mind. Lenin quotes Hobson's speculations, in a context which implies that he approves of them, if only as an extreme possibility:

The greater part of Western Europe might then assume the appearance and character already exhibited by tracts of country in the South of England, in the Riviera and in the tourist-ridden or residential parts of Italy and Switzerland, little clusters of wealthy aristocrats drawing dividends and pensions from the Far East, with a somewhat larger group of professional retainers and tradesmen and a large body of personal servants and workers in the transport trades and in the final stages of production of the more perishable goods; all the main arterial industries would have disappeared, the staple foods and manufactures flowing in as tribute from Asia and Africa. (quoted in *Imperialism*, pp. 540–1)

This is, indeed, a possible outcome, but it is not what happened. It is precisely the complaint of the underdeveloped countries today that they have been excluded from 'all the main arterial industries', and it is a major concern of more recent Marxist theorists to explain why the major industries have remained centred in the old heartlands of imperialism and have not developed to any great degree in the underdeveloped countries. Capital export went, in practice, mainly into the development of raw material production for export from the underdeveloped areas to the manufacturing centres of the advanced countries. This is the development predicted by Hilferding and by Bukharin.

I stress this point for two reasons. Firstly, because it brings out how large is the gap between Lenin and recent Marxist writers, even those who sincerely regard themselves as his disciples, and, secondly, because the tradition that derived from Lenin led Marxists astray for a long time.

Regarding capitalism as being in the last throes of decay and dissolution, they were quite unable to explain or to cope with its unexpected capacity not only to survive, but also to advance.

In theoretical terms, however, the crucial failing in Lenin's pamphlet is its failure adequately to theorise the place of the nation state in the world economy. Lenin has sections headed: 'the division of the world among capitalist combines' and 'the division of the world among the great powers', but *there is no theoretical connection established between them*. This is an extreme example of the methodological weakness of Lenin's pamphlet that has already been mentioned; he describes a number of trends without fully explaining how they are connected.

In discussing the division of the world among capitalist combines, Lenin says:

> As the export of capital increased, and as the foreign and colonial connections and 'spheres of influence' of the big monopolist combines expanded in all ways, things 'naturally' gravitated towards an international agreement among these combines, and towards the formation of international cartels. (*Imperialism*, p. 501)

This is followed by accounts of the various attempts to form such cartels, in the electrical industry, the oil industry and so on.

The next section goes straight on to discuss the division of the world between the great powers, and again the emphasis is on a factual account of the way the world has been divided. The central point is that the world had, for practical purposes, been divided already, and that any change had to be by redivision, which would inevitably mean conflict. This was the essential point Lenin wanted to make against Kautsky and it is, in that context, a strong point.

The question that is left open, however, is: who is it that is dividing the world? The implicit answer is: the national groups of finance capital. This invites the further question: why should blocs of finance capital form on a national basis? (This was the central question that Bukharin tackled.) Perhaps because Bukharin had already dealt with this question, perhaps because it was not relevant to his immediate concerns, Lenin does not try to answer. He takes it for granted, with such remarks as: 'Monopolist capitalist combines, cartels, syndicates and trusts divide among themselves, first of all, the home market, seize more or less complete possession of the industry of a country' (*Imperialism*, p. 500). Yes, but why? Why is a 'country' a relevant unit in this context? Lenin gives no answer.

One criticism of the Bukharin-Lenin analysis deserves mention here. It is often argued that their thesis is refuted by the fact that Britain, the country with the largest colonial empire, was relatively late in reaching the stage of monopoly capitalism. This line of criticism is, at least in part, an example of the semantic confusion caused by different uses of the term 'imperialism'. For Lenin, in particular, imperialism did not specifically refer to the possession of colonies. He explicitly recognised that earlier stages of capitalism also involved colonial expansion, but for different reasons and with different results (*Imperialism*, p. 517). It would, however, be legitimate to criticise Lenin (not Bukharin) for taking England as exemplar of the parasitism and decay characteristic (he says) of imperial centres in the monopoly stage of capitalism. British firms as a group had a monopoly in the colonies, but individual (industrial) firms did not. It is not, in any case, difficult to account for the British empire in the nineteenth century in Marxist terms; Marx's own discussions of British rule in India have already been described.

To summarise, Lenin did not provide a full analysis of the key links in his argument. The connections between monopoly, capital export and the division of the world remain obscure. He did, however, write a powerful descriptive account of a world divided between great rival empires. Within these, two tendencies operated; on the one hand, the export of capital led to the internationalisation of capitalist production and the extension of capitalist relations of production to the furthest corners of the world, while on the other hand, power was concentrated into the hands of great blocs of finance capital and wealth channelled to parasitic rentier classes.

III   The labour aristocracy

In their writings on imperialism, Lenin and Bukharin were grappling with the most immediate political problems of their time. With the outbreak of the First World War, the mass of workers in each of the main belligerent countries had supported the war effort of their 'own' states. The working classes of Europe were, at that very moment, killing each other on the battlefields. This horrifying fact ran completely counter to Marx's prediction:

> The working men have no country. . . . National differences and antagonisms between peoples are daily more and more vanishing,

owing to the development of the bourgeoisie, to freedom of
commerce, to the world market, to uniformity in the mode of
production and in the conditions of life corresponding thereto.
(*Manifesto*, pp. 79–80)

The theory of imperialism explained why there should be antagonism
between the ruling classes of different countries, between the
beneficiaries of the 'state capitalist trusts' or 'monopoly capitalist
combines'. It still remained to explain how the proletariat could be
infected by the rise of aggressive nationalism.

Hilferding, writing before the war, saw imperialism as directly opposed
to the interests of the working class, even in the dominant countries. His
point was that the close links between the state and capital show up the
class character of the state, and lead the proletariat to adopt a stance of
opposition to the state and to imperialism.

This over-optimistic estimate could no longer be sustained at the time
when Bukharin and Lenin were writing. They argued that sections of the
working class in the dominant countries did benefit from the monopoly
position their capitalist masters had in the world market, and that this
explains the support that the imperialist powers were able to gain from
the working-class movement. They also argued (though not in detail)
that this gain accrued to only part of the workers, and that it was merely
a relative gain: workers employed by a monopoly in an advanced country
did better than those in a weaker position, but all would do better in a
socialist society.

The main argument that Lenin, in particular, relied on, however, was
that imperialism made war inevitable, and that the horrors of war totally
wiped out any gains the workers might get from monopolistic privilege. I
will discuss this argument in the next section.

Bukharin sets the context like this:

The first period of the war has brought about, not a crisis of
capitalism . . . , but a collapse of the 'Socialist' International. This
phenomenon, which many have attempted to explain by proceeding
solely from the analysis of the internal relations in every country,
cannot be more or less satisfactorily explained from this angle. For
the collapse of the proletarian movement is a result of the unequal
situation of the 'state capitalist trusts' within the boundaries of
world economy. (*IWE*, p. 161)

His argument is fairly straightforward. There is always a tendency in capitalist economies for workers to identify with their employers, on the basis that: 'the better the business of our shop, the better for me'. The evolution of trades union struggle has largely wiped out this attachment to a particular enterprise or industry and replaced it with an awareness of the need to unite against the capitalist employers. At the same time, however, the formation of 'state capitalist trusts' has created a basis for solidarity between classes on the national level, the 'so called working class protectionism with its policy of safeguarding "national industry", "national labour", etc.' (*IWE*, pp. 162–3).

The competitive struggle has been transformed into a struggle in the world market between 'state monopoly trusts'. The stronger trusts gain monopoly profit. They also gain extra profit by exploiting native labour in the colonies. These extra profits are the basis for the payment of increased wages. The workers in the dominant countries therefore gain from the success of 'their' states in the competitive struggle.

Lenin's arguments follow the same lines, but are rather broader and less specific. He is more insistent that it is only a section of the workers who gain, and also emphasises the possession of colonies more strongly, quoting Engels, who had discussed the reactionary political stance of the English working class as early as 1858. The significance of this, though Lenin does not bring it out, is that Engels and Lenin are pointing to the emergence of a 'labour aristocracy' *before* the rise of monopoly (in the sense of control of a market by a single enterprise or organised group of enterprises). This seems inconsistent with Lenin's own comment 'the economic possibility of such bribery, whatever its form may be, requires high monopolist profits' (*Imperialism*, p. 540).

Let us first consider the case of an enterprise which gains high profits because of its monopoly control of markets. It is clearly *possible* for such a firm to pay higher wages to its workers than it would be able to without a protected monopoly position. There is, however, nothing in its monopoly position that *compels* it to pay higher wages. If workers are effectively organised in trades unions, then they can struggle for higher wages, and the sheltered economic position of the employers may reduce their resistance to this pressure. Alternatively, a firm may decide to pay higher wages in order to forestall trades unionism or to gain the loyalty of its workers. The gains are very likely, in this case, to go to a privileged minority, with the management using the policy of 'divide and rule'. Workers' gains may be in terms of better working conditions, shorter hours or better conditions of work rather than in higher wages.

Against this must be set the possibility, emphasised by Hilferding, that a larger firm with greater financial resources may be in a stronger position to *resist* wage claims and to suppress trades unions, especially if it can call on state support in these conflicts.

The stronger economic position of large monopoly firms may thus lead to better or worse conditions for workers, depending on the precise balance of forces. Lenin, in particular, seems to suggest a conscious policy of the ruling class in his repeated use of the word 'bribe' to describe the gains of the workers.

There is a difficulty, however. All the classical Marxists tended to overstate the extent to which monopoly had triumphed. In fact, it was still the exception rather than the rule for a single firm or organised cartel to have complete control over the market for some product even within the protected boundaries of a single advanced country, and in the world market as a whole, price competition was very far from being suppressed. This difficulty is compounded by Lenin's insistence on tracing the history of the 'labour aristocracy' back to nineteenth-century England, when markets were certainly competitive in the sense that there were many competing firms.

We must, therefore, look at the case where a particular country has a monopoly position in the production of some commodity, either in the world market or in colonial markets, but where there are many small firms competing with each other within the country concerned.

The main point is that no single firm can afford to concede higher wages unless its competitors do. The fact that the firms in the industry have a *monopoly as a group* makes little difference when there is *competition within the group*. The only way that workers can gain is by a general wage increase across the whole industry, and this can only be achieved by some force that operates at that level. A general shortage of labour in the industry is one such factor (which might be the product of its success in gaining control of markets), a strong trades union organisation is another, and the intervention of the state is a third. Marx discussed this latter possibility in relation not to wage increases, but to statutory limitations on hours of work. Emmanuel's theory of 'unequal exchange' follows the same lines, with trades union action as the driving force (see chapter 9). Very much the same considerations apply where the industry has a technical lead over its overseas competitors, and thus an advantage in productivity. This was probably the main factor in the dominant position of British capitalism in the nineteenth century.

Lenin also seems to suggest (the text is not very clear on this) that profits from investment abroad provide a further basis for the bribing of the working class. This is much more dubious. In general the firms that receive profits from abroad will not be the ones that employ the workers to be bribed in the home country. The recipients of profits from British investment abroad were mainly individual rentiers, and it is hard to see any plausible mechanism by which the money was transferred to the 'labour aristocracy'. Rentiers, it is true, employed servants, but these were generally among the worst paid sections of the working class. Butlers and housemaids do not make a very plausible basis for the Second International.

It is true that there are many interconnections that I have not discussed, which provide some basis for working-class support for imperialism. Protected markets, for example, may improve security of employment. Workers producing luxury goods have at least a short-run interest in the prosperity of the buyers of such goods, and so on. These sorts of connections provide a basis for talking of 'national prosperity' and of a 'national interest', in the way that Bukharin does, but to deal with them adequately would require a detailed analysis which neither Bukharin nor Lenin provides.

Both Bukharin and Lenin correctly identified skilled workers as the better off stratum of the working class, and therefore tended to identify them as the beneficiaries of imperialism. In fact, differentials between skilled and unskilled workers were of great antiquity, and it is not clear that skilled workers, as such, did particularly well out of imperialism. To analyse this point further would require an analysis of the world division of labour in terms of the labour process. One could argue that the work done by unskilled workers is more easily transferred to establishments in colonies where cheap labour can be employed, and that skilled workers are more protected from this kind of competition.

It should also be pointed out that the export of capital works counter to the workers' interests, at least in the longer run. It creates jobs abroad at the expense of jobs at home although it may, in the short run, encourage the production of capital goods for export and thus keep up employment in the industries concerned.

To sum up, Bukharin and Lenin observed that the living standards of some workers in some advanced countries had risen significantly, and that they no longer had 'nothing to lose but their chains'. At the same time, the countries where this was happening were also those which were coming out on top in the struggle for world dominance. Our authors concluded, probably rightly, that there was a connection between these facts, but they were not able fully to specify the mechanisms at work. It cannot be said that we have got much further since.

They deserve great credit for recognising that a 'national interest' does exist, at least to a certain degree, and that sectional and nationalistic sentiments among the working class have a real material basis. This is a crucially important fact.

The idea of a 'labour aristocracy' has been much discussed. There can be no doubt that stratification of the working class is a very important topic for study. Subsequent work on the subject has tended to move away from basing it in the possession of colonies and of a monopoly position in the world market. This is another field in which much remains to be done.

IV 'Ultra-imperialism' and the polemics against Kautsky

In the years before the First World War, the centre of gravity of the socialist movement and of theoretical Marxism was in Germany, in the German Social Democratic Party. The dominant figure, both in theoretical debates and in practical politics, was Karl Kautsky. Around Kautsky grew up a tradition of Marxist thought which was, in its time, the established Marxist orthodoxy (though it is difficult to remember this today when, with the benefit of hindsight, we tend to focus on Lenin and the other Bolsheviks). At the time, the various Russian groupings seemed relatively insignificant.

The leaders of the German Social Democrats had a long tradition of support for free trade, which they associated with low prices and, in particular, low food prices. When Hilferding built his analysis of the rise of monopoly around the role of tariffs, and the connection between protection and monopoly, he was working firmly in this tradition. In arguing that the rise of finance capital had unified the capitalist class and that finance capital had definitely seized control of the state, he broke sharply from the orthodox approach, which was still rooted in the idea that state policies were the outcome of a clash of interests representing different fractions of capital. Kautsky and his school regarded imperialist policies as expressing the interests of financial capital and of certain monopoly groups, but he held that sections of industrial capital still retained an interest in peace and free trade. The social democrats hoped that by throwing the weight of the working class into the scales against imperialism and militarism, the balance could be tipped in favour of peace.

Immediately before the First World War, Kautsky came up with a further reason for optimism about the prospects for peace, in the theory of *ultra-imperialism*, that is, the possibility that the major powers would find it preferable to agree to exploit the world jointly, rather than fighting over the division of the world. A similar line of argument had been advanced earlier by Hobson (as Lenin points out), using the term 'inter-imperialism'.

The importance of this argument in the theoretical framework of the social-democratic centre was that this new policy alternative would draw its support from those sections of the ruling class who would otherwise have an interest in supporting imperialist policies, and would thus strengthen the political forces working for peace and weaken those prepared to risk war. This idea played an important part in lulling the working-class movement into a false sense of security on the eve of the First World War, and thus contributed to the débâcle of the Second International on the outbreak of war.

When the war broke out, Kautsky transferred his hopes for peace to the post-war period. In a key article, published soon after the start of the war, he wrote:

> What Marx said of capitalism can also be applied to imperialism: monopoly creates competition and competition monopoly. The frantic competition of giant firms, giant banks and multi-millionaires obliged the great financial groups . . . to think up the notion of the cartel. In the same way the result of the World War between the great imperialist powers may be a federation of the strongest, who renounce their arms race.

> Hence from the purely economic standpoint it is not impossible that capitalism may still live through another phase, the translation of cartellisation into foreign policy: a phase of ultraimperialism, which of course we must struggle against as energetically as we do against imperialism, but whose perils lie in another direction, not in that of the arms race and the threat to world peace. (Kautsky, 1970, p. 46)

Kautsky argued that this policy of 'peaceful', joint exploitation of the world by the united finance capital of the great powers would be forced on them by the threat they faced from the oppressed colonial peoples and from their own proletariat.

The way this theory was posed, and the way in which it was attacked by the left, reveal a great deal about the concepts of imperialism current at the time and shared by both sides in this debate. Kautsky is arguing that the stress may shift from conflict between imperialist powers to maintenance of a world system of exploitation. It is surely the latter, the world-wide suppression of colonial peoples by the metropolitan bourgeoisie, which is generally understood by the term 'imperialism' today, but Kautsky was careful to distinguish it from imperialism as the term was then understood, and to give it a different name. The very suggestion that such a shift was possible aroused vehement hostility from the left.

For both sides, inter-imperialist rivalry leading to war was the very essence of imperialism. As I suggested at the beginning of this chapter, the concept of imperialism has shifted its meaning between then and now.

In describing ultra-imperialism as 'peaceful', it is clear that Kautsky did not mean that exploited peoples or the proletariat at the centre would be treated with kid gloves. He simply meant that the ruling classes of the major capitalist powers would not go to war with each other.

There are three different issues that arise in considering the theory of ultra-imperialism. Firstly, does it make sense on a purely theoretical level as a possible tendency in capitalist development? Secondly, if so, was this tendency in fact dominant at the time of the First World War, or, alternatively, was it reasonable to expect it to become dominant within a fairly short time? Thirdly, does this theory have anything to offer us in understanding the world today?

There is no space here to deal fully with the second of these questions, since detailed historical and empirical material would be required. Those who criticised Kautsky at the time could, of course, only consider the first two of these questions. The third question will be taken up in chapter 12.

The central reason for left-wing opposition to the theory of ultra-imperialism is, however, obvious. Lenin and his allies thought that a socialist revolution was on the cards for the near future, and they wanted to argue that war and misery were the only alternative to revolution. In the context of the First World War, idle dreams of the possibility of lasting peace after the war were clearly a diversion from the real issues.

Both Bukharin and, especially, Lenin wrote about imperialism primarily to challenge Kautsky's view, and to repair the damage done to the international socialist movement by the capitulation of the parties of the Second International at the outbreak of the war. As far as they were concerned the intimate connection between capitalist development, imperialism and war was the central theoretical basis of their stand against abandoning the struggle for socialism for the duration. No compromise on this issue was possible.

Lenin vehemently rejected any idea of ultra-imperialism: 'development is proceeding towards monopolies, hence towards a single world monopoly. . . as completely meaningless as is the statement that "development is proceeding" towards the manufacture of foodstuffs in laboratories' (*Imperialism*, p. 530).

Bukharin is more moderate; in the abstract a world trust is thinkable, but in reality it cannot come about. He advances two reasons for this. Firstly, any agreement between 'state capitalist trusts' must be disrupted by uneven development. The strong will not in any case accept agreements since they will hope to gain more without. Secondly, if the proletariat become strong enough to prevent aggressive policies, as Kautsky hoped they might, they would be strong enough to establish socialism. Hilferding, who wrote before Kautsky's theory of ultra-imperialism was devised, put the same argument, but did not come to any conclusion as to whether force or peaceful division of the market would prevail, though he thought that agreements were only likely to be temporary.

The first of Bukharin's arguments rests on the assumption that national blocs of capital, each exploiting exclusive possession of a national economic territory, must remain the basic units between which any ultra-imperialist peace would be made. However, in addition to the reasons which Bukharin put forward for the formation of nationally based 'state capitalist trusts', there is a counter-tendency, also arising from factors included in his analysis.

For Bukharin, as for Hilferding, an important motive for capital export is the desire to penetrate the protected markets of other nation states from within. Over a long period of time, this can result in the interpenetration of different national capitals, with the same group of firms operating within each national economic territory. In this case a struggle to enlarge one nation's territory at the expense of others becomes economically pointless. To give an example, there would be no point in Ford or General Motors seeking to extend their markets by sponsoring

US annexation of parts of the EEC, when they are securely established in the European industry already. In the same way, tariff barriers between different markets become a hindrance rather than a benefit once multi-national firms are well established.

As for the second argument, that if the working class is strong enough to compel the adoption of peaceful policies it will also be strong enough to overthrow capitalism, this seems an extremely schematic argument which does not do adequate justice to the complexity of political developments. All of our authors anticipated socialist revolutions in the advanced countries within a fairly short period of time. We have, in fact, seen the emergence of a socialist bloc, and of Third World liberation movements which pose a massive threat to world capitalism, forcing the major capitalist states onto the defensive, together with a political absorption of the working class into a re-shaped political system. It is clear that the orthodox objections to the theory of ultra-imperialism no longer have the same force.

I am not here arguing that Kautsky's theory is correct as applied to our own times, only that the arguments that Lenin and Bukharin put against him are not decisive on a purely theoretical level. The First and Second World Wars provide strong evidence that rivalry leading towards war was the dominant tendency at the time when they were writing, but here, as elsewhere, they allowed themselves to be drawn by the pressures of debate into overstating their case.

V Summary

Bukharin combined the analysis of the *internationalisation* of capitalist relations of production (Marx, Luxemburg) with Hilferding's analysis of the formation of blocs of finance capital to show why these blocs formed on a *national* basis. The competitive struggle continues, in the era of finance capital, but it now takes the form of military and political rivalry between 'state capitalist trusts'. Lenin's *Imperialism* follows the same lines on a lower level of abstraction, providing a forceful descriptive account of imperialism. Both argued that capital export accelerated development in underdeveloped areas (though Bukharin was more cautious in his predictions), both discussed how workers in imperialist centres gain some (limited) advantages from the success of 'their' nations, thus explaining the material basis of working-class nationalism, and both thought that inter-imperialist rivalry made inter-imperialist war inevitable. They had relatively little to say about the impact of imperialism on underdeveloped countries, but Lenin expected an acceleration of capitalist development in backward areas.

Part III

Modern Marxist theories
of development
and underdevelopment

6 · Baran

I The context

The last three chapters have dealt with the theories of imperialism developed in the period from 1900 to 1920. I now turn to theories put forward after the Second World War, since the period between the wars produced no notable innovations in the Marxist theory of imperialism. The success of the Russian revolution and the defeat of revolution in western Europe widened the rift between social democrats, who now abandoned their Marxist heritage, and communists, who stood by the Russian revolution and came to accept the leadership of 'the party of Lenin'. This division was institutionalised with the formation of the Third International, the 'Comintern', and of separate communist parties in the various countries of Europe.

The rise of Stalin in Russia was followed by the imposition of a grey orthodoxy in matters of theory, not only in Russia, but in all of the communist parties. Most Marxists accepted the imposition of this discipline because they could see no alternative, while the few centres of independent Marxist thought that did exist were isolated and condemned to impotence. The victory of Fascism in most of continental Europe further disrupted any serious development of Marxist theory. I will not discuss the various textbooks of Marxism produced in the Soviet Union; they reproduced Lenin rather mechanically and tended, as far as imperialism is concerned, to draw on the weaker aspects of Lenin's writing, stressing the 'overripeness' of capitalism and interpreting it in an underconsumptionist sense. (See Kemp, 1967, chapter 7 for a discussion of some of these works.)

In the early 1920s, before Stalin had consolidated his power, there were notable advances in economics in Russia, but they were, naturally, directed mainly to problems of socialist planning and post-revolutionary economic policy. The importance of these debates and the originality of

131

the ideas produced can hardly be overstated, but they did not contribute to the theory of imperialism.

Marxist economics, understood as the study of capitalist (not socialist) economies, was kept alive through this period by a handful of writers working in isolation in the West, to whom we owe a great debt of gratitude. Maurice Dobb, in England, wrote a number of valuable works, but had little new to say about imperialism. (See Dobb, 1940, chapter 7 and Dobb, 1963, pp. 311 ff.) Paul Sweezy, in America, produced a textbook of Marxist economics, *The Theory of Capitalist Development* (Sweezy, 1942), which is an important bridge between the classical Marxist writings and more recent work.

After the Second World War, things did not immediately improve. Stalinist orthodoxy remained unshaken, while the 'cold war' was the excuse for continued repression in the West. The post-war boom enabled the working class in the West to be incorporated into the established system to a greater extent than ever before. Both the advanced capitalist countries and those of the Soviet bloc appeared locked in political immobility and intellectual cynicism.

In the underdeveloped countries, however, previously almost ignored by Marxists, things were stirring. The Chinese revolution destroyed the idea that only workers in relatively advanced countries could make a revolution, and independence movements emerged throughout the continents of Asia and Africa.

Paul Baran's *Political Economy of Growth* (Baran, 1973, cited below as *PEG*), published in 1957, marked an important shift in Marxist theory, both in its theoretical content and in the problems to which it was addressed. Baran stigmatised monopoly capital as a cause of stagnation, in both the advanced and the underdeveloped countries. Rivalry and war had receded into the background in the new circumstances of American dominance. At the same time, he was the first major Marxist theorist to treat underdeveloped countries as worthy of study in their own right. (Lenin, it is true, had written on the *Development of Capitalism in Russia*, but Russia was a semi-developed rather than an underdeveloped country.) Baran differed from his predecessors essentially in regarding the development of capitalism in underdeveloped countries as a different process from that which the advanced countries had gone through in an earlier period of history. This approach has become fundamental to subsequent Marxist thinking about underdevelopment.

Sweezy, in 1942, had argued that capitalism has an inherent tendency to stagnation as a result of lack of demand, a problem exacerbated by the rise of monopoly, and had traced the lack of demand to the low level of consumption of the mass of the population. This 'underconsumptionist' argument derives from Hobson, though it is also a possible interpretation of Lenin and of passages from Marx. It recurs throughout the history of Marxism, but in Sweezy and in Baran it is brought to the centre of the picture and connected up with similar ideas from Keynesian economics. This will be the topic of the next section.

Sweezy had retained the stress on inter-imperialist rivalry, a line which made sense during the Second World War, when he explained Fascist expansionism as a manifestation of this rivalry. He did, however, prepare the ground for a later shift of emphasis, by explaining the intensity of rivalry in terms of a particular historical situation: the rise of Germany and the USA and their challenge to British world domination. It was thus a product of particular circumstances, which could change.

Throughout their careers, Baran and Sweezy worked closely together, a collaboration which culminated in their joint work, *Monopoly Capital* (1968). It is rather unprofitable to try to determine which was the original author of the general line of thought that they represent. From the *Theory of Capitalist Development*, through the *Political Economy of Growth* to *Monopoly Capital*, there is a consistent development, starting very close to classical Marxism, but evolving into something distinctively different.

As Marxist economics revived in the 1960s, Baran and Sweezy provided an important starting point, especially in America and in the Third World. The journal, *Monthly Review* (edited, with others, by Sweezy), nurtured a whole school of writers who followed in their footsteps.

II Monopoly and stagnation

Baran and Sweezy were, as remarked above, 'underconsumptionists', in the sense that they thought that capitalist economies were characterised by a chronic lack of demand because of the restricted purchasing power of the workers. I have already discussed, and rejected, this general stance (chapter 2). Sweezy really put forward two arguments. In the *Theory of Capitalist Development* he argued that continuous expansion in a capitalist system is logically impossible if one takes account of various tendencies described by Marx. This argument applies at all stages of capitalist development. He also argued that it was unlikely that *monopoly* enterprises would carry out enough investment to sustain demand. This second argument is the one developed by Baran. They are combined, in a rather different form, in *Monopoly Capital*.

Sweezy's first argument runs as follows: with the development of capitalism, the share of wages, and hence of wage earners' consumption, in total output falls, while the concentration of capital into fewer hands means that a falling share of total profit is consumed. Consumption therefore absorbs a falling share of total output. (This prefigures the 'law of rising surplus' set out in *Monopoly Capital*.) If we restrict our attention to a very simple model, similar to that used by Marx in constructing the schemas of reproduction, then the falling share of consumption must be matched by a rising share of investment in new means of production as a fraction of total output. Both consumption and investment increase over time, but if demand is to expand in line with output, investment must rise faster than consumption.

Sweezy then argues that new means of production are only required to expand the capacity to produce consumer goods (this point is implicit, not explicit), and that there is a technically fixed ratio between the new means of production needed and the additional consumer goods output that is produced, so the two can only expand in step.

This implies a contradiction between the requirements that investment should increase faster than consumption, to maintain demand, and the technical requirement that they increase at the same rate. Sweezy therefore concludes that demand will fail to match output, unless some way is found of absorbing output in unproductive uses (military spending, etc.) or through capital export.

The flaw in the argument is obvious; Sweezy assumes that means of production can only be used to produce consumer goods. If there were a falling share of consumption in output, then this could be balanced by an accelerating rate of growth with an increasing fraction of investment going into the industries that produce means of production. There is no assurance that this will happen, of course, but if sufficient profitable investment opportunities exist then the opportunity for an acceleration of accumulation will be taken up. The prospect of profit is the engine that drives capitalism, not the expansion of consumption.

If we reject Sweezy's underconsumption analysis, we are left with the rate of investment, itself determined by investment opportunities, as the central determinant of whether the gap between output and consumption will be filled. Sweezy has a further argument here, distinct from the underconsumption argument, and it is this second line of argument that predominates in Baran's *Political Economy of Growth*, and in their later joint work, *Monopoly Capital*. I shall concentrate on Baran's formulation of the argument since it seems to me more complete than those in the other works cited.

Baran argues that investment is determined by two main motives: to introduce new techniques of production and to expand output. A monopoly will tend to hold back on the introduction of new techniques, because these threaten to make its existing equipment obsolete, while it will not want to expand output because it would have to cut prices to generate the corresponding extra sales, thus reducing its profits.

Baran, in particular, stresses the contrast between competitive capitalism and a capitalism dominated by monopolies. In competitive capitalism, any firm which holds back on cost-reducing innovations will be driven out of the market by the low prices of its competitors, and competitive firms will invest to expand output because they are each trying to expand their share of the market, heedless of the effect on the total output and hence the price. Any firm that holds back on expansion will fall behind its competitors, will find itself with higher costs and without the resources to introduce new methods of production. (He also describes the waste resulting from the rather random pattern of expansion under a competitive system, but it is clear that he regards competition, on balance, as a force for development.)

There is a noticeable shift here from the classical Marxist position. The classical Marxists regarded the *tendency* towards monopoly as a factor *intensifying* competition, not suppressing it, although it is true that they were not wholly consistent in this. Baran and Sweezy, by contrast, argue that the competitive struggle virtually vanishes when there are only a few large firms operating in each market, since these will generally prefer to adopt a 'live and let live' policy towards each other. Hilferding had discussed this possibility in a rather open-minded fashion, but Lenin and Bukharin had rejected it as part of their rejection of 'ultra-imperialism'.

There is something of a paradox here. While the classical Marxists, especially Bukharin, tended to talk as if each national economy was dominated by a single 'state capitalist trust', their thoughts were influenced by the fact that concentration had not gone that far in reality. The main form of monopoly was the relatively fragile cartel agreement between rather a large number of firms, liable to break down into furious competition. Baran and Sweezy, writing later, stressed that there were typically several firms, not just one, in each market, but that they were few enough and established enough to maintain a stable 'balance of power'.

It is necessary, however, to evaluate the theoretical argument. Will monopolies in general invest less than competitive firms would do? I do not believe that Baran and Sweezy establish this central point satisfactorily.

Consider technical innovation first. There has been a massive debate on the effect of market structure on technical advance, and although this debate is not settled, no clear empirical evidence has emerged of the superiority of competitive markets. Any greater incentive that small firms may feel to innovate is offset by their reduced capacity to do so. (See, for example, Hay and Morris, 1979, chapter 13 and references cited there.).

On the level of theory, the case is not clear cut anyway. Both a monopoly and a competitive firm have an incentive to minimise their costs: there is, therefore, an incentive to adopt any innovation that reduces costs. In both cases it pays to introduce new equipment and throw away the old only if the total cost of production with the new equipment is lower than that direct cost of production on the old (since the capital cost with the old equipment is already sunk: the alternatives are to throw it away, or to go on using it as long as it gives any return at all towards the capital costs). Baran is aware of this (*PEG*, pp. 198–9) but introduces other arguments resting on the risk of committing capital and the limited supply of capital to the firm. He argues that these will lead monopolies to hold back where competitive firms are forced to go ahead. One can argue, on the other hand, that large firms devote much resources to the deliberate search for new methods of production and new products to market, and thus have more opportunities to innovate, even if they are slower in taking up some of them.

What Baran's argument comes down to in the end is not that monopolies will slow down technical change in the long run, but that they will introduce new techniques less wastefully and thus with a lower rate of investment. Whether this helps or hinders capitalist development depends on an assessment of whether, in the long run, capitalist expansion is more often slowed by lack of demand or by lack of resources to take up all the technological opportunities open to it. In other words, the way monopolies respond to technical change only leads to a shortfall of demand in a framework in which a shortfall of demand is a problem anyway.

The main weight of the argument must thus fall on the assertion that monopolies will hold back on the expansion of output in order to protect their monopoly profits. This is a *static* argument applied to an essentially *dynamic* problem. For a *given* level of costs and of demand, there will be a particular price and a particular output which give a monopoly the maximum profit. It will continue to produce this output, and will not invest for expansion, as long as the given conditions remain the same. To analyse investment we must look at the causes of *changes* in costs and demand. The static model cannot help us here.

A similarly static model of a single competitive industry can be constructed. Again, with given costs and demand there is a determinate equilibrium output, determined in this case by the equalisation of profit rates between industries. Any expansion of the industry would depress profits and induce an outflow of capital. In this case too, the rate of investment will be governed by *changes* in costs and demand (see Matthews, 1959, pp. 33 ff.).

For the determinants of changes in demand, we must look outside the single industry, and look at the economy as a whole. The expansion of one industry generates demand for means of production and also creates jobs, thus expanding demand for consumer goods. The expansion in demand, if not offset by contraction elsewhere, has a cumulative effect. Other industries step up investment, and this generates further expansion. This cumulative process will work through whether the economy is competitive or monopolistic, though not necessarily in exactly the same way. The same process works in reverse when demand contracts.

The result is that a capitalist economy moves through a sequence of booms and slumps, and does so in a timespan short by comparison with the periods involved in discussions of secular growth. The major factors determining the overall rate of investment over a long period of time must therefore either be forces that manifest themselves slowly but steadily through boom and slump, or forces that actually work through the mechanism of the cycle, through the relative strength of boom and slump and through the limiting factors that halt a boom or a depression. The desire of monopolies to avoid spoiling a given, static, market by overexpansion does not fit the bill at all.

It has to be admitted that nobody has a really satisfactory theory of the determinants of investment, or of their relation to the predominance of monopoly or competition in the economy. In default of any theory, we must turn to the evidence.

Baran, writing in the 1950s, looked for evidence mainly to the period before the Second World War. The depression of the 1930s, the deepest and most prolonged in history, made it easy for him to find examples of the failure of monopoly capitalism. We are now, in the 1970s and 1980s, in another depression, but the 'long boom' of the 1950s and 1960s suggests strongly that monopoly capitalism is not incompatible with growth. The 'long boom' was a period of rapid growth in the world capitalist economy which far outstrips any such episode in the epoch of competitive capitalism. Baran and Sweezy should have realised this when they wrote *Monopoly Capital* in the 1960s, but they seem to have been misled by an excessive concentration on the American economy. It was, of course, Japan and continental west Europe that were the main centres of growth.

III Growth and surplus

Sweezy's *Theory of Capitalist Development* was constructed within an essentially classical Marxist framework. Baran, in his *Political Economy of Growth*, introduced major changes in the conceptual framework, in particular with his treatment of *'economic surplus'*, and this new apparatus was substantially retained in *Monopoly Capital*.

The idea of an economic surplus goes back before Marx to the English 'classical' economists and the physiocrats. They thought essentially in terms of a physical surplus, available to society or to the state, over and above the part of output needed to maintain the population and the capital stock intact. This surplus or 'net product' could be used for accumulation, for military purposes or for the development of culture. (See, for example, Ricardo's *Principles*, 1971, chapter 26.)

Marx transformed this idea into an expression of class relations; surplus labour is the labour that an exploited class has to do to produce goods for its exploiters. In a capitalist society, this takes the form of *surplus value*. Corresponding to this we can define a *surplus product*, consisting of all the goods which are appropriated by the capitalist class, either for their own consumption, for new investment or for the use of unproductive workers and hangers-on of one sort or another.

Baran reverts, essentially, to the classical, i.e. the pre-Marxist, definition, and this for very much the same purposes as those of the classical economists: he wishes to discuss the 'nature and causes of the wealth of nations'. More specifically, he sees growth in the physical volume of output as a process that can be described on a purely physical/technical level, with the social relations of production acting as either a spur to this development or a brake holding up the process of growth.

He defines economic growth as 'increase over time in *per capita* output of material goods' (*PEG*, p. 128). To measure growth, we must have some way of aggregating the output of material goods; Baran discusses this, but decides to assume that 'increases of aggregate output can somehow be measured' (p. 129). The relevant point here is not the technical problems of measurement, but the fact that Baran conceptualises growth in this essentially *quantitative* way, by contrast with earlier Marxist writers whose focus was on *qualitative* change in the social relations of production. In some ways this represents a step forward, since ideas like the 'development of the forces of production' and 'increases in the productivity of labour', which are central to a Marxist analysis of capitalism, are essentially quantitative in character. There is, however, a corresponding danger that qualitative changes will be overlooked and that socialism may be seen solely as a means to more rapid growth.

Baran has a very simple theory of the determinants of economic growth. He lists a number of factors generating growth (pp. 129–31), but emerges with *new net investment in means of production* as the dominant factor. Since net investment has to come out of the economic surplus, this enables him to conclude that it is the *size* and *use* of the economic surplus that is the key factor in economic growth.

To fit into Baran's framework, net investment must be defined in a way that diverges from Marx's concept of capital accumulation. Baran defines net investment as the net addition to the stock of means of production in use in the society concerned. This is the same definition as that used by bourgeois economics. Marx, on the other hand, defined capital by reference to a specific social relation, so that capital accumulation, for Marx, includes the wages advanced to new workers, but excludes any additions to means of production used in non-capitalist sectors of the economy. Marx includes, under the heading of primitive accumulation, the transformation of means of production (and consumption goods) into capital by transfer from a non-capitalist to a capitalist sector. In Baran's framework, this is not investment, and its only significance lies in the changes in the use of the surplus that may follow from it.

Baran's purpose is to argue that capitalism was, at one stage, a (moderately) efficient engine of growth, but that it is so no longer, and that socialism would do the job better. To argue this he needs a framework which conceptualises growth independently of social relations, in order to be able to compare growth in socialist and capitalist systems. This is, in a way, fully consistent with the perspective of classical Marxism: he is arguing that capitalism has become a fetter on the development of the forces of production and has thus come to the end of its historically allotted span.

Baran introduces three different concepts of the surplus, none of them corresponding to Marx's concept (though he tends, in using them, to blur the distinctions, and end up rather close to Marx's concept after all).

He defines the *actual surplus* as the difference between current net output and current consumption. Since virtually all uses of output other than investment in new means of production are to be counted as consumption, the actual surplus is equal to net investment plus any outflow (or minus any inflow) of funds across the boundaries of the country concerned. Note that this does not mean that surplus necessarily determines investment; if investment is insufficient to absorb the (potential) surplus, then output will either fall or be used for current consumption. In a capitalist system goods will not be produced if there is no demand for them.

For the world as a whole, the actual surplus must equal net investment (plus additions to stocks of gold, which can be ignored), so any discrepancy for one country must constitute a transfer of surplus for investment in another country. In a capitalist world, this transfer can come about either by an export of capital (which remains the property of the capitalists of the capital exporting country) or by the flow of profits, dividends and interest into or out of a country as a result of previous acts of investment. It can also take the form of flows of 'tribute' directly extracted from its colonies by a dominant power.

The *potential surplus*, on the other hand, is the amount that a totally growth-oriented society could devote to investment without reducing current consumption below some minimum necessary level. It is thus 'the difference between the output that *could* be produced in a given natural and technical environment with the help of employable productive resources, and what might be regarded as essential consumption' (*PEG*, p. 133). There are considerable conceptual and practical difficulties of measurement here, but Baran avoids using the concept in a quantitative way, being content to indicate that a large gap exists between the potential surplus and the actual level of investment.

Baran spends some time discussing which kinds of *labour* are productive and which are unproductive. From the point of view of the definitions, it is more relevant to think of the way in which different *products* are to be treated, since the definitions of surplus are cast in terms of the output and use of products. Put simply, any outputs that Baran disapproves of ('that would be absent in a rationally ordered society') are to count as part of actual consumption, but not of necessary consumption. They thus account for part of the gap between the potential and actual surplus. (I cannot resist the thought that the working class might, in a 'rationally ordered society', allot themselves a chromium-plated Cadillac each, if only to show their independence of puritanical intellectuals. I would not like to defend this thought against less frivolous comrades, but it does point to the difficulties of a concept of surplus based on what is 'rational' rather than on the exploitation of one class by another.)

The third concept of surplus is the *planned surplus*, a concept relevant only to a socialist society which plays little part in the further development of Baran's arguments. It is the difference between an 'optimal' level of output (perhaps less than the maximum possible output because of shorter working hours, etc.) and an 'optimal' level of consumption. It thus represents the outcome of a deliberate and conscious collective choice between consumption and investment.

Baran's procedure is now fairly obvious: the planned surplus represents the use that a rational society would make of its potential surplus. In a capitalist society, the actual surplus falls short of the potential surplus, and it is the size and use of the surplus, the relation between actual and potential surplus, that will be the focus of Baran's investigation.

IV The advanced countries

Baran's discussion of the advanced capitalist countries is really a discussion of America, though he does not say so. Virtually all of the examples and evidence that he gives are American, and the whole story makes much more sense in that context than it would as applied to, say, Japan or West Germany. It is worth noting that the concept of a 'nation state' or a 'national economy' is taken for granted as being the relevant unit of analysis, with no serious discussion. It gradually becomes clear, as Baran introduces such concepts as the surplus, the level of investment and so on, that we are to understand these as aggregates at a national level.

The essence of his argument as far as the advanced capitalist countries are concerned turns on a contrast between competitive and monopoly capitalism, though it is presented, rather confusingly, in terms of a contrast between the *idealised model* of competition held by the classical economists and the *reality* (as Baran sees it) of monopoly capital. Still, he admits that this idealised model 'indicates, at least approximately, the essential principles of the mechanism that has actually provided for . . . an unprecedented development of productive forces' (*PEG*, p. 165).

According to this account, competitive capitalism maximises the surplus by depressing workers' consumption to a minimum, encouraging thrift on the part of capitalists, and eliminating unproductive spending. The surplus is directed mainly into investment because of the competitive pressures to innovate and to expand. Competitive capitalism is thus a powerful agent of growth.

The evolution of the surplus under monopoly capitalism proves rather difficult to pin down:

> The economic surplus generated under monopolistic capitalism is, however, as large as is possible in the only relevant sense of the notion, that is, taking into account the prevailing level of output, the market mechanism responsible for the distribution of income under capitalism as well as the more or less steady rise of conventional standards of subsistence. (*PEG*, p. 177)

In other words, it is what it is. It is, however, large and rising. Baran seems here (it isn't very clear) to be using a concept of surplus as the total of profit and other property income. He has returned, in other words, to Marx's concept, though in terms of prices and not values.

He focuses on the *use* of the surplus, arguing that monopolies will tend to invest less than they might, so that there is a chronic lack of demand unless other stimulating factors take over. I have already described (and rejected) this picture of monopoly as a cause of stagnation, which is really the heart of Baran's case against monopoly capitalism.

If surplus is not used, however, it will not be realised in money terms at all. Goods that cannot be sold will not be produced. The resulting unemployment will also lead to a reduction in consumption, reducing total sales and total output still further. The central problem for monopoly capitalism, therefore, is to avoid a slump of the dimensions of the 1930s or worse. This is achieved, at least some of the time, in Baran's account, by the absorption of the surplus in various forms of waste, some of them a response to the lack of demand, some a fortuitous result of other developments in capitalism.

Because of the chronic lack of demand, sales effort is stepped up and part of the potential surplus is diverted into advertising, wasteful product differentiation and so on, thus partly relieving the lack of demand that underlies it. (This argument is more fully developed in *Monopoly Capital* than in the *Political Economy of Growth*.) Another part is devoted to a proliferation of unproductive activities within the giant firm, for reasons not directly connected with the lack of demand, but tending, all the same, to relieve it.

More important in absorbing the surplus is *state spending* which absorbs large chunks of the potential surplus in various wasteful ways, notably through military spending. Baran discusses the possibility that the state might devote surplus to useful purposes, but concludes that this is impractical on political grounds. The ruling class is, firstly, ambivalent about state spending; it wants demand to be maintained, which requires that the surplus be used, but at the same time wants to retain ownership of the surplus and resents parting with it in taxes. Secondly, there is fierce opposition to any collective provision that affects capitalist interests by competing with private provision. The state will, in any case, not aim at real full employment, since a certain amount of unemployment is necessary to maintain labour discipline and keep wages down. These arguments enable Baran to accept the substance of a Keynesian analysis of unemployment while rejecting the Keynesian argument that state intervention can produce a stable and conflict-free capitalism.

In the same way, Baran rejects the argument that an increase in wages or in transfers to the poor could relieve the problem by raising consumption. This was Hobson's prescription, and Baran joins with Lenin in arguing that this way out is not possible in a capitalist framework. Baran's whole theoretical position is very close to that of Hobson.

Military spending, with related forms of expenditure, such as spying, military aid to allies, and so on, emerges as one of the few forms of state spending which can absorb the surplus without harming the interests of any powerful fraction of the ruling class. Military spending is, in Baran's analysis, intimately tied up with imperialism.

Baran does not give a definition of imperialism, nor is it clear from his use of the word exactly what he means by it. He uses the word broadly to indicate a policy and an ideology of expansionism (cf. Bukharin) rather than a stage of development (cf. Lenin). It does not necessarily imply a policy of formal territorial expansion, but includes more general policies designed to forward the interests of the country's citizens and, specifically, its giant corporations, all over the world. It does not necessarily seem to imply rivalry between imperialist powers (though Baran does mention rivalry in a rather muted form; *PEG*, pp. 242-3).

To put it very briefly, Baran gives an account of the origins of imperialism which follows along broadly classical Marxist lines, but argues that its effects in the advanced countries are mainly felt through the military and other spending involved, and, in effect, that imperialism ends up virtually as an excuse for state spending. This at first sight surprising conclusion needs further examination.

The export of goods does not help with the absorption of surplus, since it must be balanced by a corresponding import of goods or export of capital, otherwise the balance of payments is disturbed and will compel a readjustment (by revaluation of the currency or by other means). This does not prevent individual enterprises from seeking to alleviate their own problems of deficient demand by seeking export markets.

The export of capital, on the other hand, compels a balancing export of goods (to keep the balance of payments in line), and thus does help to absorb surplus. At the same time individual monopolistic enterprises, unwilling to expand at home for fear of spoiling the market, are anxious to expand abroad. The world market is not as thoroughly carved up as are national markets (*PEG*, p. 240), though the same desire to avoid competition that holds them back at home is at work here too (p. 239). Baran is very ambivalent here. On the one hand, he needs to explain capital export as an important link in his argument, but on the other hand, he wants to retain the picture of monopoly as a force holding back investment on a world as well as a national level. For reasons which will be examined later, he maintains that underdeveloped countries only offer very limited scope for investment. In this he stands opposed to the classical Marxists who anticipated substantial development in the more backward parts of the world.

In any case, as his critics have pointed out, the export of capital only helps to absorb surplus in a very temporary way. Baran argues elsewhere that the return flows of profits and dividends, which augment the surplus, soon outweigh the outflow of capital. This does not really damage his argument, since it is individual corporations that decide to invest abroad, and they are trying to maximise their profits.

Baran argues that these corporations call for, and get, government support for their activities abroad, in the form of pressure on the government of the 'host' country, by military, economic and diplomatic means, and that this requires massive spending on the maintenance of a military establishment, on foreign aid, technical assistance and so on. It is this that is the real significance of imperialism:

> What matters here is not whatever increases in income and employment an imperialist country may derive from foreign trade and investment. These need not be very large, even if of vast importance to the individual corporations involved and the groups associated with them. In fact, as long as the advantages *immediately* related to foreign economic activities represented the major consideration promoting imperialist policies, their political foundations as well as their ideological justification were inevitably somewhat shaky.

> The issue appears in an altogether different perspective when not merely the direct advantages of imperialist policies to the society of an advanced capitalist country are taken into account but when their effect is visualised in its entirety. The loans and grants to so-called friendly governments, the outlays on the military establishment . . . all assume prodigious magnitudes. . . .Thus the impact of this form of utilisation of the economic surplus on the level of income and employment in an advanced capitalist country transcends by far the income- and employment-generating effect of foreign economic activities themselves. The latter assume actually only incidental significance compared with the former – an errant stone setting in motion a mighty rock.
> (*PEG*, pp. 245–6)

At first sight it is difficult to accept this argument. It is surely irrational to incur all the real risks (of war, for example) involved in an imperialist policy purely to gain the benefits of state spending which could be gained anyway by redirecting state spending to more useful ends. This is precisely Baran's point; it is irrational but it happens, because capitalist politics is not rational, and because certain powerful interests do gain from this policy while others would be threatened by any alternative policy.

The argument is in fact a neat inversion of an old radical critique of colonialism. It has often been argued that the possession of colonies gives advantages to a favoured few, but that on balance the costs to the 'nation' exceeded the benefits. Radicals have therefore argued that the people as a whole should oppose imperialist policies. Given his under-consumptionist stance, Baran can argue that the 'costs' of imperialism are, in fact, benefits, since they help to maintain demand and employment by absorbing the surplus. There is thus a coincidence of interests between the direct beneficiaries of imperialism and the mass of the people (as long as the only alternative to monopoly capitalism with imperialist policies is monopoly capitalism without these policies).

Baran mentions Lenin's idea of a 'labour aristocracy' in this context, but it is clear that his ideas are not the same as Lenin's. All that he takes from Lenin is the possibility that 'the policy of imperialism may actually be of benefit to the ordinary man in an imperialist country' (*PEG*, p. 245). Lenin, however, saw these benefits as a sharing of monopoly profits in the form of higher wages for a minority of the working class; Baran sees them primarily as improving the employment prospects of the working class in general.

Baran's case depends, firstly, on the general presumption that monopoly capital has difficulty in absorbing the surplus and that waste is therefore, paradoxically, good for monopoly capital and for the population as a whole (so long as the basic framework remains unchanged), and, secondly, on the existence of a particular political constellation that permits some forms of state spending while barring others. Both of these presumptions looked more plausible in America in the 1950s and 1960s than they would in other places and at other times. I, for one, would be reluctant to accept Baran's account as a general theory. A Marxist interpretation of history must involve both general theories and consideration of the specific circumstances in which they work themselves out. It is important to keep the two separate, something Baran does not always do.

V The world economy and the origins of underdevelopment

Baran divides the world economy into two parts: the advanced capitalist countries and the underdeveloped countries. The countries of the 'socialist camp' are largely left out of the picture and only discussed as models for others to follow. As long as they engage only in planned and balanced trade with the rest of the world, they have little direct economic effect on the world capitalist economy. Countries in an intermediate stage of development are also largely ignored.

The interrelation between advanced and underdeveloped countries can

be summarised under three headings: trade, flows of surplus and political
–military influence. Trade flows serve to provide cheap sources of
primary products to the advanced countries, while the development of
industry in the underdeveloped areas is discouraged by the competition
of manufactured products imported from the advanced countries.
Surplus flows, in the form of profits and dividends, deprive the underdeveloped countries of much-needed resources for investment (though
they might not be used even if they were available), while adding to the
problems caused by an excessive surplus in the heartlands of monopoly
capital. The political influence of the advanced countries helps to
maintain governments in power in the underdeveloped areas which are
well disposed to foreign investors and which hold back indigenous
development. All these forces, as they affect the underdeveloped areas,
will be discussed in more detail in subsequent sections.

To set up this bipolar model of the world system, Baran must explain
the reasons for the massive discrepancy in accumulated capital, in wealth
and in power between the two sections into which the world is divided.
The high level of development in the heartlands of capitalism is no
problem; according to Baran, competitive capitalism is a force for rapid
development, and there was a long period when these economies were
dominated by competitive capitalism. The difficulty, then, is to explain
why the same process did not work elsewhere.

Baran argues that before the period of European colonialism, there was
'everywhere a mode of production and a social and political order that
are conveniently summarised under the name of feudalism' (*PEG*,
p. 268). Despite differences between different areas, this order 'had
entered at a certain stage of its development a process of dissolution and
decay', which created the possibility of capitalist development. In this
he differs from Marx (chapter 2) who thought that there were major
differences between European feudalism and the 'Asiatic' mode of production.

The three pre-conditions for capitalism that Baran identifies are: an
increase in agricultural output accompanied by the displacement of
peasants from the land, a growth of commodity production and of the
division of labour, and the accumulation of capital by merchants and rich
peasants.

Of these, he assigns strategic significance to the third, the
accumulation of capital in the form of merchant capital, on the grounds
that the other two were proceeding at a roughly even pace everywhere.
The development of merchant capital in Europe was the basis of

European expansion, and of a process in which European capital siphoned off the surplus of the rest of the world.

The world economy, therefore, starting from a state of near parity between its different parts, was differentiated into a rich and a poor section by a redivision of surplus. This explanation is set out mainly in terms of a comparison of the history of India, massively looted and exploited by its British conquerors, with that of Japan, which remained independent and became a major capitalist power in its own right. The argument is wholly consistent with his whole approach in which development is seen in essentially quantitative terms and is determined by the size and use of the surplus.

In addition to the redivision of surplus, Baran also stresses the importance of state support as another essential element in capitalist development. Independent states, such as those of Europe and Japan, took measures to protect new industries from competition, to provide infrastructure, and so on, while the colonial administrations of subject territories systematically discriminated against local producers who might compete with those in the ruling country.

Baran's work represents a move towards seeing capitalist development as the development of one area at the expense of others. Ultimately this can lead to a view of history as a zero sum game, a struggle for the division of a fixed world income. It would be unfair to accuse Baran of taking this position, given his stress on the progressive character of competitive capitalism and its creation of 'an unprecedented development of productive forces, . . . a gigantic advance in technology, and . . . a momentous increase in output and consumption' (*PEG*, p. 165). His successors, however, notably Frank, have moved further in this direction, and away from the classical Marxist analysis.

VI Underdeveloped countries today

Whatever the origins of underdevelopment, Baran argues that a fairly uniform and characteristic social and economic structure has come into existence in the underdeveloped countries, and that this structure blocks their further development.

The main elements of this structure are: a large and very backward agricultural sector characterised by small-scale peasant production and a parasitic landlord class; a small but relatively advanced industrial sector, partly foreign owned, producing for the restricted local market; a number of enterprises producing for export, typically foreign owned and producing primary products; and finally a large sector of traders, including large-scale merchants who control foreign trade and have close links with foreign capital, as well as petty traders who penetrate into the remoter rural areas.

Baran calls this a 'capitalist order' (*PEG*, p. 300), but the agricultural sector is *prima facie* characterised by pre-capitalist relations of production. Baran does not in fact differentiate at all clearly between capitalist and pre-capitalist modes of production in his discussion; the correct way to draw this distinction has since become a matter of fierce debate.

Read in terms of an 'articulation of modes of production', Baran's description would amount to identifying a capitalist urban industry and export sector and a predominantly pre-capitalist rural sector, with merchant capital forming the principal link between the two. This is, I think, how Amin interprets it. On the other hand, we could regard these as being different levels in a 'chain of metropolis-satellite relations' in which towns are satellites of the imperialist countries, and the villages are satellites of the towns, as Frank does. Baran's rather descriptive and practical approach leaves the way open for a number of different interpretations; he was the pioneer who made the internal structure of underdeveloped countries into a central issue in Marxist theory.

The starting point of his analysis is, naturally, the *economic surplus* in underdeveloped countries. He argues that the surplus, while small in absolute terms because of the low level of output, is large in relative terms because mass consumption is depressed to the lowest possible level. The economic surplus is therefore large enough to permit a fairly rapid rate of growth, although from a low starting point. The explanation for the lack of growth in underdeveloped countries therefore must lie in the use of the surplus, not in its size. Baran rejects the idea of a 'vicious circle of poverty', the idea that poor countries remain poor because their poverty prevents them from saving.

He puts forward, essentially, a double explanation for the lack of productive investment in these countries. Firstly, the surplus is not available for investment because it is either drained away to the advanced countries or absorbed in unproductive uses, and secondly, even if the surplus were not diverted in these ways it would not be used for investment, because the incentive to invest is too low.

Baran does not separate these two arguments, and so does not explain why he puts both forward. Presumably, if the surplus were available for investment but was not invested, this would show up in a chronic lack of demand, falling prices, and an outflow of capital, while if the investment opportunities were there without the available surplus, there would be a permanent boom and a capital inflow. With both a low available surplus for investment and a low incentive to invest, there is a sort of low-growth equilibrium. The two arguments are, in any case, not wholly separable since the low incentive to invest is, in some instances, the cause of the diversion of surplus into other uses. Savings and investment decisions are not entirely separated.

I shall follow Baran in going through the different sectors in turn, looking at the generation and use of surplus.

The largest sector in most underdeveloped countries is agriculture. Baran describes two ways in which agricultural production may be organised: small-scale peasant production or a system of large estates. These may be combined in different proportions in different areas.

Where subsistence peasant farming predominates, productivity is very low because of the small scale of production and the archaic methods used. Despite this, a large fraction of total output is taken by landlords, demonstrating the existence of a substantial surplus. Peasants do not invest in improved methods of production, because they cannot afford to (the surplus is being drained away from them), and because there are, in any case, few opportunities for mechanisation as long as the land is subdivided into very small holdings.

Landlords do not invest in improvements because they cannot be sure of getting a return in the form of higher rent, because the smallness of holdings makes many forms of investment impossible, and because the surplus that they control is largely absorbed by 'the necessity of maintaining the style of life appropriate to their status in society' (*PEG*, p. 304). What savings they do carry out are diverted into money-lending or into the acquisition of additional land, and thus, presumably, into consumption by the impoverished peasants who are driven to borrow or to sell off their land.

Here it is clear that it is the *social relations of production* that are the obstacle to development, and that these are essentially pre-capitalist relations. This point has been argued more explicitly and forcefully by a number of subsequent writers.

Where there are large estates worked by hired labour, where, in other words, agriculture is capitalist (Baran does not say this), investment is deterred because labour is cheap and machinery relatively expensive, while the returns on investment in agriculture are typically uncertain and slow to materialise. Here we see a different argument; capitalism in underdeveloped areas suffers from various difficulties which hamper its full development. This line too has been followed by a number of writers; the harmful effect of low wages on development has been the special concern of Emmanuel (chapter 9).

An agrarian reform is not the answer if all it does is to relieve the burden of rent on the peasants and to subdivide large estates. Since they are so poor, the peasants will spend the increased income on consumption, and the barriers to progress caused by the subdivision of the land will remain or be worsened.

The advanced capitalist countries avoided this trap by the development of capitalist agriculture, which centralised agricultural production, expelled large numbers from the land, raising productivity and providing an industrial proletariat, and provided, simultaneously, a market for industrial products and a supply of agricultural products to feed the industrial workers. (See Marx's account of primitive accumulation.)

Baran argues that agrarian reforms can only succeed in the context of industrial development and of a state policy designed to encourage the expansion of capitalist industry. They are not, by themselves, any answer and may make matters worse. The exact reasons why the capitalist road in agriculture can only be followed if there is simultaneous industrial development are not clear. It is true that the labourers expelled from the land by the emergence of capitalist agriculture will only find jobs in industry if there is industry to employ them, but need that be any concern of the capitalist farmer? Capitalist agriculture has in fact developed fairly rapidly in many underdeveloped areas since the time when Baran wrote, with a corresponding growth of urban unemployment.

An important part of the surplus accrues to 'merchants, money lenders and intermediaries of all kinds', a group who I will categorise collectively as merchant capital (in order to connect his argument with that of other writers, I use terminology that Baran avoids).

Merchant capital can exploit the many opportunities for monopoly profit in the 'disorganised and isolated' markets of underdeveloped countries, but at the same time these monopoly profits attract new recruits to this stratum from *déclassé* landlords, rich peasants and so on. The intensified competition leads not to an erosion of monopoly profit but to the creation of ever-smaller and more local monopolies. The result is a large, parasitic stratum of traders, absorbing large parts of the surplus despite the relative poverty of many of its members. The subdivision of merchant capital, like the subdivision of land, is a barrier to progress. Baran recognises that large-scale merchants exist too (just as large plantations do in agriculture); they are deterred from investing their profits productively by the relatively low returns on productive investment and the attraction of alternative uses of funds.

Baran's description of the parasitic hold of merchant capital is convincing (see *PEG*, pp. 308–13), but his explanation of this state of affairs is sketchy. In the advanced countries too there was a stage in which merchant capital dominated, but it was thrust aside by industrial capital. The explanation for the persistent hold of merchant capital in the rural areas of the underdeveloped world must be in the lack of development of both agriculture and industry, especially, in Baran's account, the latter. Frank makes mercantile exploitation the main element in his analysis (see chapter 7).

Baran's explanation for the lack of industrial development is the crux of his explanation of underdevelopment, and has several interconnected elements. Competition from abroad stifles infant industries, the narrowness of the market discourages development, and what industrial development there is rapidly takes a monopolistic form and becomes a barrier to further progress. These handicaps applied, to a certain degree, to present advanced countries in the initial stages of their growth, but were overcome with resolute state support; the lack of equivalent support from the state is a further factor in holding back similar development today.

In his discussion of industry, Baran's arguments depend on a lack of *incentive* to invest, rather than on a shortage of surplus to provide the resources for investment. This seems inconsistent with his emphasis on the transfer of surplus to the imperialist countries in his explanation of the origins of underdevelopment. The inconsistency is not very serious; it provides two alternative explanations. Subsequent writers have drawn on both accounts.

Competition from abroad is a factor many Marxists (and others) have emphasised in explaining lack of industrial development; one could go back to Marx's account of the destruction of the Indian (handloom) textile industry in the epoch of the industrial revolution. Amin has developed this argument in more detail, so I will postpone discussion of it to chapter 10. Competition from abroad can, in any case, be prevented by protection. State support is therefore the critical factor here.

The narrow home market is a result of the generally low level of output and income. Baran does not here put forward an underconsumptionist argument: it is the low *general* level of development, rather than the poverty of the producers as such, that is to blame. His argument is slightly odd, though. 'Under such circumstances there could be no spreading of small industrial shops that marked elsewhere the transition from the merchant phase of capitalism to its industrial phase' (*PEG*, p. 314). Surely. a narrow market does not prevent the spread of *small-scale* production; it is rather a barrier to the development of *large-scale* industry.

The real importance of the narrow market, to Baran, is that larger-scale production leads to an early development of monopoly, and monopoly is the real villain of the piece throughout his argument.

> Completing swiftly the entire journey from a progressive to a regressive role in the economic system, they [industrial firms] became at an early stage barriers to economic development rather similar in their effect to the semi-feudal landownership prevailing in underdeveloped countries. . . . Monopolistic industry on one hand extends the merchant phase of capitalism by obstructing the transition of capital and men from the sphere of circulation to the sphere of industrial production. On the other hand, providing neither a market for agricultural produce nor outlets for agricultural surplus labour and not supplying agriculture with cheap manufactured consumer goods and implements, it forces agriculture back towards self sufficiency, perpetuates the idleness of the structurally unemployed and fosters further mushrooming of petty traders, cottage industries, and the like. (*PEG*, pp. 315–16)

I have already described Baran's argument that monopoly deters investment, and its weaknesses. The case he puts forward may be stronger in an underdeveloped country where a large part of total demand derives from a rather static and inflexible agricultural sector, since, as I have argued above, it is the expansion of the market that must be the main stimulus to development in a monopolistic system.

Foreign firms catering for the domestic market are even more likely to operate on a large scale and to have a monopoly position. The fact of foreign ownership makes no difference to the stifling effect of monopoly on investment. They are additionally charged with sending surplus abroad and with importing many of the things they buy. Neither charge is very convincing (and Baran lays little emphasis on them). Foreign firms would presumably re-invest their profits locally if it were profitable to do so, and would similarly buy goods locally if they were cheaper or better. (Baran has something of a tendency to emphasise the nationality of firms even where it seems irrelevant.) More important is the political backing these firms can get from their home countries and the fact that by displacing local businessmen they retard the formation of a national bourgeoisie.

There are also firms producing for export, mainly producing primary commodities and mainly foreign-owned. Baran's case against these as sources of development turns partly on a claim that they typically pay out only a small part of their revenue in wages, that the surplus is correspondingly high and is predominantly taken out of the country. There is thus little stimulus to consumer demand (which might stimulate investment) nor is there a large contribution to the local investible surplus. I will reserve the main discussion of these questions for later chapters; again Baran is the source of ideas that have been developed further.

Baran also regards the political influence of foreign-owned firms as particularly important. This leads on to his analysis of the state in underdeveloped countries. Since the state absorbs surplus on a large scale, if it is to be a net contributor to economic growth it must provide correspondingly strong support for domestic expansion, above all for industrial expansion. Baran argues that much investment in 'infrastructure' by the state in underdeveloped countries benefits only foreign firms producing for export, and therefore makes little or no contribution to economic growth.

VII The state and politics in underdeveloped countries

Baran considers three different kinds of governments that exist in the underdeveloped countries: colonial administrations, 'comprador' regimes and 'New Deal' governments. This division looks slightly less relevant now than at the time when Baran was writing, since decolonisation has almost eliminated formal colonial rule. They all rest on a similar basis in class structure and class interests, so it is best to start by looking at these interests.

The class structure of the underdeveloped countries is characterised, firstly, by the enormous weight of *foreign capital*, both in its economic and political power within the country concerned and and, above all, by its ability to call on the support of the government of its home country. Baran's characterisation of the place of imperialism and militarism in the advanced countries themselves has already been discussed. Foreign capital is opposed to economic development because it would threaten the cheap supplies of labour that it enjoys, and because it would involve higher taxes and a diversion of state economic support to the promotion of internal development to the neglect of the 'needs' of the export sector for specialised infrastructure. Secondly, there is a powerful bloc of *mercantile interests* attached to foreign capital, enterprises that act as suppliers, agents, subcontractors, etc., as well as those who handle import and export business. These Baran calls the 'comprador' bourgeoisie. In representing their own interests, they represent, to a large extent, the interests of foreign capital as well. Thirdly, there are feudal or semi-feudal *landed interests*, who have their own reasons for opposing any disturbance in the *status quo*, as well as for allying with foreign capital. Finally, *industrial capital*, although it has a relatively small weight in the economy, is concentrated into a few powerful monopolies which will oppose any developments that threaten their monopoly position.

These are not the only class forces: workers, peasants and intellectuals have their own interests, opposed to those of the ruling oligarchy, and must be repressed or somehow bought off (or both), while a progressive industrial bourgeoisie, though weak, may exist.

It is clear that there are many possible alignments that could arise from this complex web of classes and class fractions, and Baran's importance in the development of the political analysis of underdeveloped countries is, as in other aspects of his writing, largely in the possible lines of analysis suggested by his work.

His own stress is mainly on the role of foreign capital, and the imperialist states that lie behind it, in stifling development. This makes sense, since if we take away the element of foreign dominance we are left with very much the same classes and fractions as were contending for power in the advanced countries at an early stage in their development. We may doubt Baran's presumption that mercantile and feudal classes must be uniformly hostile to development; they were not always so in the countries where capitalism first emerged.

Colonial territories are, of course, directly dominated by foreign capital, interested in cheap labour, natural resources and cheap government. No more need be said. 'Comprador' governments are described by Baran as being essentially the same as colonial administrations, except that the job of government is farmed out to local interests that can be relied on to support their paymasters (or be thrown out if they give trouble). The only real difference that results is that privileged sections of the local population get hold of substantial chunks of the surplus which they squander ostentatiously. His main examples are oil sheiks (before OPEC, of course). One can think of many such puppet governments today, though I suspect that they are not as frequent or as totally under the thumb of the imperialists as they were.

The third group, of 'New Deal' governments, is more interesting. Baran describes, without very deep analysis, the formation of a popular coalition to demand independence. At the time he was writing, only a few colonial territories had achieved formal independence, and they were at an early stage in their development; Baran names India, Indonesia and Burma – a group notable for the subsequent divergence of their paths. Baran does not wholly rule out the possibility that some of these countries may achieve genuinely independent economic development along the lines followed by Japan, but he points out the enormous difficulties in so doing.

The central point is that it is not solely foreign capital whose interests are threatened by economic development. There are powerful interests within the country which also have much to fear. Once independence is attained, the nationalist movement splits into a right and a left wing, and the outcome depends on the precise balance of forces.

If popular pressures for reform are strong, Baran argues, then this is likely to lead to a rapid reconciliation between reactionary local interests and foreign capital; independence will become a sham and the pretence of democracy will be abandoned. Again, it is not difficult to think of examples. The prospects for capitalist development are better where the working class is weak and the industrial bourgeoisie relatively strong.

Although capitalist development is not impossible, Baran regards it as unlikely and anticipates that it will at best be slower than the potential surplus makes technically possible. The only sure road to development, for him, is by the complete overthrow of capitalism and the adoption of socialist planning. He advocates what is essentially a Soviet model of development with the surplus in agriculture being used to develop heavy industry first and with consumer goods industries following on afterwards.

Since Baran defines development in quantitative terms, and makes a clear prediction that monopoly capitalism will slow growth in both advanced and underdeveloped areas, one might try to test this prediction against the facts. It does not fare well. In almost every country in the world, growth of total output has been more rapid, since the Second

World War, than in any previous epoch. Industry has grown more rapidly in underdeveloped than in advanced countries (Warren, 1973). *Per capita* output in underdeveloped countries, especially in the agricultural sector, has, it is true, grown at a rate much less than might have been hoped, but even here it is doubtful whether any previous period has a better record. It might be argued that Baran was comparing monopoly capitalism with socialism, which would have done even better, but this is not my reading of him. The prospects for capitalist development will be discussed further in chapter 12.

VIII Summary

Baran argues that monopoly leads to a diversion of the surplus of output over necessary consumption away from productive investment towards wasteful uses. It is thus a cause of stagnation in both advanced and underdeveloped countries (an argument that is theoretically weak and conflicts with the facts). Underdeveloped countries are dominated by foreign capital with its local hangers-on, and by mercantile and landlord interests. All are hostile to development. Baran's importance is in having directed Marxists' attention to the analysis of underdeveloped countries, and in having provided many of the ideas that were built on by subsequent writers.

7 · Frank, Wallerstein and the 'dependency theorists'

Andre Gunder Frank's most influential book, *Capitalism and Underdevelopment in Latin America* (Frank, 1969a, cited below as *CULA*), starts with a sentence which sums up his position admirably. 'I believe, with Paul Baran, that it is capitalism, both world and national, which produced underdevelopment in the past and which still generates underdevelopment in the present' (*CULA*, p. xi).

It is essential to realise how drastic a break with the classical Marxists this is. Contrast the quotation from Frank, above, with these quotations from Marx and from Lenin:

> National differences and antagonisms between peoples are daily more and more vanishing, owing to the development of the bourgeoisie, to freedom of commerce, to the world market, to uniformity in the mode of production and in the conditions of life corresponding thereto. (Marx, *Manifesto*, p. 80)

> The export of capital affects and greatly accelerates the development of capitalism in those countries to which it is exported. While, therefore, the export of capital may tend to a certain extent to arrest development in the capital exporting countries, it can do so only by expanding and deepening the further development of capitalism throughout the world. (Lenin, *Imperialism*, p. 498)

The classical Marxists expected the development of capitalism to lead to a growing uniformity in methods of production and in the standards of living of the bulk of the population throughout the world. Both Marx and (especially) Lenin emphasised the unevenness of this process, but they did not anticipate a growing gulf between advanced and underdeveloped areas. This is, of course, all part of Marx's view of the 'historic role' of capitalism in promoting the development of the forces of production and thus creating the material preconditions for socialism.

On the facts, Baran and Frank are clearly right; a huge gulf in

158

productivity and in living standards has opened up between the advanced capitalist countries and the rest of the world during the last hundred years. This does not necessarily mean that the explanations that they have proposed for this development are correct, nor does it mean that this trend is still operative today, or that it is bound to continue.

Many theories put forward in the 1960s and 1970s are built around the idea that capitalism necessarily produces cumulatively growing differences between advanced and underdeveloped areas, and that development in 'peripheral' countries is possible only if they make a complete break with the world capitalist system. These conclusions have, however, been reached by a number of different routes.

In this chapter I will discuss the work of Andre Gunder Frank and Immanuel Wallerstein, who have much in common. They both argue that capitalism can only be analysed *on a world scale*, and they define capitalism as a *system of monopolistic exchange*, which acts to transfer surplus from subordinate areas to the imperialist centres. This system governs the distribution of political power, the forms of organisation of production and the class structures of different areas, and has existed essentially unchanged from the sixteenth century. This approach is quite different from that of the classical Marxists, for whom relations of *production* were primary. I will also discuss the 'dependency theorists', who put forward a rather similar case, but with more emphasis on the economic mechanisms at work today.

Frank's work has typically taken the form of essays which have been made more widely available by being collected together and published in book form. The most important collections are *Capitalism and Underdevelopment in Latin America* (*CULA*, 1969a, first published in 1967) and *Latin America: Underdevelopment or Revolution* (*LAUR*, 1969b). *Lumpenbourgeoisie: Lumpendevelopment* (*LL*, 1972) was a reply to his critics, and represents a minor modification and restatement of his position. *Dependent Accumulation and Underdevelopment* (*DAU*, 1978) represents a further shift on some issues, and is influenced by other writers, notably Amin, who are discussed in later chapters of this book. *DAU* contains a historical account of the world economy interspersed with more theoretical essays. As a brief history it is one of the best available. I shall concentrate on the earlier works, since they have become a part of the intellectual history of the period, even where Frank has subsequently changed his opinions. Frank has been criticised by Laclau (1971), among others.

Wallerstein's *The Modern World System* (*MWS*, 1974a) is the first instalment of a promised four-volume analytical history of the capitalist world economy, and covers the period from 1450 to 1640. A more accessible introduction to his views is to be found in an article (1974b) which is included, with others, in a useful collection, *The Capitalist World Economy* (*CWE*, 1979). Wallerstein's views (and those of Frank) have been critically analysed by Brenner (1977).

I will give summaries of Frank's analysis (section I) and of Wallerstein's (section II) before looking in detail at some key issues: their conception of capitalism (section III), the metropolis-satellite relation as conceived by Frank (section IV), and the effects of transfers of surplus (section V). Finally, I will discuss the concept of 'dependence' (section VI).

I Frank's account of the 'development of underdevelopment'

Frank does not give an explicit definition of 'capitalism', and his conception of it is very unclear. What is clear is that his use of the concept is formed by his insistence that underdevelopment is a product of capitalism and by his consistent opposition to 'dualist' interpretations of Latin America.

In essence, Frank identifies capitalism with a system of (world-wide) links of *exchange*, characterised by monopoly and by exploitation. He is effectively forced to this definition, since he wants to argue that the 'development of underdevelopment' has been going on in Latin America since the Spanish (and Portuguese) conquests, i.e. since the sixteenth century, and that the process has been unchanged in its essentials ever since. What other characteristics of the economic system could he point to that have been operating in Latin America over such a long span?

He also (implicitly) argues that any part of the world which is affected in any fundamental way by 'capitalism' (i.e. by exchange) is to be regarded as 'capitalist'. He has little difficulty in showing that the effects of the capitalist world economy have penetrated so deep into Latin America that no part of the continent has been unaffected. Even areas substantially devoted to self-sufficient subsistence farming (such as north-east Brazil – see e.g. *CULA*, pp. 153–4) are the product of the decay of earlier export industries. He argues convincingly that *latifundias* (large estates worked by peasant cultivators) originated as a response to commercial opportunities even where they have subsequently declined into almost self-sufficient isolation.

This aspect of his argument is directed against theories of *dualism* as applied to Latin America. These theories attempt to preserve the idea of capitalism as a progressive force, a force for development, by asserting that the economy of an underdeveloped country is divided into two essentially independent sectors. The one is modern, progressive and capitalist, while the other is archaic, essentially untouched by capitalism and feudal. The 'backward' or 'traditional' sector is characterised by local self-sufficiency and independence from the world market. Development, on this analysis, requires a transfer of resources from the feudal to the capitalist sector and a general transformation or 'modernisation' of feudal agriculture and of social and political structures. Dualist models of various sorts have been put forward by Marxist as well as non-Marxist writers, but Frank's main targets here are bourgeois sociologists and political scientists rather than economists. (See his scathing attack, 'Sociology of development and underdevelopment of sociology', *LAUR*, pp. 21–94.)

Frank demonstrates, with a wealth of factual and historical information, that no part of Latin America has been left untouched by market relations. This has not been disputed; the debate since has focused instead on the conceptual issues involved, which will be discussed in section III.

Incorporation into the world capitalist system leads to development in some areas and to the 'development of underdevelopment' elsewhere. *Underdevelopment*, according to Frank, is not an original state; he calls the state of affairs before capitalist penetration *undevelopment* (though he pays little attention to it, since he argues that all vestiges of older forms have long since been remade by capitalism).

The 'development of underdevelopment' occurs because the world capitalist system is characterised by a *metropolis-satellite* structure. The metropolis exploits the satellite, so that surplus is concentrated in the metropolis; the satellite is directly impoverished and is cut off from potential investment funds so that its growth is slowed down. More important, the satellite is reduced to a state of *dependence* which creates a particular sort of local ruling class which has an interest in perpetuating underdevelopment, a 'lumpenbourgeoisie' which follows a 'policy of underdevelopment' or 'lumpendevelopment' (*LL, passim*). The origins of these arguments in Baran's writings are obvious, and are freely acknowledged by Frank.

Frank's main original contribution is in the idea of a *chain* of metropolis-satellite relations. He describes it as follows:

The monopoly capitalist structure and the surplus expropriation/appropriation contradiction run through the entire Chilean economy, past and present. Indeed, it is this exploitative relation which in chain like fashion extends the capitalist link between the capitalist world and national metropolises to the regional centres (part of whose surplus they appropriate) and from these to local centres and so on to large landholders or merchants who expropriate surplus from small peasants or tenants, and sometimes even from these latter to landless labourers exploited by them in turn. At each step along the way the relatively few capitalists above exercise monopoly power over the many below, expropriating some or all of their economic surplus, and to the extent that they are not expropriated in turn by the still fewer above, appropriating it for their own use. Thus at each point, the international, national and local capitalist system generates economic development for the few and underdevelopment for the many. (*CULA*, pp. 7–8. Similar statements may be found throughout Frank's work, e.g. *CULA*, pp. 146–8, about Brazil)

This 'chain' of metropolis-satellite relations has existed, according to Frank, since the sixteenth century, and changes since then represent only changes in the forms of dominance and exploitation of the satellite and are not changes of substance. He calls this the principle of *'continuity in change'*. I shall criticise this argument on the grounds that changes in the forms of dominance may have important effects (section IV).

Frank particularly stresses the *political* consequences. The ruling classes in underdeveloped countries owe their position to their place in a 'chain' that runs from the countryside to the imperialist metropolis, and thus have an interest in maintaining it.

This colonial and class structure establishes very well defined class interests for the dominant sector of the bourgeoisie. Using government cabinets and other instruments of the state, the bourgeoisie produces a *policy of underdevelopment* in the economic, social and political life of the 'nation' and the people of Latin America. (*LL*, 1972, p. 13)

This seems to me to be much the strongest part of Frank's argument, and it is at its best in his historical analysis of the crucial turning point in Latin American history, the period after independence in the nineteenth century. At this time there was a bitter conflict between the 'Europeans', the advocates of free trade, and the 'Americans', the advocates of protection for domestic industries. The 'Europeans' were, of course, led by the merchants who handled the export and import trades and by the agricultural export interests, and they were the stronger party precisely because the preceding centuries of dependence had created an economy dominated by those groups that stood to gain from continuation of the system.

Free trade made imported manufactured goods available cheaply to the export agriculturalists, and the weakness of the local currency increased the value of exported products in terms of the depreciated currency, transferring income to those who sold goods for export. Local manufacturing industry was unable to compete with imports without protection, so perpetuating the imbalance (*LL*, p. 61).

State policy was geared to the needs of the export sector in other ways as well: taxes, distribution of land, immigration policy, ports, railways and so on. Frank summarises: 'the ''European'' lumpenbourgeoisie built ''national'' lumpenstates which never achieved real independence but were, and are, simply effective instruments of the lumpenbourgeoisie's policy of lumpendevelopment' (*LL*, p. 58).

He contrasts this with the United States, which did not offer suitable conditions for export agriculture except in the south.

> Consequently, the class structure which developed there, based at the start on small farmers, did not present any obstacle to a development policy which permitted the Northern bourgeoisie to become strong enough to use independence to promote integrated development, to defeat the planter/exporters of the South in the Civil War, to impose a policy of industrialisation and arrive at their own industrial 'take-off' point. (*LL*, pp. 58–9)

More recently, in *DAU*, he has added the argument that New England was a 'sub-metropolis' from an early stage, running a very profitable (and elegantly self-contained) 'triangle' of trade: rum to Africa, slaves to the sugar plantations of the West Indies, and molasses home to be processed into rum.

Another piece of evidence for his case is the pattern of development in the period from 1929 to the early 1950s. With links between Latin America and the world metropolis disrupted by the depression and then by the Second World War, the area experienced the 'biggest independent industrialisation drive since the post independence 1830s and 1840s'

(*LL*, p. 76). The political hold of 'metropolitan allied export interests' was weakened, and industrial and regional interests forced themselves into the government.

The resulting burst of industrialisation, however, was limited mainly to 'import substituting' production of finished consumer goods and led to a new dependence on imports of 'an ever greater volume of raw materials and capital goods as inputs for national manufacturing' (*LL*, pp. 85–6). The foreign exchange to pay for these still depended on raw material exports, and development was brought to a halt by the fall in raw material prices after the Korean War. The new industrial bourgeoisie was compelled to turn back to encouraging export industries and to attracting foreign capital to try to fill the gap.

This episode seems to be, and to a certain extent is, a striking confirmation of Frank's argument. The links are weakened, and development follows. This development is inadequate, because of the inheritance of dependence. When the metropolis recovers, the links of dependence are re-established. We should note, however, that the word 'dependence' is being used in several senses. It has previously been used to mean involvement as a satellite in a chain of metropolis-satellite relations. Now it means a need to import raw materials and capital goods. This 'new' form of dependence will be discussed in section VI below.

It seems to me that the essential truth at the heart of Frank's argument is that *state policy* is a critical element in economic development, that state policy is the outcome of conflict between classes and fractions of classes with conflicting interests, and that those classes and fractions that benefit from an existing economic structure will both have an interest in perpetuating it and be in a strong position to succeed. This idea is, of course, to be found in Baran and, in rather different contexts, in other Marxist writings. Frank has applied it with great success to the analysis of Latin American history.

Frank presents these arguments in a distinctive way, which seems to me to be an important source of weakness. His normal procedure is to make brief, sloganistic assertions, and then to justify and expand on these by giving a series of historical examples, frequently quoting at length from other writers or from original sources. The problem with this style of argument is that it leaves no room for systematic theoretical exposition; one is left repeatedly saying: yes, it happened like that in those cases, but *why*, and must it be the same *everywhere*? In addition, crucial terms (development, underdevelopment, metropolis, satellite, capitalism, and so on) are never explicitly defined. The reader is left to infer their meaning from the essentially descriptive uses that they are put to. It seems to me that Frank often allows these terms to have a spectrum of meanings rather than a single precisely defined sense, blurring the logic of some of his most important assertions.

II Wallerstein: the world system

I shall summarise Wallerstein's arguments briefly, since they have a great deal in common with those of Frank. He insists that any social system must be seen as a *totality*. Nation states, in the modern world, are not closed systems and cannot be the subject of analysis as if they were.

> We take the defining characteristic of a social system to be the existence within it of a division of labour, such that the various sectors or areas within are dependent upon economic exchange with others for the smooth and continuous provisioning of the needs of the area. (*CWE*, p. 5)

The only kinds of social system that have existed are *'mini-systems'* (closed local economies), *'world empires'* (defined by the extraction of tribute by a central authority) and *'world economies'* (connected by market exchange). A 'world' system does not necessarily have to cover the whole globe; it is defined as a 'unit with a single division of labour and multiple cultural systems'. A world economy, then, is a world system without a single central authority.

The modern world system is capitalist, since it is a world economy (as defined). Wallerstein simply equates the two: 'Capitalism and a world economy (that is, a single division of labour but multiple polities) are obverse sides of the same coin. One does not cause the other. We are merely defining the same indivisible phenomenon by different characteristics' (*CWE*, p. 6).

The capitalist world system is divided into three tiers of states, those of the *core*, the *semi-periphery* and the *periphery*. The essential difference between these is in the strength of the state machine in different areas, and this, in turn, leads to transfers of surplus from the periphery to the core, which further strengthen the core states. State power is the central mechanism since 'actors in the market' attempt to 'avoid the normal operation of the market whenever it does not maximise their profit' by turning to the nation state to alter the terms of trade.

At least in origin, the core-periphery division is explained by a sort of technological determinism. Western Europe specialised in manufacture and animal raising. These activities require relatively high skills, and are better carried out by relatively well-paid free wage labour. The resulting social structure is the foundation of relatively strong states, able to manipulate markets to their advantage: the 'core' states. Hispanic America (mining) and Baltic east Europe (grain) specialised in activities requiring relatively little skill, hence capitalists chose (via state intervention) forms of coerced labour, and a difference of interests emerged between the manufacturing and primary product export interests. As a result the local states were weak, and readily subjugated by the core. They thus became 'peripheral'.

Once in existence, the core-periphery division is maintained by the ability of the core states to manipulate the workings of the system as a whole to suit their needs (within limits). They deliberately weaken peripheral states or eliminate them altogether by conquest, and also alter the workings of markets by imposing monopolistic restrictions, protecting their own industries and forbidding corresponding protection in the periphery, and so on.

The 'semi-periphery' is a sort of 'labour aristocracy' of states or geographical areas. Without it, a world system becomes polarised and liable to revolt, while an intermediate tier diffuses antagonisms. I find this argument hard to accept. Was the creation of a semi-periphery deliberate? The particular cases Wallerstein cites (Italy in the sixteenth century, Russia later, including the USSR) do not seem to have been deliberately created by the core states, and in any case, given that the core is (necessarily) divided into distinct national states, who is there to oversee the interests of the system as a whole? However, the idea of a semi-periphery is a fruitful one. Standing somewhat to the side of the core-periphery links (not intermediate links in a chain, as in Frank), the semi-periphery constitutes, so to speak, a site for change. New core states can emerge from the semi-periphery, and it is a destination for declining core states. In Frank's account it is hard to see how any change in the hierarchy can come about, so that each case has to be explained on *ad-hoc* grounds.

At this stage, one might well ask what has happened to relations of production and to classes in the ordinary Marxist sense. Wallerstein seems to regard anybody who produces for profit in the market as a capitalist. He argues that labour power is indeed a commodity but 'wage labor is only one of the modes in which labor is recruited and compensated in the labor market. Slavery, coerced cash-crop production, sharecropping and tenancy are all alternative modes' (*CWE*, p. 17). Marx's concept of capitalism in terms of a relation between free labour and capital is ruthlessly ditched. 'Class analysis' amounts, in Wallerstein's view, to the analysis of the interests of 'syndical groups' within particular states, and is legitimate provided we look at the 'structural position and interests in the world economy' of these groups. At the same time, classes have no permanent reality and are no more fundamental than 'ethno-nations'. That, at least, is my interpretation of some more than usually opaque passages in Wallerstein's writings. (See *CWE*, pp. 24, 224-6.)

The central point, which has been the subject of much debate, is that 'modes of labour control' (wage labour, slavery, etc.) are secondary results of the functioning of a world system defined by the existence of market links. The situation in the core is such that free wage labour tends to be chosen (by the ruling class, with state support) while in the periphery more coercive systems are used. When pressed for an explanation of this, Wallerstein refers to his detailed work in *MWS* for particular reasons which apply to particular areas in the sixteenth century.

Overall, Wallerstein's primary assertion is that a world system must be analysed as a whole. Few are likely to disagree. However, what he offers beyond this seems to me to amount to little more than a series of definitions and phrases together with a mass of detailed material that often seems to have little connection with his overall generalisations. What is lacking is a level of *theory* that would connect the two. A formidable apparatus of scholarship (*MWS* is one of the most heavily footnoted books I have read) and a fondness for obscure jargon (e.g. 'nomothetic propositions') are no substitute.

III 'Capitalism' and 'feudalism': Laclau's critique

Both Frank and Wallerstein define capitalism as a system of exchange relations, and do so specifically in order to include, within their analysis of capitalism, relations of exploitation such as those between landlords and peasants, which do not involve wage labour in the strict sense.

This approach has been criticised by Laclau, in an article which has been the starting point for much debate (1971, reprinted in Laclau, 1977). He states his essential point as follows:

Of course, Frank is at liberty to abstract a mass of historical features and build a model on this basis. He can even, if he wishes, give the resulting entity the name of capitalism. . . . But what is wholly unacceptable is the fact that Frank claims that his conception is the Marxist concept of capitalism. *Because for Marx – as is obvious to anyone who has even a superficial acquaintance with his works – capitalism was a mode of production.* The fundamental economic relationship of capitalism is constituted by the free labourer's sale of his labour power, whose necessary precondition is the loss by the direct producer of ownership of the means of production. (Laclau, 1977, p. 23)

He goes on to cite quotations from Marx which indicate that Marx regarded exchange, and the development of merchant capital, as perfectly consistent with the persistence of pre-capitalist modes of production. I have already described this aspect of Marx's analysis.

Laclau suggests that we should distinguish between 'modes of production' and 'economic systems'. He defines a mode of production as 'an integrated complex of social productive forces and relations linked to a determinate type of ownership of the means of production' (p. 34), and goes on to define the feudal and capitalist modes (the only two he regards as relevant):

The feudal mode of production is one in which the productive process operates according to the following pattern: 1. the economic surplus is produced by a labour force subject to extra-economic compulsion; 2. the economic surplus is privately appropriated by someone other than the direct producers; 3. property in the means of production remains in the hands of the direct producer. In the capitalist mode of production, the economic surplus is also subject to private appropriation, but as distinct from feudalism, ownership of the means of production is severed from ownership of labour power. (p. 35)

Laclau is then in a position to define an 'economic system' as 'the mutual relations between the different sectors of the economy, or between different production units, whether on a regional, national or world scale' (Laclau, 1977, p. 35). The point here is that 'an economic system can include, as constitutive elements, different modes of production.' In particular, feudal production for exchange is not ruled out. Frank's evidence that supposedly feudal areas of Latin America have been deeply influenced by exchange relationships becomes irrelevant, and Laclau can assert that: *'to affirm the feudal character of the relations of production in the agrarian sector does not necessarily involve maintaining a dualist thesis'* (Laclau, 1977, p. 32).

Wallerstein meets Laclau's criticism head on: 'The substantive issue, in my view, concerns the appropriate unit of analysis for the purpose of comparison. . . . Sweezy and Frank better follow the spirit of Marx if not his letter' (*CWE*, p. 9). The essence of his reply is that the system must be viewed as a totality, and that the only totality that actually exists is the world economy.

This brings out what I regard as the key point very well. Both Frank and Wallerstein are looking for *descriptive generalisation*, based directly on the observed facts. Marx, by contrast, insisted on the necessity of *abstraction*. The capitalist mode of production was not, for Marx, a directly observable empirical thing (which the capitalist world economy is); it is instead a *conceptual object*, the product of thought. The aim is to pick out key relationships and examine them in isolation before elaborating the analysis to deal with the complexities of the real world. Wallerstein's reply, therefore, misses its target, since Marx was not looking for a totality that really exists.

However, an appeal to the authority of Marx only settles the issue for dogmatists. Laclau is right to say that Marx defined a mode of production in terms of relations of production, but it remains to be shown that this approach gives better results in explaining reality than any other. I shall argue below that major weaknesses in Frank's analysis follow directly from his neglect of relations of production. If this is accepted, then it strengthens Laclau's case. On the other hand, Laclau's own explanation of underdevelopment and of the persistence of pre-capitalist modes is most unconvincing.

Laclau says '[Frank] shows us *how* the advanced countries have exploited the peripheral countries; what he at no times explains is *why* certain nations needed the underdevelopment of other nations for their own process of development' (Laclau, 1977, pp. 35–6). And again: 'if we want to show that . . . development generates underdevelopment, what we have to prove is that the maintenance of pre-capitalist relations of production in the peripheral areas is an inherent condition of the process of accumulation in the central countries' (Laclau, 1977, p.37).

There is a clear logical fallacy here. Laclau is saying that if development requires underdevelopment, then underdevelopment will happen, but not otherwise. This is the crudest kind of functionalism; whatever is necessary for capitalism will happen. It cannot be sustained. If underdevelopment were necessary for development, it might still fail to happen, either because owners of metropolitan capital, not having understood Marx, fail to realise the necessity, or because they lack the means to enforce their wishes. On the other hand, underdevelopment might not be necessary, but it could happen all the same, just as an innocent bystander might be killed in a shoot-out, without his death being necessary to anybody. Then again, underdevelopment might contribute to development without being necessary to it, it could be the jam on the bread. I stress this point, perhaps too heavily, because this logical fallacy is all too common in Marxist writings.

Laclau tries to show the necessity of underdevelopment to development through the falling rate of profit, a theory that I have already criticised (see chapter 2). He argues that the organic composition of capital rises in the advanced countries, bringing down the rate of profit and this must be offset by expansion into areas where the organic composition of capital is low. My criticism here is that, even if true, this would not explain the persistence of pre-capitalist modes; rather, one would expect investment in underdeveloped areas to lead to the replacement of pre-capitalist modes by capitalism (as Lenin, for example, expected).

Brenner (1977) develops Laclau's critical points and adds a very thorough critique of Wallerstein, while advancing quite different positive arguments. His central point is that capitalism is unique, above all, for the way in which it promotes technological development, increased productivity and hence increased profits (through relative surplus value). This tendency to develop the forces of production is one of the main conclusions which Marx derives from his analysis. Brenner shows that other modes of production ('modes of labour control' in Wallerstein's terms) do not have the same dynamic. At the same time, Brenner argues, 'modes of labour control' are not freely chosen by ruling classes. They are the result of class struggle.

Different parts of the world economy, therefore, have their own tendencies that derive from the modes of production installed there. This does not mean that they evolve independently of each other, but that analysis should start from the workings of distinct modes of production, and then go on to analyse how they interact with each other.

It should also be noted that once we regard increasing productivity as the essence of capitalist development, then the prosperity of the 'core' or 'metropolis' does not have to be at the expense of anybody else;

development is not necessarily the 'other side of the coin' of under-development (which is not to deny that international flows of surplus can and do take place). This emphasis is not, of course, new; it is a reassertion of the classical Marxist perspective.

IV The chain of metropolis-satellite relations

Frank's most distinctive contribution is the idea of a 'chain of metropolis-satellite relations'. As a description it fits the facts well, as Frank shows in great detail. Relations of dominance and surplus extraction exist not only between the direct producers and their immediate exploiters, but at all levels in the world system. The idea is important to Frank, since the 'chain' serves both to channel surplus to the metropolis and to create the class interests that sustain underdevelopment. As an analysis, however, it raises more questions than it answers. I shall criticise Frank primarily for conflating very different kinds of relations on the basis of purely superficial similarities. In particular, I shall argue that merchant capital and modern monopoly capital are quite different in their relation to production and in their economic and political effects.

Frank's essential idea is of an *exchange* relationship in which the metropolis has a monopolistic position because each metropolis has several satellites, while each satellite confronts only one metropolis. The concept of monopoly used here is the familiar conception of the economics textbooks: a single seller (or group of sellers acting collusively) facing a multitude of small buyers or, conversely, a single buyer facing many sellers. The monopolist is then free to set the terms of exchange to his own advantage, and capture any surplus controlled by the other party.

Frank, however, generalises the idea to cover any monopolistic relationship: 'the source or form of this monopoly varies from one case to another' (*CULA*, p. 147). One can say, for example, that landlords monopolise access to the land, capitalists monopolise the means of production, and so on. But if one does not distinguish between different forms of monopoly, and in particular between class monopolies and individual monopolies, between monopoly control of the means of production and monopoly in exchange, then the assertion that exploitation is the result of monopoly becomes an empty tautology.

If one looks at the 'upper' levels of the hierarchy that Frank describes (the international and inter-regional links of the chain), I think there are two distinct kinds of monopolistic relations involved. The first, and the one that fits Frank's account best, is the monopolistic system of *merchant capital*, established in Latin America by the Spanish and Portuguese conquests and dominant there into the twentieth century. Merchants collect together products for export and for inter-regional trade, and distribute foreign and urban products. They are generally not directly involved in production, or, where they are, their activities in organising production are secondary. Mercantile monopoly may be associated with either pre-capitalist or (small-scale) capitalist relations of production. The second kind of monopoly, which Frank does not distinguish clearly, is modern *monopoly capital*, characterised by large-scale capitalist production. In underdeveloped countries, this typically appears in the form of multi-national companies, though national monopolies also exist. In contrast to merchant capital, modern monopoly capital exercises direct control over production and normally introduces fully capitalist production relations and the most modern technology. To confuse these two seems to me to be a major mistake. This confusion runs right through Frank's work. It is true that there are some cases that are hard to categorise, for example cases where multi-national firms are engaged in buying agricultural products from small-scale producers, or where they organise production on a relatively primitive technical basis (e.g. plantation agriculture). Examples are banana and sugar 'empires' in Central America and the Caribbean, British tea companies in India and Ceylon, Unilever in West Africa and so on. However, the existence of borderline cases does not invalidate the classification.

At the 'lower' levels of the hierarchy, close to or at the level at which the direct producers are exploited, Frank mentions merchants, landlords and (occasionally) capitalists. These must be clearly distinguished from each other – this is the major point of Laclau's critique. Frank argues that it is often difficult to disentangle these relationships in practice, but this surely makes it even more essential to be clear in analysis.

I am not arguing that these different exploitative relations exist independently of each other. In each different historical period they have interacted and reinforced each other – this is what gives Frank's account its descriptive verisimilitude. I hope to show that these distinctions are important in understanding the workings of the resulting economic systems.

The next major point to note is that Frank identifies an *economic* hierarchy of individuals or classes (the 'relatively few capitalists above' exploiting 'the many below') with a *spatial* or *geographic* hierarchy (world and national metropolises, regional centres, local centres). This coincidence of economic and spatial relations is characteristic of some, but not all, systems of exploitation.

Merchant capital tends to create a geographical hierarchy where it is gathering together the output of scattered production units for export in bulk, or for bulk supplies to urban centres. This is the case that fits Frank's picture best: the economic and geographical hierarchies coincide.

Modern monopoly capital is often administered through a superficially similar geographical hierarchy. The head office is in a major world centre, regional offices or local subsidiaries are established in large cities, while productive activities are located wherever manpower, markets and raw material supplies dictate (see Hymer, 1972, and Chandler and Redlich, 1961). This hierarchy of administration is not, however, in any real sense a 'chain of metropolis-satellite relations'. The intermediate levels of management are no more than agents of the corporation; they have no independent economic base. The real relation of exploitation is a direct wage relation between the workers and the corporation as a unit of capital.

Another kind of hierarchy is created by the existence of subcontractors, etc., subordinate to the large corporations. This was discussed by Hilferding and is still important (see Friedman, 1977). This structure is similar to that of merchant capital in that it involves exchange relations, but different in that the units involved are producing units, and are often located within a single urban area.

All of these hierarchical structures differ from competitive capitalism, which is characterised by a 'chain' with only one link: the relation between workers and capitalists. Frank is, no doubt, right to emphasise that the advanced capitalist countries went through a phase in which hierarchical structures were displaced by competition in crucial sectors of the economy, while the underdeveloped countries missed out on this stage.

There are superficial similarities between Frank's 'chain' (and also Wallerstein's core-periphery relation) and the classical Marxist theories of imperialism. Lenin says that finance capital 'spreads its net' over the world, and Bukharin talks of a 'few consolidated, organised economic bodies' confronting an agrarian periphery. However, for Bukharin and Lenin, all this was part of a *process* of internationalisation that was transforming the world system by simultaneously concentrating power and wealth at the centre and also developing production and creating a true proletariat in the periphery. Where Frank and Wallerstein see an essentially static system of redistribution persisting for centuries, the classical Marxists saw a process of development that was transforming the world.

The essential difference between these views is to be found in the classical Marxist emphasis on the relations of production. Frank is only able to argue that the 'chain' has remained essentially unchanged by ignoring the real changes in the relations of production involved in the displacement of merchant capital by modern monopoly capital.

V The transfer of surplus from satellite to metropolis

Frank's purpose in describing the 'chain of metropolis-satellite relations' is to argue that it is the cause of the 'development of underdevelopment'. This latter phrase is not very clearly defined, but part of its meaning seems to be a *quantitative* retardation in the growth of output, employment and productivity. The other aspect of its meaning is a *qualitative* deformation of the economic structure.

In this section I will discuss the argument (used, in rather different forms, by Baran, Frank, Wallerstein and others) that the transfer of surplus from the satellite to the metropolis leads to a retardation of development in the satellite.

The first step is to examine the concept of surplus. Frank refers to Baran's definitions (chapter 6 above), but there are additional difficulties in using this definition within Frank's analytical framework. Baran defines surplus in terms of the difference between output (actual or potential) and consumption (actual or necessary). For a self-sufficient producing unit, the surplus is the *physical* excess of what is produced over what is consumed. Frank, however, is explicitly concerned with production units that are not self-sufficient, but are involved in a network of exchange relations. In this case, goods will be consumed that are not produced within the unit concerned, and we must have some system of *valuation* to measure production and consumption in comparable units. This problem was a major preoccupation of the English classical economists, one that Marx inherited from them and tackled by using labour values. Neither Frank nor Baran suggests any solution to this problem. It is not a mere technicality; if one wants to argue that there is exploitation in exchange, one has to compare the prices that are actually paid with some reference set of 'correct' prices. At the prices actually paid, obviously, a peasant receives goods equivalent to those that he sells.

I know of no simple or universal solution to this problem, which greatly reduces the usefulness of the concept of surplus. Labour values seem to me to be useful only within a relatively homogeneous system in which competition imposes a certain uniformity in levels of technique by eliminating inefficient producers. This is the context implied by Marx in his discussion of value. As Frank rightly emphasises, the world economy is not now, nor has it ever been, homogeneous in this sort of way, so that the concept of surplus can only be used in a rather loose and qualitative fashion.

If we accept a concept of surplus, we must still ask: what are the effects of a transfer of surplus from satellite to metropolis? Here Frank's conflation of the economic and geographical dimensions of exploitation adds powerfully to the confusion. To say that one region extracts surplus from another suggests strongly that some physical goods are being seized from one place and shifted to another. Within a system of exchange, however, what is happening is that an exchange of goods of unequal *value* (in some sense) is taking place, and that control over the use of certain value magnitudes is being transferred from individuals (or groups) who live in one place to individuals (or groups, or corporate bodies) who live (or have their head offices) in another. Without analysis of the *use* of the surplus, this tells us nothing about the geographical location of new investment, and the whole point of Baran's concept of surplus is that surplus represents potential investment and hence economic growth.

As a starting point, consider what determines the geographical pattern of investment in a fully developed (ideal) capitalist system. Here, investment will be directed into the activities that yield the highest profits (this is what leads to the formation of a general rate of profit, see Marx, *Capital*, III, ch. 10). In geographical terms, this implies that investment will be located where costs are lowest (allowing for transport costs), and this will presumably mean, other things being equal, that investment will go to low wage areas, i.e. underdeveloped areas. I do not argue that these ideal conditions have ever existed, nor am I arguing that an allocation of investment according to profitability would be desirable. The real point is that the geographical pattern of investment need not correspond at all to the geographical distribution of the owners of the surplus. If anything, the super-exploitation of underdeveloped countries should mean *more* rapid development there, and this is exactly what the

classical Marxists expected. A large part of Frank's argument is therefore misdirected; the transfer of surplus from satellite to metropolis
cannot in itself explain the lack of development in the satellite. To
explain that one must analyse the factors that govern the *use* of the
surplus.

Part of Frank's answer to this criticism would no doubt be to refer to
his discussion of the distortion of the satellite's economy as a result of
economic dependence; this will be discussed in the next section. One can
also, however, argue that the structure of the chain of metropolis-satellite
relations impedes the return flow of investment from metropolis to
satellite. Here, the distinctions between merchant capital and modern
monopoly capital drawn in the last section are relevant.

In the case of a mercantile hierarchy, there are very real barriers to the
productive use of the surplus in the satellite. The production units are
separate from the capitalist enterprises that exploit them. If mercantile
profit is ploughed back into the expansion of the mercantile enterprise
itself, this does nothing to expand actual production. Where production
is in the hands of pre-capitalist producers, there may be no way in which
investment funds could be channelled into production, at least without
transforming the social relations of production, a task which merchant
capital may have neither the means nor the desire to undertake. Where
production is organised in small capitalist firms or in pre-capitalist units
which can absorb money capital productively (for example, slave
plantations), the problem is that investment funds will not be
forthcoming unless production is profitable, and production is not
profitable if the potential profits are being creamed off by mercantile
middlemen. Baran discusses these issues; Frank does not have any
theoretical analysis of them.

In the case of modern monopoly capital, especially in its highest form,
the multi-national company, the case is different. It has been argued by
many commentators (e.g. Hymer, 1972; Adam, 1975) that multi-
national companies have a 'global perspective', that is, they look over
the whole world in selecting sites for investment, potentially profitable
markets, etc. They have no special reason to concentrate investment in
their home countries, indeed they have become multi-national precisely
because they have not done so in the past. The investment decisions of
the multi-national companies should approximate more closely to the
'pure' capitalist pattern than those of any preceding form of capital.

Frank does cite evidence to show that the outflow of profit from Latin
America to the USA in various forms has greatly exceeded the return

flow of investment funds from the USA. This is not really surprising, since it is generally true that only a small part of profit is re-invested, whether the profits are generated in advanced or underdeveloped countries, by local or foreign capitalists. In all these cases, a large fraction of profit is consumed. This is an indictment of *capitalism*, but not particularly of *foreign* capital. Baran argues that monopoly capital is particularly prone to waste the surplus. I have criticised this view, and in any case it is a charge directed against *monopoly* capital, rather than against foreign or multi-national corporations as such. In Frank's treatment of foreign firms, nationalist rhetoric often supplants sober analysis.

My conclusion, then, is that the extraction of (control over) surplus from the satellite by the metropolis is not, in itself, an explanation for lack of development in the satellite. This must be explained by looking at the *use* of the surplus. Of course, the fact that the surplus is in different hands may be relevant to determining its use, but it is not the only factor. In particular, the relations of production and of exchange are crucial factors. Where production is in the hands of multi-national corporations, the scope for productive use of surplus is far greater than it is where production is precapitalist and surplus is captured by merchant capital. In all cases, however, the incentives and opportunities provided by the economic environment are critically important.

VI The concept of 'dependence'

Frank uses the term 'dependence' in a variety of senses (as noted above). One is political; the ruling class in a dependent country is enmeshed in a chain of exchange relations, so that its position depends on maintaining the chain. A second, rather different meaning is associated with a school of radical Latin American economists, the 'dependency theorists'. Frank can be regarded as a member of this school, although his approach is rather different from theirs on some issues. They do, however, largely coincide in their analysis of current forms of dependence. The point is that even a 'nationalist' government cannot successfully promote capitalist development because of the constraints imposed by the international environment.

Dos Santos (1970) defines dependence as follows:

By dependence we mean a situation in which the economy of

certain countries is conditioned by the development and expansion of another economy to which the former is subjected. The relation of interdependence . . . assumes the form of dependence when some countries (the dominant ones) can expand and be self sustaining, while other countries (the dependent ones) can do this only as a reflection of that expansion.

My first quarrel with this definition is with the assertion that the dominant countries enjoy independent (self-sustaining) development. I do not believe that any part of the world economy can now be regarded as independent, and the historical record seems to me to confirm this view (consider, for example, the effects of the 'oil crisis' of the 1970s). It is often argued that 'metropolitan capital' or 'the dominant countries' have shaped the world to fit their needs. This kind of argument needs to be treated with extreme care. Capital, in the abstract, cannot 'act' at all; it is a process, a relation, which has its own impersonal laws of motion. These have shaped both dominant and dominated countries. The state machines in the dominant countries have sought consciously to shape the world to suit the interests of their national capitals, but within narrow constraints imposed by the conditions they found and by the rivalry between them. For these reasons, I would prefer to speak of relations of interdependence and dominance rather than of dependence, since the latter formulation implies that some countries are (economically) independent.

What constraints are imposed on the 'dependent' countries? Dos Santos and other dependency theorists argue that development is restricted by the narrowness of markets, by balance of payments constraints, and by 'technological dependence'. I will postpone discussion of the last of these to chapter 12.

The story runs as follows: underdeveloped countries produce a narrow range of staple raw materials for export (this is the result of earlier stages of development). Incomes are very unequal and much of the surplus flows out of the country, so that the mass market for consumer goods is limited in size. 'Import substituting' industrialisation involves capital intensive techniques, so that employment is low, as are wages, leaving a large part of the population 'marginalised', either unemployed or in low productivity traditional activities. (The concept of 'marginalisation' has much in common with dualistic theories, except that here it is the lack of dynamism of the modern sector that excludes people, forcing them back into low productivity activities, where theories of dualism originally saw the modern sector as held back by the traditional sector.) The market remains narrow, further constricting development. Furtado (1973) suggests a further factor: consumption patterns among the elite are copied from those of more advanced countries, and the result is to bias demand towards imports or towards goods which, by their nature, are produced by capital intensive methods, reinforcing the problem. Modern production methods require imported capital goods, imported components and materials. Multi-national companies remit profits abroad (openly or by devious means). The balance of payments is therefore a constant problem, halting growth, and compelling the retention of traditional export industries as foreign exchange earners.

Consider, first, the problem of narrow markets. There are two issues here: the absolute size of the market, and its rate of growth. A small market will limit the opportunities for use of modern large-scale techniques; there is no doubt that small underdeveloped countries are at a disadvantage here, though larger underdeveloped countries (Brazil, India, etc.) are not. Production for the potentially almost unlimited export market can overcome both this problem and the problem of a slowly growing market. Relatively slow growth in the market for consumer goods is the result not of a *high* rate of exploitation, but of a *rising* rate of exploitation. Correspondingly, the market for means of production could expand relatively rapidly. This is the standard argument against underconsumptionism, an argument that Frank has accepted in his more recent work (*DAU*, chapter 5). It is argued, however, that means of production are predominantly imported, so that the growth of local industry is limited by the slow growth of the market for consumer goods. All of these arguments therefore hinge on assumptions about the pattern of international *specialisation*. Exports (which generate income, and hence demand) are assumed to be confined to traditional exports. Production for the local market is assumed to be limited to consumer goods. To give these arguments a solid foundation requires an *explanation* of the pattern of specialisation.

What of the balance of payments? The argument here can be put in a very simple algebraic form. Let domestic production (measured at current prices) be Y, and assume that a fraction m of this is imported (as means of production) and a fraction d of the revenue is paid out abroad as profits, royalties, etc. Let (traditional) exports be X. Balance of payments equilibrium requires that export earnings, x, equal payments abroad, $(m+d)Y$. Hence the maximum level of Y consistent with balance of payments equilibrium is given by $Y = X/(m+d)$. One could clearly elaborate this model enormously; m and d may depend on the rate of exploitation, the division of demand between different sectors, the capital intensity of methods of production used, and so on. The point is that the whole argument depends on the values of X, m and d. If it is possible to produce non-traditional exports and to diversify production, cutting down imports of means of production by producing them locally, then X can be increased and m reduced, and development is no longer rigidly constrained. Again, it is the pattern of specialisation that has to be explained.

It is worth noting that the limitation of markets and the balance of payments constraint are not independent of each other. Suppose that domestic production (Y) is limited by demand. The demand for locally produced goods is equal to export demand (X) plus local demand for locally produced goods. Suppose that all of local income is spent; local demand for local goods is then equal to local income minus imports, i.e. $Y(1\text{-}d)\text{-}mY$. Then

$$Y = X + Y(1\text{-}d)\text{-}mY$$

which reduces to exactly the same equation as that for balance of payments equilibrium. The balance of payments constraint can only bite if there is an attempt to spend more than income, either through private sector credit creation or through a government development programme financed by credit creation. It is the latter form that has plagued national governments attempting 'independent' development. Note, finally, that the above arguments apply equally to dominant and subordinate countries.

I conclude that the dependency theorists have provided a useful analysis of the *consequences* of a given pattern of international specialisation, but that we need an analysis of its *causes*. Emmanuel (chapter 9 below) supports the dependency theories with an analysis of international *prices*. Amin (chapter 10 below) has tackled the problem of explaining international specialisation, though I shall argue that he has not provided a complete analysis. In chapter 12, I will present Warren's case for arguing that the existing pattern of specialisation is breaking down.

VII Summary

Both Frank and Wallerstein define capitalism in terms of a network of exchange relations, on a world scale, that channel surplus from satellite (periphery) to metropolis (core). Both insist that the internal structure and development of different parts of the world economy is primarily determined by their place in the whole, and that the organisation of production at a lower level (enterprise, sector, nation state) is secondary. Both assert that development and underdevelopment are opposite sides of the coin, that each is the result of the other. My main criticism of both is that there is little connection between their grandiose general statements and their (often very illuminating) discussion of particular historical cases. What is lacking is real theory. I have suggested that theories based on the Marxist analysis of relations of production could fill this gap, though I have not provided such a theory in this chapter. Writers discussed in other chapters have provided elements of such a theory, though there is much yet to be done.

Nevertheless, Frank and Wallerstein have made an important contribution by insisting on the importance of underdevelopment and the necessity of analysing it in terms of the development of a *world* system.

The 'dependency theorists' have more modest aims. They have shown how development can be stifled by limited markets and by balance of payments problems, but their analysis rests on an implicit assumption of a predetermined pattern of specialisation between different countries. This assumption has to be justified.

8 · Rey and Arrighi

During the 1960s there was a huge upsurge of interest in Marxism, and by the end of the decade it was bearing fruit in the form of published work. Perhaps half of the total volume of Marxist writing on imperialism surveyed in this book was published within a few years, around 1970. Given the timescale of research and publication, this means that it was all being written at the same time. The broadly chronological order of discussion that I have adopted so far breaks down.

In this chapter I will discuss the work of two writers, P. P. Rey and G. Arrighi. Both of these writers have studied African societies in terms of an interaction ('articulation' is Rey's term, which has since been widely adopted) between different sectors characterised by different relations of production. Both, therefore, use a framework broadly similar to that proposed by Laclau (simultaneously) in his critique of Frank. Both adopted this approach in order to be able to analyse the politics of the areas concerned in terms of the class conflicts and class alliances created by the impact of capitalism (foreign and domestic) on indigenous social structures. Although they have much in common, Rey and Arrighi arrive at distinctly different conclusions.

I will start with Rey, since he has been more concerned to emphasise the general conceptual and theoretical issues involved. I will first discuss these general issues and outline Rey's account of capitalist development (section I), then go on to his main case studies, of Europe and Congo-Brazzaville (sections II, III) and attempt a critical assessment of his work (section IV). Finally, I will turn to Arrighi's contribution (section V).

Rey's main works on imperialism are: *L'Articulation des modes de production*, which makes up the bulk of *Les Alliances de classes* (Rey, 1973, cited below as *Alliances*), in which he sets out his main theoretical perspective and discusses the transition from capitalism to feudalism in Europe, and *Colonialisme, néo-colonialisme et transition au capitalisme* (Rey, 1971, cited below as *Colonialisme*), in which he sets out a detailed study, based on his own fieldwork, of the transition from the 'lineage mode of production' to capitalism in Congo-Brazzaville. *Capitalisme négrier* (Le Bris, Rey and Samuel, 1976) is a collection of studies of migration by African workers, both within Africa and between Africa and France. The 'theoretical introduction', by Rey, is a good concise summary of his views. One of the starting points for Rey's work was a debate among Marxist anthropologists about the nature of social relations in the part of Africa which Rey studied; for these debates see Meillassoux (1964), Terray (1972) and Rey (1975), as well as *Colonialisme*, part 1. There are useful discussions of Rey's work in English in articles by Bradby (1975) and Foster-Carter (1978).

Arrighi's most important contributions, some of which were written in collaboration with John Saul, are collected in *Essays on the Political Economy of Africa* (Arrighi and Saul, 1973, cited below as *EPEA*; page references are to this collection, though the original articles are listed in the bibliography). The best known of these papers is 'Labour supplies in historical perspective: a study of the proletarianisation of the African peasantry in Rhodesia', which is rightly regarded as a classic.

I The 'articulation' of modes of production

The upsurge of Marxism in the 1960s was accompanied by a 'return to Marx' and by a movement to purify Marxism by expelling the contaminating influence of bourgeois economics and sociology. This current of thought was particularly strong in France, where it was led by Louis Althusser, the communist philosopher, and his followers. Rey subsequently rejected their more 'structuralist' formulations in favour of a greater stress on class struggle (see the second essay in *Alliances*), but was heavily under their influence at the time he wrote the main works surveyed here.

The part of their work most relevant to the development of the theory of imperialism is the distinction they drew between a *mode of production* and a *social formation*. The best statement of these concepts and their interrelations is to be found in Balibar's essay 'The basic concepts of historical materialism' (Althusser and Balibar, 1970, part III), and in the glossary included in the English translation of the same book.

Put simply, they insist that a mode of production (capitalism, feudalism, etc.) is an abstract, timeless concept. It would be wrong to look for a real example, to assert, say, that England in 1850 was a capitalist mode of production. A mode of production is defined by a particular, exactly specified, relation connecting two classes (in the case of class, as opposed to classless, modes); it must be defined and analysed in the most precise and rigorous fashion. A social formation is also a conceptual construction, but of a more concrete kind; a real society can be thought of as a social formation. (There are some tricky philosophical issues here, concerning the relation between knowledge and reality, which I will not pursue.) Both mode of production and social formation must be analysed from the point of view of their *reproduction*, that is to say that their different components must be related in such a way as to interlock to produce a functioning system which can maintain itself in existence, at least for a time. For a critical discussion of these concepts, see Cutler, Hindess, Hirst and Hussain (1977).

What is most relevant in understanding Rey's work is the idea that a social formation may contain more than one mode of production. This parallels Laclau's idea that an 'economic system' may contain several modes of production. Althusser and Balibar insist that one mode of production normally dominates the others, defining a dominant or ruling class, except during brief stages of transition when a dominant mode is being supplanted.

Rey was very strongly influenced by this school of thought. His concept of the 'articulation of modes of production' is firmly set in a classical Marxist analysis of transition, analysed in an Althusserian style. The classical Marxists conceived of modes of production as *stages of development* which succeeded each other in turn. However, one mode of production cannot replace another overnight, so there must be a long process of transition in which the old mode of production first dominates, while allowing the new to grow up, then the new mode comes to dominate, while the old persists for a further period. Rey's originality is in insisting that this process takes so long that transition is the normal state of affairs, and in analysing the process with the same rigour as is usual in the discussion of 'pure' modes of production.

Two modes of production cannot be seen as coexisting within a transitional social formation entirely independent of each other, just sitting side by side. (That would be dualism in its crudest form.) There is an interaction, in which each affects the workings of the other, so that the evolution of a transitional social formation cannot be understood by analysing the logic of one mode of production in isolation. The two modes of production are in contradiction, in the sense that one will replace the other, but at the same time, during the period of transition, each must be reproduced, so that the conditions of their reproduction must be compatible with each other. The process goes through successive stages characterised by the dominance first of one mode, then of the other. This process is what Rey calls the 'articulation' of two modes. Other writers have extended the term rather loosely, to refer to the coexistence of modes even where no transition is involved.

In all the cases which Rey is concerned with, the expanding mode is capitalism. He follows Luxemburg in insisting that capitalism always has, in itself, an inherent tendency to expand at the expense of the pre-capitalist societies in which it originated and which it finds around itself. This insistence on what Foster-Carter (1978) calls the 'homofience' of capitalism (literally, 'having the same effect') places him definitely in the classical Marxist tradition and leads him to reject any explanation of underdevelopment in terms of restrictive behaviour by capitalists, of the sort proposed by Baran, Sweezy and Frank:

> Let us cease to reproach capitalism with the one crime that it has not committed, that it could not think of committing, constrained as it is by its own laws always to enlarge the scale of production. Let us keep firmly in mind that all the bourgeoisies of the world burn with desire to develop the 'underdeveloped' countries.
> (*Alliances*, p. 16)

His position is thus diametrically opposed to that of Frank, for whom capitalism causes underdevelopment.

Why then have some areas advanced, while others have not? If capitalism by itself has the same effect everywhere, the difference must be found in the other half of the articulation, in the pre-capitalist modes that are the 'medium and soil' (Luxemburg) of capitalist development. Rey criticises Luxemburg for failing to take the internal workings of these modes seriously. Capitalism, he argues, has prospered where it succeeded feudalism, while 'generally speaking, non-western countries, apart from Japan have shown themselves and still show themselves to be wretched environments for the development of capitalist relations of production' (*Alliances*, p.11).

Rey proceeds by considering the conditions required for the expanded reproduction of capital. The first requirement is a class of free wage labourers, so the articulation with the pre-capitalist mode must be such as to exclude a growing section of the population from pre-capitalist production (or at least to ensure that they have to spend a part of their time or a stage in their lives working for a wage). Rey also argues that capitalism is relatively very slow to establish itself in agriculture, and especially in the production of basic foods. The capitalist sector must, therefore, obtain means of subsistence for its workers from pre-capitalist agricultural producers by exchange.

In the heartlands of capitalism, where capitalism succeeded feudalism as the dominant mode, these needs were met by the expulsion of peasants by feudal landlords and the sale of a surplus product extracted as rent. To make his account consistent, Rey has to redefine feudalism (to include the extraction of rent from free peasants); his analysis will be discussed more fully in the next section. The point is that feudal landlords, acting in their own interests, simultaneously serve the interests of the emerging capitalist class, so that an alliance between the old and new ruling classes is possible. Extra-economic coercion is used (to expel peasants) but this coercion comes from the pre-existing ruling class.

In the rest of the world, however, the pre-capitalist modes that existed differed from feudalism in that they did not evolve naturally in such a way as to meet the needs of capitalism, and capitalist relations of production could not arise from within. These areas could (and did) engage in *exchange*, through the medium of merchant capital, and were thus drawn into the world market, but the effect of exchange was to reinforce the hold of the pre-capitalist ruling class and reinforce the resistance of these societies to the implantation of capitalist relations of production. This is really the most crucial part of Rey's argument; he has argued it in detail only for one case, that of a particular area in Congo-Brazzaville (section III), and it is not at all clear that the argument generalises to other areas. I shall argue that Rey's method of investigation is very valuable, and should be widely copied, but that his conclusions must be regarded as unproven.

Since the preconditions for capitalist production did not arise naturally in most parts of the world, they were imposed by external force. In order to open up the resources of these areas for capital, it was necessary to displace the existing ruling class and reorganise indigenous societies. Direct military and administrative coercion was used to recruit workers and to compel villagers to plant, harvest and sell cash crops (especially food crops). Rey calls this system of administrative coercion the *colonial mode of production*.

This mode of production plays, however, only a temporary role. Once the pre-capitalist framework has been transformed to fit the needs of capital, it can be left to itself, and capitalist reproduction and growth can be assured by primarily economic means and by a state with a political base within the area concerned. Formal decolonisation becomes possible without threat to the economic interests of capital. This is the *neo-colonial* pattern characteristic of the underdeveloped world today. The expansion of capitalist relations of production is, however, hindered by the persistence, even in a modified form, of the pre-existing modes of production. These modes of production must persist since, according to Rey, capitalist mechanisms cannot, for a long time, assure the reproduction of the system on their own.

From this account Rey deduces his central political conclusions. Capitalism and the restructured pre-capitalist modes of production need each other and sustain each other. It is therefore impossible to struggle for the abolition of pre-capitalist forms of oppression without at the same time seeking to overthrow capitalism, while anti-capitalist revolutions (Russia, China) have been able to abolish these archaic restrictions in a very short space of time.

On a world scale, the development of capitalism went ahead in previously feudal areas, but was blocked elsewhere. Capitalist and non-capitalist areas were linked by exchange handled by merchant capital. Pre-capitalist societies do not, however, necessarily respond in a flexible fashion to the needs of the capitalist sector (through market signals) since exchange does not alter the basic relations of production and does not provide any strong stimulus to a more rational organisation of production. There are thus good reasons for capitalist expansion into non-capitalist areas, but at this stage the means were lacking.

This blockage was broken when central capitalism had reached the stage of the development of finance capital, according to Rey, because it was only at this stage that capital acquired the capacity to impose capitalist relations of production from the outside. He is not very clear on this; I take him to mean that capital export on a large scale became possible, and that this was necessary for the capitalist development of the rest of the world because of the absence of indigenous capital. European states did, in fact, reorganise the mode of production in colonial territories much earlier (e.g. Latin America from the sixteenth century), but the modes of production they imposed were pre-capitalist, not capitalist. Rey's whole chronology seems to be geared to the case of Africa. The epoch of finance capital is thus also the age of imperialism and colonial conquest, but for reasons rather different from those proposed by Lenin. (See Michalet, 1976, for a reinterpretation of Lenin on similar lines; Michalet and Rey differ on most other points.)

Gathering the story together, it goes as follows. Capitalism emerged in previously feudal areas, and went through a whole process of development there (the capitalism-feudalism articulation) with a corresponding massive development of the forces of production, while the rest of the world was drawn in to relations of exchange without any transformation of either relations or forces of production. The rise of finance capital was the signal for forcible conquest and transformation of 'underdeveloped' areas, and this could be followed (after quite a long time) by decolonisation, leaving capitalist relations of production dominant, but with development still retarded by the persistence of pre-capitalist modes alongside capitalism.

The whole dynamic of Rey's theory of imperialism comes from the out of step development of capitalism in previously feudal areas and in the rest of the world. Where he differs from most other writers is in seeing the difference as not merely quantitative, but as the result of differences in the mode of production itself.

This account clearly draws heavily on the work of the classical Marxists. The similarities and differences between Rey's account of the history of capitalism and that of Rosa Luxemburg are obvious. Both emphasise the role of coercion in the expansion of capitalist relations of production, but Rey distinguishes sharply between the role of coercion in the transition from feudalism to capitalism (where the coercion is the work of the feudal ruling class itself) and in other transitions (where coercion is exercised from outside), and he also distinguishes between the transformation of a 'natural economy' into a commodity-producing system (which need not involve coercion, at least in establishing the limited commodity production that merchant capital needs to generate profitable external trade) and the transformation of relations of production by the creation of a proletariat.

His argument has obvious (and acknowledged) roots in Marx's treatment of primitive accumulation, of the Asiatic mode of production and of merchant capital. The aspects of Marx's work that Rey has built on had, however, been substantially neglected in the whole intervening period, so that to point to these origins in Marx is not to decry Rey's contribution.

More important, Rey has extended the ideas of both Marx and Luxemburg by providing an explanation for a 'neo-colonial' stage following colonialism. This connects the present stage of development of imperialism to its predecessors and to a coherent account of the whole history of capitalism. There are, however, difficulties with Rey's theories, which will be discussed below.

II The articulation of feudalism and capitalism

Rey's starting point is a critique of Marx's theory of absolute rent (see *Capital*, III, ch. 45). Absolute rent is the rent paid to a landlord on even the least fertile land (differential rent being that paid on better land, according to its quality). Marx deals with this in a framework of three classes: landlords, capitalist tenant farmers and wage workers. The landlord, he argues, will require some rent before he will allow a tenant to use even the worst land. Rey points out that if the landlord's only alternative is to leave the land idle, he will accept the most infinitesimal rent as better than nothing, so Marx's argument explains absolute rent at the price of making it utterly insignificant. Rey also argues that this conceptualisation of rent is unsatisfactory in that it is not based on relations of production: either it is the result of wholly juridical relations (legal ownership of land) or of a relation between two non-producing classes (landlords and capitalists). Neither of these is acceptable to Rey, who takes a very austere view of the kinds of relations compatible with Marxist theory. This theoretical austerity is characteristic of Marxists influenced by Althusser; the rest of us do not have to accept it.

Rey takes a bold line in rectifying these difficulties. Following a rather obscure hint in Marx's 'Introduction' to *A Contribution to the Critique of Political Economy* (Marx, 1976, p. 40), he proposes to identify 'capital' with the capitalist mode of production and 'landed property' with the feudal mode. Rent is then an effect of the articulation of feudal and capitalist modes, and not something integral to the capitalist mode of production itself. More specifically, the feudal mode of production is identified with a *class relation* between landlords and peasant cultivators, who are exploited in the form of rent. As long as a landlord has the option of renting land to peasants on terms determined by this feudal relation, then a capitalist farmer must offer at least an equal rent to obtain the use of the land. It is thus the persistence of feudal (landlord-peasant) relations of production alongside capitalist agriculture that determines the existence and level of absolute rent.

This argument gives a foundation in economic theory for Rey's conception of the articulation of two modes of production. The coexistence of two modes of production involves four classes (not three as in Marx's theory of rent): capitalists and workers in capitalist production, landlords and peasants in feudal agriculture. These modes do not simply coexist; there is an interaction, which matters to the dominant mode (capitalism) as well as to the subordinated mode of production. Rey argues that the persistence of feudal relations (i.e. of private ownership of land by non-producing landlords) not only affects distribution, but plays a central role in the reproduction of capitalist relations of production (by excluding workers from free access to land) and in the expansion of capitalism (by expelling peasants to add to the proletariat). This is the real significance of Rey's discussion of rent; the treatment of rent itself is of secondary importance.

Rey then goes on to set this analysis of the capitalism-feudalism articulation in an historical context by dividing it into stages. The first stage, the emergence of capitalism, is explained by the transformation of agriculture and the expulsion of peasants. The basic outlines are similar to those of Marx's account of primitive accumulation, but where Marx interprets the transformation as a simultaneous creation of capitalist industry and capitalist agriculture, Rey sees it in terms of a rise of capitalist industry interacting with a restructured feudal agriculture. The feudal mode is still dominant at this stage, capitalist production is at the stage of 'manufacturing' (in Marx's terms) and the social formation is held together by merchant capital.

Landlords played the essential role here. Firstly, they expelled peasants, thus creating a proletariat. The reason Rey gives is specific to England; the conversion of estates to sheep farming, prompted by the Flemish demand for wool. Secondly, they compelled peasants to produce for the market by demanding rents in cash, thus creating a market for capitalist (industrial) products and a supply of agricultural raw materials and food. Thirdly, the backing of the landlord-dominated absolutist state was essential. At the same time, the expansion of capitalism served the interests of the landlords by expanding the demand for agricultural products, thus permitting higher rents. Rey thus sees the emergence of capitalism as a product of the dynamic of feudalism itself. There is no essential conflict between capitalist and feudal orders, but instead a coincidence of interests between capital and landed property.

Once capitalism is well established, we go on to the second stage of the articulation of feudalism and capitalism, the stage where industrial capital dominates. During this stage, the division of labour between industry (capitalist) and agriculture (partly peasant) is established, so that peasant producers are forced into competition in the market. Rey argues:

> At the same time, capitalist production is not yet completely
> assured of victory on this battleground or even, in some branches,
> cannot yet compete at all. As a result, the expropriation of the

peasants is not yet assured by these means, and capitalism, to obtain extra labour power needed for expanded reproduction . . . must turn to extra economic means. One of these can be to keep landed property alive, where it still exists, and to continue the process of expropriation . . . another can be taxes and mortgages on small peasants where . . . landed property no longer exists or no longer plays the role of expropriator in the service of capital.
(*Alliances*, pp. 80–1)

The third, and final, stage of the feudalism-capitalism articulation is reached when capitalist production becomes competitive with peasant production in all branches of agriculture. The peasantry is finally destroyed and cannot reconstitute itself, any more than artisan production can survive in industry. Capital's need for landed property is over. This stage, according to Rey, has hardly been reached anywhere except perhaps in the USA and so we need not bother with it.

Looking over this account of the feudalism-capitalism articulation (transition), Rey is arguing that the interests of capitalists and landlords largely coincided in *production* (separation of workers from means of production, expansion of markets for industrial and agricultural products) and only diverged in *distribution* (since rent is a deduction from profit). He concludes that there is a natural *alliance* between capitalists and landlords. It seems to follow (Rey is not entirely explicit) that bourgeois revolutions were unnecessary. One can see why he should wish to argue this, to contrast the 'peaceful' transition from feudalism to capitalism with the violent means used by capitalism to establish itself in other social formations. Perhaps the break with the Marxist tradition is not as great as it seems, since this tradition has always stressed that capitalist *production* grew up in a feudal milieu (otherwise how could there be a bourgeoisie to conduct a bourgeois revolution); the bourgeois revolution, it is said, was necessary to replace the *political superstructures* of feudalism.

III The slave trade, colonialism and neo-colonialism

Rey's analysis of the impact of capitalism outside its homelands rests essentially on a single example: his study of 'lineage' societies in Congo-Brazzaville. This goes into great detail (*Colonialisme* runs to some 520 pages) and I can only give a very oversimplified summary of it here. A full judgment of it would require specialist knowledge of the area which I do not possess. It can have few equals in its combination of rigorous and creative Marxist theory with detailed study of a pre-capitalist society and of its penetration by capitalism.

What Rey wants to demonstrate is, firstly, that he can define a *lineage mode of production* (in a strictly Marxist sense), which was dominant before the installation of capitalism in the area studied and, secondly, that the history of the area can only be understood by looking very carefully at the workings of both modes of production involved and their interaction. Specifically, he argues that the lineage mode of production was very well suited to generating a supply of slaves for export during the period of the slave trade, rather poor at producing goods for export, and quite incapable by itself of generating either a proletariat or a marketable supply of food to support a proletariat. These facts conditioned the history of its interaction with capitalism.

According to Rey, the lineage mode of production defines two classes: chiefs (or elders) and their dependants (or juniors). Each chief has a group of dependants, and individuals are allocated to positions in the system by (real or notional) kinship relations. Subsistence production is carried out in groups of various sizes; the chief's subsistence being produced mainly inside his own household.

Groups are connected together by a network of exchanges, carried out by the chiefs. It is the chiefs' role in these exchanges, that defines the class status of chiefs and the lineage mode of production. 'Prestige goods' obtained in previous exchanges or produced by the surplus labour of dependants are exchanged, by reciprocal gifts, for each other, for slaves (until 1920) or for women (as brides for members of the group, for whom a 'bride price' or '*dot*' is paid).

Other writers have described this (or similar systems) as primitive-communal, i.e. classless. Rey presents a very careful definition of class:

> We shall speak of class conflict in any society in which a particular group controls a surplus product, the partial or total use of which is for the reproduction of the relations of dependence between the direct producers and this group. (Rey, 1975, p. 60)

He argues that capitalism too is defined by an exchange relation (the sale of labour power) and that in the capitalist mode, as in lineage societies, the surplus product may not be devoted to the personal consumption of the ruling class. It has been argued that chiefs (elders) are not a distinct class, because juniors succeed in their turn, but Rey replies that the majority of the population (slaves and their descendants, women, most free males) are excluded.

Slavery and the exchange of slaves are clearly of vital importance to the history of this area. It should be understood that slavery within lineage societies was something quite different from slavery in the plantations of the Americas. When an offence was committed (theft, witchcraft, etc.) the offender could be handed over to the chief of the offended group, so that enslavement always took an individual outside his group of origin. The receiving chief could either pass the slave on in a further exchange or settle him in his own group. Once settled, he was no longer saleable and acquired a status little different in practice from other members of the group. Slave production, therefore, did not exist, nor did a permanent status of chattel slavery. Rey argues that this 'circulation of men' together with the 'circulation of women' (as wives) functioned to redistribute population from overpopulated to underpopulated groups, in a society in which population was the main resource.

It is easy to see how this system fitted in with the slave trade. It is often argued that commodity exchange with merchant capital has a dissolving effect on pre-capitalist societies, and one would think at first sight that the export of literally millions of slaves (from Africa as a whole) over a period extending from the sixteenth to the late nineteenth century would have had the most appallingly destructive effects. Rey argues, on the contrary, that lineage societies remained in good shape during this period, since the trade in slaves was no more than an extension of the normal functioning of these societies.

European slave traders acquired slaves through the kingdoms of the coastal areas, each of which monopolised one of the few usable harbours. These kingdoms were hierarchical lineage societies, and traders bought slaves through agents who were themselves chiefs of important lineages. In this way trade with Europeans was assimilated to the system of exchanges between chiefs.

Coastal lineage societies received considerable revenues (in commissions etc.) from the slave trade which could be used to acquire slaves over and above the number exported. These surplus slaves could be settled and incorporated into the society; Rey asserts that: 'Throughout the whole period of the slave trade the kingdom of Loango enriched itself both in goods and in men' (*Colonialisme*, p. 279).

Much the same goes for lineage societies further into the interior of the country. These served as a transmission belt, through which slaves moved towards the coast while the European products obtained in exchange moved inwards. The category of 'prestige goods' came, during this period, to consist almost exclusively of European products. The wealth and power of the dominant chiefs increased and the network of exchange relations between them was extended rather than being undermined. 'The depopulation of lineage societies [was] slowed down by the mechanisms of control over the circulation of men, and above all compensated by the mechanisms of reinsertion of a part of the slaves who came into them' (*Colonialisme*, p. 279).

The main areas of depopulation were far inland, in areas without a lineage structure or where the lineage mode of production was weak, and failed to provide for a net acquisition of slaves.

This, then, is a particular illustration of Rey's general thesis that exchange relations with capitalism do not necessarily break down pre-capitalist societies or pave the way for the establishment of capitalist relations of production.

As the slave trade declined (for reasons external to Africa), European merchants tried to develop trade in products as a substitute. This trade had gone on alongside the slave trade, but on a relatively small scale, and it persisted into the colonial period. The products involved were primarily ivory and rubber, products of hunting and gathering, which were obtained in traditional and extremely wasteful ways which threatened to destroy the natural sources of these products.

In 1898–1900, the French state, having taken formal authority over the area, tried to establish 'rational' production for export by dividing the territory between 'concessionary companies' (*sociétés concessionaires*). This episode is important in Rey's argument, since the failure of this initiative is his main piece of evidence for the incapacity of capitalism to establish itself by primarily economic means. The concessionary companies found that they had, in fact, to deal with the local chiefs, since French colonial power had not, in practice, been imposed in the area.

Attempts to introduce capitalist production proved unprofitable since wages (paid to the chiefs) were high, supplies of labour power could not be ensured and neither could provisions for the workers. The companies ended up simply continuing the traditional patttern of trade from trading posts in the interior instead of at the coasts. This trade took the form of barter and was restricted in volume, since lineage society met only its needs for prestige goods through exchange. The subsistence of the local population continued to rest on traditional production outside the sphere of the market. Because of the wasteful methods of production, supplies dried up, and when rubber prices fell in 1913 the companies retreated back to the coast and effectively ceased to exist.

The period from the completion of military conquest (1920) to 1934 was characterised, according to Rey, by the dominance of a *colonial mode of production*, defined by the forced recruitment of labour and the forced sale of products. This must, however, be seen as only a stage in the process of the installation of capitalism as the dominant mode of production. It is the first stage in the articulation of capitalist and lineage modes of production, corresponding to the stage of primitive accumulation in the homelands of capitalism. The previous contacts between capitalist and lineage societies were wholly external. The centrepiece of this period was the construction of the Congo-Ocean railway by forcibly recruited labour, an enterprise that cost fifteen or twenty thousand lives.

> In the beginning, after the failure of the concessionary companies, a 'subsistence' society only exchanging with commercial capital to meet its needs for prestige goods. Afterwards, in the period from 1934 (or even 1932) to to-day, 'free' sale of labour power . . . and continually growing sale of products. This is because, during the period of construction of the [Congo-Ocean] railway, workers who had lived in the self sufficient subsistence economy became simultaneously wage earners and buyers; while the men who remained in the villages and above all the women became sellers of provisions. The unity of the producers and consumers was broken. . . . During a first stage workers on the one hand, products on the other were obtained by force, because the society did not know what to do with the money that was forced on it in 'payment' . . . But soon enough the situation was reversed and money became the intermediary, not only for goods, but also for . . . the bride price.
> (*Colonialisme*, pp. 365–6)

Rey does not argue that the colonial mode of production was set up deliberately for the purpose of transforming lineage society, though the administration certainly had in mind a 'civilising mission' (for civilisation read capitalism). Rather they were compelled by circumstances.

> In 1921, the administration were forced by facts to use the only form of intervention which was adequate to the scale of their projects: the reorganisation of the mode of production itself. . . .

We consider that a very large number of economic and even technical choices which were made had the essential function of transforming the social mode of production (whether or not that was the conscious aim of those in charge – G. Sautter does not judge them to have been intelligent enough to have consciously attempted such an intervention). (*Colonialisme*, p. 367)

The major way in which the lineage mode of production was adapted to the needs of capitalism was the monetarisation of the *dot* ('bride price'). Rey stresses that this is not a genuine price, nor are women commodities. The point is that the social relations of the lineage mode of production are expressed in money form, just as money rent is, according to Rey, a monetary expression of a feudal relation of production.

Money circulating among chiefs of lineages as bride-price payments is generally not diverted to other purposes. At the same time, the chiefs require young men to make money payments to them as a contribution to the bride price. The sums of money available for payment in the form of bride price thus continually increase and the level of the bride price has inflated correspondingly. This, according to Rey, serves a double function. The young men are forced either to work for wages or to sell products in order to pay their share. In this way the lineage relation of production, the control of the chiefs over the circulation of women, serves the needs of capitalism by forcing products and, above all, labour power on to the market. Simultaneously, the inflation of the bride price keeps it out of reach of a wage earner unless it is augmented by the accumulated hoard of the chief, so that the chiefs keep their hold; the lineage relation of production is maintained.

During the colonial period, the political structure of lineage society was first disregarded and disrupted, then reconstituted, in much the same way as the economic-social structure. The traditional system of chiefs was absorbed into the administration, and the previous patterns of dominance between tribes, clans and lineages largely reappeared. Rey traces the way that the nascent indigenous bourgeoisie and the political leadership of the independent state of Congo-Brazzaville are derived from the same group who controlled and profited by the slave trade, a 'comprador' group with centuries of experience in acting as intermediaries between capitalism and native society.

The stage is set for the neo-colonial period, which corresponds to the second stage of the capitalism-feudalism articulation. In this stage, capitalism can see to its own reproduction by purely economic means, but needs a pre-capitalist mode alongside it to provide a source of additional labour power and also to provide food for the capitalist labour force. We have seen how lineage society was reconstituted in the colonial period so as to fit these needs.

There is less to be said about this period than about its predecessors, since the capitalist mode of production now dominates, and the workings of capitalism are relatively well understood. In the Congo-Brazzaville this stage got fully under way in the 1950s, after an interlude of twenty years in which its preconditions had been established, but in which first depression and then world war held up development.

The dominant motive force in this period is investment by metropolitan finance capital in the export sector. Only metropolitan capital has the means to invest on a large scale: the colonial period had created a suitable environment for capitalism, but had not formed any substantial capitalist class. The transformation of the lineage mode had ensured the availability of plentiful and cheap labour power, and the natural resources of the region were now open to capitalist exploitation. The external market dominated, since the internal market, created by the separation of producers from the means of production, was primarily a market for food, supplied by local small-scale production.

The most important assertion that Rey makes about the neo-colonial period is that development is still held up by the persistence of a pre-capitalist (lineage) mode of production. This is no longer a matter of labour scarcity, but of the dominance of 'tribalist' politics in the newly independent state of Congo-Brazzaville (though this is asserted rather than demonstrated):

The reinforcement of the lineage system is undoubtedly an obstacle to 'development'. Many well-intentioned European observers believe that the capitalist states of the West could, from a technical point of view, have an interest in supporting the development of an efficient modern bureaucracy as against the tribalist bureaucracy. They forget one thing, that capitalism is not interested in the *technical* aspect of development (production of use values), but in the social aspect (development of capitalist relations of production and above all the extraction of surplus value). (*Colonialisme*, p. 462)

For this reason, capitalist states support tribalism and maintain the lineage mode of production and, in other areas, maintain other pre-capitalist forms. 'Throughout the world, capitalism to-day plays a fundamentally counter-revolutionary role: it keeps the most archaic forms in existence; it restores them when they are threatened (see for example the sultanates of Chad)' (*Colonialisme*, p. 463).

We thus arrive, by a completely different route, at rather similar *political* conclusions to those of Frank. Pre-capitalist forms of exploitation are maintained by capitalism and stand or fall with it. Capitalist expansion will not remove the burden of these 'archaic forms' except at a snail's pace. The revolutionary struggle must confront capitalism head on, and must not compromise itself by limiting its assault either to pre-capitalist abuses or to foreign capital alone. Only a socialist revolution can remove the double burdens that the workers of under-developed countries suffer, and the victory of the revolution will sweep away pre-capitalist forms as well as the capitalist mode of production.

IV   A critique of Rey

At the most simple level, one might take from Rey only the assertion that a careful analysis of pre-capitalist systems is necessary to understand the history of their displacement by capitalism, a process which is still going on in many parts of the world today. It is surely impossible to disagree with this, though it must be said that most Marxists have tried to analyse history in terms of the internal dynamics of capitalism alone. Accepting this point, alone, implies a major research programme.

Rey, however, claims much more than this. He wants to show, firstly, that the process of transition can (and must) be analysed in terms of the defining relations of production of the modes involved, in a strictly Marxist sense, and, secondly, that the general pattern of development in other areas is similar to that in Congo-Brazzaville, so that his account of colonial conquest, of decolonisation, and of the continuing retardation of development can be generalised. I will argue that a final judgment on these claims cannot yet be made.

Rey's account of the capitalism-feudalism articulation follows fairly well-trodden paths; the novelty is in the interpretation that he proposes. The traditional Marxist definition of feudalism identifies it with the personal servitude of the producing peasant. On this definition, feudalism (serfdom) was effectively extinct in western Europe when capitalism first appeared; instead of an articulation, one is left with a gap. Laclau's definition in terms of 'extra-economic coercion' might solve this problem (though one would have difficulty drawing a line between economic and extra-economic coercion), at the expense of widening the feudal mode to cover areas outside Europe. Laclau's intention, after all, was to argue that Latin American agriculture is feudal. Rey's own definition, which identifies feudalism with the relation between peasant cultivator and private landowner, is necessary to his argument, since he wants to demonstrate that 'feudalism' has persisted up to the present time in Europe.

I will not try to pass judgment on Rey's definition as such; definitions can only be judged by their functioning within a whole framework of analysis. The problems involved in distinguishing capitalist, feudal and other modes in agriculture will be discussed further in chapter 11. The main difficulty seems to me to be in Rey's argument that 'under-development' is caused by the persistence of pre-capitalist modes *other than feudalism*. In particular, how can Latin America be excluded from the areas dominated by feudalism? Rey does make some passing comments on the *latifundia* system in Brazil (*Colonialisme*, pp. 356–9). This system, he argues, is an articulation of two modes of production: 'A mode of production close to the system of ground rent, which only applies to cash crops, and a "traditional" mode of production in which the owner of the *latifundia* does not intervene and which is devoted to subsistence crops' (*Colonialisme*, p. 356).

The point here is that the landlord does not provide for the subsistence of the labour force, and thus has no interest in expelling surplus peasants to reduce costs. Rey argues that this suits *merchant* capital, by concentrating surplus labour into export production, but holds back the development of *industrial* capital. This system was established in Latin America by merchant capital and has blocked subsequent development, but was not copied in Africa, where colonial penetration came later under the aegis of industrial capital and finance capital.

The 'system of ground rent' is, of course, feudalism (as Rey defines it). Is the *latifundia* system really any different from feudalism as it existed in many parts of Europe, where peasants held individual plots on which they produced subsistence goods, while labouring to produce cash crops on the feudal lord's *demesne*? Brenner (1977) has argued that exactly such a system (in east Europe) blocked capitalist development there, and Banaji has argued cogently that European and Latin American feudalism are the same thing (see chapter 11). Rey, in fact, differs from the Marxist mainstream in regarding feudalism as a favourable environment for capitalism; he talks of capitalism being 'protected in its youth by feudalism' (*Alliances*, p. 11, see also Foster-Carter, 1978, p. 60). If Latin America has been feudal, we must either explain under-development there by some cause other than the pre-existing mode of production, or say that feudalism is not a favourable environment for capitalism, and that the origins of capitalism are to be sought in the *dissolution* of feudalism. Either would undermine Rey's overall account.

There is a further point. Although Rey speaks in general terms of the creation of a class of free labourers by 'the expanded reproduction of feudalism', the actual story he tells depends critically on a specific conjuncture: the creation of an opportunity for gain by switching production from labour intensive activities (production of grain, etc.) to an activity requiring much less labour (sheep raising). He does not explain why landlords should have gone on expelling peasants in all the homelands of capitalism over a long historical period, still less does he demonstrate that any 'internal logic' of feudalism was at work in this process. He has a surprising amount in common with Wallerstein here (if in nothing else), since both stress the way a landed ruling class responds to commercial opportunities. Brenner (1977) tells a contrasting story (see pp. 265–8).

Rey's analysis of Congo-Brazzaville is also open to criticism. Firstly, one can argue that lineage societies are in fact classless, primitive-communal systems. I do not feel qualified to judge. This criticism would harm Rey's claim that analysis must be founded on the defining relations of production of the dominant mode, but would otherwise leave his account untouched.

Secondly, one can criticise the notion of a 'colonial' mode of production, a notion which seems to me to be profoundly unsatisfactory. The idea seems to be a product of Rey's Althusserian structuralism (since rejected); there must be a dominant mode, and it cannot at that stage be capitalism since the conditions of capitalist reproduction are not yet assured. This is only a problem on the level of a local social formation; capitalism has a secure base for its reproduction in its homelands.

How can the 'colonial' mode be justified? Rey insists, in other contexts, that a mode of production must be defined by a determining relation of production, a relation between classes which reproduces the domination of one class over the other. What is this relation in the colonial mode of production? What classes does it connect? Who are the ruling class – the administrators? The colonial organisation clearly did not reproduce itself: rather it produced the conditions of capitalist domination.

It seems to me unnecessary to describe colonialism as a mode of production at all. State intervention in the economy is something perfectly comprehensible to Marxists. We can surely describe the colonial practices of forced recruitment of labour and forced sale of products as a form of state intervention generated by the *articulation* of the capitalist and lineage modes of production at a certain stage in its development. State intervention also played a role in the development of capitalism in its homelands, albeit on a smaller scale, through the laws against vagabonds, the regulation of maximum wages, etc. (see Marx, *Capital*, ch. 28). The key points are that there was no distinct class of beneficiaries of forced recruitment of labour, and that it was not intended to be a permanent arrangement.

A more serious question is whether the area in Congo-Brazzaville studied by Rey is typical even of other parts of Africa, let alone of other continents. Rey's assertion that lineage societies could absorb the impact of the slave trade and survive with their essential structures intact does not seem to apply to other parts of Africa. The destructive effects of the slave trade in many areas are fairly well documented (see, for example, Amin, 1976, pp. 319–22 and references cited there).

Arrighi (see below) found that in other parts of Africa the indigenous inhabitants were willing from the start to sell agricultural products and labour power, though only if the price was right. Forcible means were used in Southern Africa to displace the Africans from the land in order to force down the price of labour power, just as in Europe (primitive accumulation). It remains true, however, that force was used, and that it came from outside and not from an indigenous ruling class, so Rey's analysis is not wholly undermined. The fact that urban unemployment is now widespread throughout the underdeveloped world is not a serious criticism; Rey only argues that a shortage of labour power is a problem in the first stage of the articulation of capitalism with preceding modes of production, and that stage is now passed. It is the political constraints imposed by the persistence of pre-capitalist modes that hold up development now. (This, in a different terminology, is reminiscent of Frank.)

Gathering these criticisms together, it seems to me that Rey's work should be taken as indicating possible lines of research, but that until the kind of approach that he has adopted is applied to a wider range of cases, his overall perspective on imperialism must be judged not proven. What is valuable is the demonstration of how much can be learned by combining detailed research with a rigorous Marxist investigation of relations of production.

V   Arrighi's analysis of modes of production in Africa

Arrighi, like Rey, has studied the penetration of capitalism in Africa both historically and in the present day. He is less concerned with theoretical niceties, more concerned with contemporary politics, and his canvas is wider, covering the whole of Africa south of the Sahara, i.e. Black Africa. He argues that this area divides into two regions with very different histories: tropical Africa and southern Africa. In his analysis of both areas the implicit (sometimes fairly explicit) basis is an account of the articulation of the indigenous modes of production with capitalism.

From Arrighi's description, it is clear that he regards the indigenous societies of tropical and South Africa as essentially primitive-communal:

> The vast majority of the population of tropical Africa consists of independent producers. . . . Individuals can customarily acquire land through tribal or kinship rights. Only comparatively rarely is land acquired or disposed of through purchase or sale. . . . Market exchanges were . . . peripheral . . .

> Feudal elements, landowning classes and national bourgeoisies are either nonexistent or not sufficiently significant, politically and/or economically, to constitute the power base of the state.
> (*EPEA*, pp. 13–14, 141)

This indigenous peasantry, however, has been very responsive to market stimuli, both in supplying goods to the market, and in coming forward as wage labourers whenever it has paid them to do so (though not otherwise). In contrast to Rey, then, Arrighi does not see the indigenous mode of production as a substantial obstacle to capitalist development. The lagging development of tropical Africa is due to the failure of capitalist development to expand the demand both for labour power and for the products of pre-capitalist agriculture, not to a lack of either.

The main characteristics of tropical Africa derive from the limited extent to which capitalism has supplanted pre-capitalist modes of production. In the earlier stages of capitalist penetration the main demand was for unskilled labour power, and this demand was met, not by the creation of a distinct, permanent proletariat, but by migrant labourers who kept a foothold in the pre-capitalist mode of production, where their families could produce a large part of their own subsistence and where reciprocal obligations guaranteed the individual's security in illness, old age, etc. A low-wage, 'low-skill pattern developed. Arrighi argues that this migrant labour force is not a proletariat, as long as subsistence is guaranteed in the pre-capitalist sector, but remains part of the peasantry. We thus have a capitalist mode of production without any substantial proletarian class being formed.

Modern international corporations, however, adopt capital intensive methods of production requiring a smaller number of semi-skilled workers. To make it worthwhile to train workers even for semi-skilled work requires a stabilisation of the labour force, which requires, in turn, a substantial increase in wages above the level which will attract migrant labour, so that workers find it worthwhile to sever their ties with the traditional economy. At the same time, the state apparatus, taken over from the colonial powers substantially unaltered, supports an elite and a sub-elite, who are also relatively well paid. These groups, together, Arrighi calls a labour aristocracy (while admitting some unease about the term). In the absence of any substantial indigenous bourgeoisie or landowning class, this labour aristocracy forms the political basis of the state. State policies then, understandably, favour relatively high wages, and high wages encourage the maintenance of the policy of using capital intensive methods of production.

The result is what Arrighi calls 'growth without development', in which the (small) modern sector offers relatively few opportunities of employment, and also buys relatively little from the traditional sector, since the relatively highly paid proletariat proper spends its income largely on the products of the modern sector or on imports. The high demand for imports, together with the lack of a substantial capital goods sector, leads to balance of payments constraints which inhibit any acceleration of growth in the modern capitalist sector, while the pre-capitalist peasant sector stagnates for want of any stimulus from demand. The relative impoverishment of the peasantry may lead to differentiation and the formation of a 'kulak' class of capitalist farmers, but the slow growth of demand for agricultural products 'restrains the incentive for, and financial ability of, the emerging kulaks to expand wage employment so that . . . it tends to produce an impoverished peasantry without fostering its absorption in capitalist agriculture' (*EPEA*, p. 126).

This formulation is strikingly similar to Patnaik's (chapter 11 below), which refers to India. Both have much in common with the 'dependency theorists'. Arrighi is mainly concerned with the effects of a particular pattern of economic development on class structure, and he confines his analysis to Africa. He therefore does not offer a detailed explanation of why foreign investment should take the form it does. See chapter 12 for discussion of the pace of capitalist development.

Southern Africa, by contrast, is distinguished by the much larger scale of capitalist penetration in the earlier stages of capitalist development (the result of mineral discoveries) and also by the presence of a substantial settler-colonial bourgeoisie drawn by the opportunities (real and imagined) created by this early capitalist boom. The difference between tropical and southern Africa thus arises from the different opportunities that capital has found in these two areas, and not from any important difference in the pre-capitalist mode of production that existed there. Arrighi's main work here is an analysis of Rhodesia (Zimbabwe), though he argues that a rather similar process happened in South Africa.

During the early stages of capitalist penetration it proved difficult to recruit a sufficient labour force locally. This was not due to any unwillingness by Africans to respond to market incentives, but to the fact that producing goods for sale got a better cash return on effort than did wage labour at the wage rates that the mines were prepared to offer. At this stage, the African peasantry could meet their subsistence needs without participating in the cash economy; sale of either products or labour power represented a use of surplus labour time to increase living standards.

The solution to this 'problem' was, in essence, simple; the African peasantry was expelled from the land, the classic centrepiece of a process of primitive accumulation. There are, however, some distinctive aspects of primitive accumulation in Rhodesia that make it worth looking at in a little more detail.

The expulsion of the peasantry from the land could not take place at once, since there was a need for food supplies for the mining sector. This need for supplies of foodstuffs is, of course, exactly the point that Rey stresses in his discussion of the articulation of capitalism with pre-capitalist modes of production; Arrighi's case study was published in the same year as the first publication of Rey's essay on the articulation of modes of production. Most of the land in Rhodesia was expropriated at a very early stage (by 1902; *EPEA*, p. 195), but the African peasantry was left in occupation since land was plentiful but labour scarce. European owners of land initially exploited the Africans through the establishment of 'semi-feudal' relations (p. 196): the exaction of labour services, or rents in money or kind. Rent and tax charges forced Africans into the cash economy, but did not force them to sell their labour power rather than their products. Extra-territorial African workers from what is now Zambia and elsewhere were essential to capitalism in Rhodesia at this stage, which persisted to the slump of 1921–3.

During this first stage various counteracting tendencies were at work. African peasants invested in improved means of production, mainly of a 'land-using' type (draught animals, ploughs), thus increasing their capacity to produce, but at the same time they were developing new consumption habits, becoming more dependent on the cash economy and being progressively excluded from the best lands by European capitalist farmers. Thus at the same time the supplies marketed by capitalist farmers drove down the prices that Africans could get by selling their products, while their capacity to produce was reduced by land scarcity and subsequent loss of fertility due to overfarming of the land. The slump of 1921–3, when agricultural prices fell sharply, marked the turning point. From then on the African population was essentially a proletariat; dependent for its subsistence on the sale of labour power, and thus in a quite different position from that of the mass of the people in tropical Africa.

The foothold that African workers retained in the peasant economy only enabled the wage to be held down to a level which provided for the subsistence of a *single* worker, while the costs of the *reproduction* of labour power were met by the work of the remaining family members in the tribal reserve areas. After the Second World War, average African wages rose as oligopolistic industry introduced more modern techniques and 'stabilised' sections of the labour force in the fashion described above, while the wages of other sections of the proletariat remained at the single-man-subsistence level. Arrighi sums up the whole process in a much quoted sentence: 'Real wages remained at a level which promoted capitalist accumulation not because of the forces of supply and demand, but because of politico-economic mechanisms that ensured the ''desired'' supply at the ''desired'' wage rate' (*EPEA*, p. 214).

Arrighi's analysis is undoubtedly a superb application of the Marxist analysis of primitive accumulation in a particular case. I think, though, that it has often been misunderstood as illustrating some specifically *colonial* mechanism; what strikes me is how similar it is to the origins of capitalism in, say, England. The 'semi-feudal' stage, and the expulsion of peasants by the action of individual landowners converting themselves into capitalist farmers are strikingly familiar. A more interesting question is why other places where superficially similar 'semi-feudal' structures existed (e.g. the Latin American *latifundia* system) have so far evolved in a very different way. Arrighi's explanation seems to be that Rhodesia's economy expanded rapidly because of the implantation of *competitive* capitalism with a numerous *national* (i.e. settler) bourgeoisie.

The persistence of a small peasant sector subsidising the reproduction of labour power is fairly distinctive, though not unique. Should this sector be regarded as possessing a distinct (non-capitalist) mode of production? Its role is clearly completely subordinate, even if a sort of vestigial ideological-political level does persist in the tribal reserves (or is deliberately created, as in the Bantustans). This question raises again the general, theoretical issues involved in the modes of production debate (chapter 11 below).

VI Summary

Rey's theory of the 'articulation' of modes of production is a theory of the transition from one mode to another, over a long period in which the two coexist. During this period, there must be mechanisms by which the social relations of each mode are reproduced despite contact with the other. The capitalist mode of production requires the reproduction of a class of free wage labourers separated from the means of production, and this requires marketed supplies of subsistence goods during a (long) transitional period until capitalist farming is fully established. In previously feudal areas these conditions were ensured by the action of the feudal ruling class itself, and capitalism was able to develop fairly rapidly. In other parts of the world, capitalism could only be implanted by external conquest followed by foreign investment (in the absence of a nascent local capitalist class), and this accounts for the late start of capitalist development in these areas. The persistence of pre-capitalist alongside capitalist relations of production accounts for continued retardation. Archaic forms of exploitation cannot be abolished by capitalist 'modernisation', but only by socialist revolution. The main criticism of this account is that it rests on a single case study, and can thus only be regarded as a hypothesis that must be tested by further research.

Arrighi presents a similar account of the conditions for capital accumulation, but blames the persistence of pre-capitalist agriculture primarily on the slow development of capitalism and, above all, on its capital intensive nature. In tropical Africa the wage earners, as a (subordinate) part of the labour aristocracy, play a part in maintaining the political structures that support 'growth without development'. Southern Africa is distinguished by its numerous (white) bourgeoisie.

9 · Emmanuel

Arghiri Emmanuel's theory of *unequal exchange* is in complete contrast to the main traditions of Marxist thought on imperialism and the world economy, and is equally distant from conventional non-Marxist theories. It is a genuinely original contribution.

Marxists have generally identified the mainspring of imperialism either with the development of monopoly (monopoly in exchange according to Frank, in production according to Lenin) or with the expansion of capitalism at the expense of pre-capitalist modes of production (Luxemburg, Rey). Emmanuel's break with these traditions is expressed in the subtitle of his book: 'a study of the imperialism of trade'. He claims that free trade between two wholly capitalist countries can still be 'unequal', and he goes on to claim that this 'unequal exchange' is the foundation of the massive inequalities that exist in the world economy. The mechanism that he proposes to explain this inequality does not rest on any monopoly by capitalist firms, nor does it involve any exercise of state power in international relations.

What Emmanuel has done is to extend Marx's theory of 'prices of production' to the determination of international prices, making the key assumption that goods and capital are mobile internationally, while labour (power) is not, so that prices and profit rates are equalised internationally by competition while wages are not. This assumption seems at least a reasonable starting point. I shall argue that Emmanuel's theory provides a very important component of a theory of the world economy, but that it cannot be regarded as complete in itself or as a complete account of the way the world system works.

The term 'unequal exchange' is not new, and has frequently been used by other writers, usually very loosely. Unequal exchange, so called, may be ascribed to monopoly pricing, to 'transfer prices' used to evade tax by multi-national companies and so on. Alternatively, it may be argued, following Marx, that high productivity labour in an advanced country produces more 'value' (in the terms of the labour theory of

208

value) than lower productivity labour in more backward areas. The product of an hour's labour in an advanced country will then exchange for the product of a great deal more labour in an underdeveloped country. In this case 'unequal exchange' is merely a reflection of divergences in productivity that have other causes. Mandel (1975, chapter 11) seems to combine all of these arguments at once in an account which is both eclectic and lacking in rigour.

Emmanuel's theory is set out in his book *Unequal Exchange* (1972, cited below as *UE*), which also contains, in the edition cited, a debate between Emmanuel and Bettelheim. See also Amin (1977, part IV) for an interesting discussion of Emmanuel's theory. An article by Emmanuel (1974), which is really a contribution to a different debate, elaborates some of his views, especially on demand and capitalist development.

I Unequal exchange: the basic theory

The statement of the theory in the body of Emmanuel's book is modelled on Marx's solution to the transformation problem, so that international exchange is presented first in terms of labour values, which are then 'transformed' into prices of production. Following Bettelheim's criticisms of some of his statements (from a more orthodox Marxist standpoint), Emmanuel counterattacked by elaborating a consistent treatment of prices of production rather than retreating under fire. I will, therefore, present the theory in its more developed form (as set out in Appendix V to the English edition) without using labour values at all. In this section the presentation will be informal; for a more formal statement, see the appendix to this chapter.

Emmanuel defines a factor of production as 'an established claim to a primary share in society's economic product'. Criticised by Bettelheim for looking at production only in terms of monetary magnitudes and not at the material basis of these magnitudes, he replied vigorously, arguing that the social relations of production are precisely relations of property ownership, of appropriation, and hence of claims to a share of the product. 'Factors of production' are therefore classes rather than physical inputs.

He then argues that in a simple commodity-producing society (i.e. a society of 'self-employed' independent producers), labour is the only factor, the only basis for a claim on the product, and thus prices must fluctuate around labour values so as to equalise rewards in different branches of production. This tendency of price towards value is enforced by competition, that is to say, by mobility of individual producers between different activities; if the price of any product is high relative to its value then there will be an influx of new producers into that line of production, forcing down the price.

In a capitalist economy, on the other hand, there are two factors (i.e. two classes). Competition between workers (mobility of labour) will equalise wages between industries, while competition between capitals (mobility of capital) will equalise the rate of profit. *Prices of production* (i.e. equilibrium prices) are then made up of money costs (wage costs, materials, depreciation of fixed capital) plus a profit margin sufficient to give the general rate of profit on the capital invested. Prices and the rate of profit can only be determined simultaneously, since prices of materials and capital goods enter as costs, and profit must be calculated on the capital required which depends, in turn, on the price of capital goods. This is a standard problem in Marxist economics, and the algebra of a solution is now well understood. The first complete solution was the work of Bortkiewitz (see *UE*, Appendix V or any modern text on Marxist economics, e.g. Howard and King, 1975). Emmanuel's solution is modelled on that of Sraffa. The formal statement is in the appendix to this chapter.

Where Emmanuel differs from Sraffa is in anchoring the system of prices by taking a wage which is fixed in terms of the commodities it can buy, a fixed real wage. In this he follows Marx, who took the value of labour power as determined by the means of subsistence necessary for the worker to survive. I will discuss the determinants of wages later, in section II.

In simple terms we can think of the profit rate as determined, on the one hand, by the gap between what is produced and the fixed wage level, and on the other hand, by the methods of production used and hence the capital intensity of production, and we can think of prices as determined by costs (of which wages are a major component) plus profits (determined in the way just described).

Emmanuel argues, in his Appendix II, that prices of production are not 'on a lower level of abstraction' than values (as Marx and the orthodox Marxist tradition have held) but that labour values and prices of production are parallel abstractions, the first being the abstraction appropriate to simple commodity production and the second that appropriate to developed capitalism. In this his position seems similar to the 'neo-Ricardian' school of thought, as exemplified by, for example, Steedman (1977).

Turning now to the world economy, Emmanuel makes the key assumption that capital is mobile internationally, and that a single rate of profit is formed at the international level, but that labour is not mobile between countries so that workers in different countries are not (directly) in competition with each other and different national levels of wages may be formed. Products are assumed, at this stage in the argument, to be freely traded (transport costs are ignored) so that a single set of prices of production exists for the whole world.

If two countries (or groups of countries) have different wage levels there are two possible circumstances in which profits can still be equalised between them, without any product having two different prices (which is ruled out by mobility of goods and free competition).

Firstly, if they produce the same products, profits can only be equalised if the high-wage country has higher productivity so that their costs are the same (or, more strictly, so that labour and other costs plus the general profit rate add up to the same price of production). In this case wage differences correspond to, and are explained by, productivity differences.

Although Emmanuel accepts that this explanation applies to some goods, he does not treat it as the normal case. He stresses instead that there is an international division of labour in which countries (or groups of countries: advanced and underdeveloped) specialise in producing different goods.

The second possibility, then, is that two countries may produce wholly different commodities, so that they are not in direct competition with each other. This is the case in which 'unequal exchange' can occur. If one good is produced only in the high-wage country and the other only in the low-wage country, then the price of each must incorporate wage costs, so their prices reflect the differences in wages. To put it simply, the products of the high-wage country are dearer and the products of the low-wage country cheaper *than they would have been if wages were the same in the two countries*.

This is what Emmanuel calls unequal exchange. Two points should be noted here which will be discussed later. Firstly, he assumes that wages are given independently of prices: 'wages are the independent variable', so that the wage difference is the *cause* of unequal exchange. Secondly, there must be some barrier that prevents all production moving to the low-wage country and enjoying lower costs of production. The theory thus assumes a *predetermined* pattern of international specialisation.

Exchange is 'unequal' because the low-wage country has to pay more for its imports than it would if wages were the same in both countries, without getting higher prices for its own exports. It thus has to export more to get a given amount of imports. Correspondingly, the high-wage country gets more imports in return for a given amount of exports. Whether the actual amounts traded would stay the same regardless of prices is another matter; the argument is concerned only with the terms of trade.

To see how this works out, I will take a very simple numerical example, which is not supposed to be realistic; it simply illustrates the principles involved. I have deliberately set it up so that the two countries are as alike as possible.

Suppose there are two countries (A and B) and two goods (1 and 2). Country A produces only good 1, while country B produces only good 2. To start with, I assume that wages are the same in each country, and I will go on to see what difference it makes if wages in country A are increased.

I assume that the production of five units of good 1 (in country A) requires 1 man year of work together with inputs of one unit of good 1 itself and one unit of good 2 as means of production (m of p), at the beginning of the period. For good 2 (in country B) conditions of production are exactly the same, five units being produced by 1 unit of labour, and one of each commodity.

Wages are assumed to be fixed in real terms. Both in A and in B, each worker must be paid enough in wages, at the beginning of the year, to buy one unit of good 1 and one unit of good 2. For each worker he employs, a capitalist must lay out, at the beginning of the year, enough money to buy one unit of each good to use as means of production, plus a wage enough to buy one unit of each good.

A capitalist is, however, interested in profits, and to calculate profit we must know the money costs and money receipts. We cannot, in general, calculate costs without knowing the prices of the goods, and we cannot calculate the price without knowing costs and profit. What we must do is to find both simultaneously. (In this case we can get to the rate of profit directly since it is obvious that the two goods must sell for the same price; this is not so in general.)

In this particular case, all costs are in the form of capital outlays at the beginning of the year, so annual costs are the same as capital employed.

We can write:

>   selling price = cost + profit

but

$$\text{rate of profit} = \frac{\text{profit}}{\text{capital}} = \frac{\text{profit}}{\text{costs}}$$

so, writing r for the rate of profit:

>   selling price = $(1+r)$ costs.

The price equations follow directly, given that the rate of profit must be the same in both countries:

$$5p_1 = (1+r)(2p_1 + 2p_2)$$
$$5p_2 = (1+r)(2p_1 + 2p_2)$$

where p_1 = price of good 1, p_2 = price of good 2.

From these equations, it follows immediately that $p_1 = p_2$ and $r = 0.25$ or 25 per cent. The actual levels of p_1 and p_2 cannot be determined, but this does not matter; it is only the terms of exchange that count, together with the real purchasing power of the wage, which has already been fixed by assumption.

Now suppose that the wage rate in country A goes up, so that it will now buy 1.5 units of each commodity, while the wage in B is enough to buy one unit of each, as before.

Following exactly the same procedure, the price equation can be set out again:

$$5p_1 = (1+r)(2.5p_1 + 2.5p_2)$$
$$5p_2 = (1+r)(2p_1 + 2p_2)$$

From this we can deduce the rate of profit, $r = \frac{1}{9}$ or 11.1 per cent (add the equations and $(p_1 + p_2)$ cancels out), and then relative prices, $p_1 = 1.25p_2$. The low-wage country, B, now has to export 1.25 units of its export, good 2, in order to buy one unit of its import, good 1. Its 'terms of trade' (export price divided by import price) have worsened by 20 per cent. Since real wages have gone up, at least in one country, and productivity is still the same, the profit rate is reduced.

Nothing has been said about the amounts actually produced and traded; to say anything about this would require additional assumptions. The theory of unequal exchange is, in the first instance, a theory of *prices*, of the terms of *exchange*, and depends on costs per unit of each product and on the wage rate for a unit of labour power.

As an illustration, I will set out a possible outcome in terms of production, consumption and trade, of the example of pricing given above. I assume that the two commodities, goods 1 and 2, are always used in fixed proportions, one unit of good 1 to one of good 2, both as means of production, and as consumer goods bought by workers or by capitalists, regardless of their relative price. This assumption is very restrictive, and more realistic cases will be discussed later. The other major assumption, also unrealistic and introduced only to simplify the example, is of 'simple reproduction', that is, all wages and profits are assumed to be spent on consumer goods with no new net investment.

Suppose that 100 workers are employed in each country. With wages equal, as in the first set of price equations, we get the pattern of production and consumption set out in table 1.

Table 1 Sources and uses of goods; equal wages

		gross product	replacement of m of p	consumption by workers	consumption by capitalists	trade
Country A	good 1	500	— 100	— 100	— 50	— 250
	good 2	0	— 100	— 100	— 50	+ 250
Country B	good 1	0	— 100	— 100	— 50	+ 250
	good 2	500	— 100	— 100	— 50	— 250

Notes: (1) Sources of goods (production, imports) shown as +, uses as —.
(2) Assumptions as given in text.

Table 2 Sources and uses of goods; wages increased in A

		gross product	replacement of m of p	consumption by workers	consumption by capitalists	trade
Country A	good 1	500	— 100	— 150	— 27.75	— 222.25
	good 2	0	— 100	— 150	— 27.75	+ 277.75
Country B	good 1	0	— 100	— 100	— 22.25	+ 222.25
	good 2	500	— 100	— 100	— 22.25	— 277.75

In constructing the table, I have assumed that profits are consumed in the country in which they originate. With free mobility of capital this need not be so, since profits in one country may accrue to capitalists elsewhere, but this is a rather different matter from unequal exchange. I will discuss this point later.

Now compare this table with the situation where wages are higher in country A, as set out in the second set of price equations above. The results are given in table 2.

Since country A's product now exchanges at a higher price, consumption in country A can be higher without any increase in production and productivity. Instead of importing 250 units of good 2 in exchange for 250 units of good 1, they import 277.5 units and only export 222.25. Although wages have gone up in A and not B, the total profit in country A now exceeds that in B, where they were previously equal. This is because it is the *rate* of profit that is equalised, and the capital advanced is increased in A by the wage increase.

Before leaving the example, consider how the cases shown in the tables would be recorded in conventional national income measurements. These figures are normally shown in money terms, so let us suppose that the price of good 2 is fixed at $1.

In the first case each country would have a gross product of $500, and a net product (output - replacement) of $300 ($500 - $200). In the second case, country A's gross product is valued at $625 (500 units at $1.25) and its net product (net national income) at $400 ($625 - $225), while country B's gross product is still $500 and net product $275. Just looking at national income figures, therefore, gives the impression that the high wages in country A are justified by a higher level of productivity, but this higher 'productivity' is really an illusion produced by the prices at which the output is valued and is a result, not a cause, of the higher wages. Physical productivity is, of course, the same in both examples.

The 'prices of production' which have been calculated in the example are equilibrium prices, determined by the equilibrium condition that the profit rate should be equalised. Actual prices will fluctuate around these levels, but will always tend back towards them because whenever the price of (say) good 1 is above the equilibrium level, profits will be higher in country A than country B, and capital will flow towards the high profits, expanding supply and pushing the price down.

An objection to the theory that will occur to many economists is that a wage increase will lead to a balance of payments deficit, and hence to a devaluation of the currency of the country concerned. This will, however, make no difference, because of the key assumption that wages are fixed in *real* terms, as a given quantity of *commodities*. A devaluation can only affect equilibrium prices if wages are fixed in money terms, and can be reduced in real terms by reducing the value of the currency. As for the balance of payments, a deficit on the current account can only arise if domestic investment is greater than domestic saving, but the assumption is that, with freely mobile capital, any excess of investment over saving is financed by an inflow of capital, and hence any current account deficit is matched by a capital account surplus.

To give some impression of what this theory might mean in reality, consider an example given by Emmanuel (*UE*, pp. 367–8; I have made some of the calculations more explicit). His critics had pointed out that imports into the advanced countries from the Third World amounted to $25 billion, which is only 2.5 per cent of the advanced countries' national income of about $1,000 billion. In reply he argued that if wages account for 50 per cent of the cost of these imports, and if wages in the Third World would have to increase by twenty times in order to bring them up to the level of those in the advanced countries, then the price of Third World exports would have to increase roughly tenfold (there would be repercussions on profits to take into account), to $250 billion, 25 per cent of the advanced countries' national income, a very considerable amount. One can, of course, doubt whether anything like the same volume of trade would take place at these prices; Emmanuel's argument is concerned only with prices, and not with the amount traded.

One point that should be stressed is that it does not matter what kind of goods are produced in the high-wage country, or group of countries, so long as they do not face competition from low-wage producers. There is no presumption that these are manufactured goods, or high technology goods, or anything of the sort, though they might be. An example which Emmanuel gives is the price of timber; since wages in Sweden, Canada and other timber exporting countries are high and rising, these products have sold at high and rising prices, while African hardwoods have not.

II Wages

The key factor in Emmanuel's theory of international prices is the difference in wages between advanced and underdeveloped countries. Emmanuel clearly needs to complete his theory with an account of wage determination.

The essential thing is that wages must be independent of market forces over the time span required to establish equilibrium prices; since otherwise wage costs could not provide the underpinning for an equilibrium set of prices that the market adjusts to. This rules out any market theory of wages. Neither can he accept the position of the classical economists (Ricardo, Malthus) in which wages are determined by physical subsistence needs, since there is no reason for these to differ markedly between countries.

Instead he starts from Marx's famous, if rather cryptic, statement that the 'quantity of commodities necessary for the worker' contains a 'historical and moral element' (which may therefore differ between countries and over time), but 'nevertheless, in a given country, at a given period, . . . is also given'. This can be interpreted as meaning that the real wage is very resistant to downward pressure in the short run, even over decades or more, since workers have adopted a certain pattern of life and entered into commitments which cannot easily be changed (the historical element). So, for example, the physical layout of cities may compel certain spending on transport, the physical character of the stock of housing may be such that it requires certain spending on maintenance, heating, etc., if workers are to function as workers at all. Another factor is the moral element, that, once a certain standard of life has been accepted as normal, there will be great resistance to changing it. This given standard of living acts as a centre of gravity around which the wage may fluctuate according to market influences, but these fluctuations are too short-lived to be incorporated into it (hence wages are the independent variable). Emmanuel assumes that 'historical and moral' factors operate relatively uniformly on wages within a single country, but not between different countries, which is why he presents unequal exchange as a process that operates between different countries. On a purely analytical level, the pricing model he has described could just as well describe relations between high- and low-wage industries within a single country.

However, he must still explain why the 'historical and moral' element changes over time and why it is different as between countries. His explanation is that trades union pressure and political action can change the level of the equilibrium wage by sustained action over a long period of time. Economic development does tend to raise wages, but not directly. Rather economic development, by centralising workers, by creating needs for higher levels of skills and so on, makes conditions more favourable for trades union and political action to raise wages. Emmanuel argues that high wages also favour development, for reasons which I will examine later, so that a vicious/virtuous circle is set up in which relatively high wages lead (after a relatively long lag) to higher wages still, and so on.

Emmanuel's model thus divides economic forces into three groups which act over different time scales. In the short run, prices and wages fluctuate around their equilibrium levels. In the longer run, equilibrium prices are determined in the way that has been described, while equilibrium wages are relatively fixed and act as the 'independent variable'. Given an even longer timescale, wages cease to be independent and are part of the vicious/virtuous circle of wage levels and development. In this longer timescale there is no equilibrium state, since the process is cumulative.

Is this account of wage determination acceptable? The difficulty in forming a judgment is that although Emmanuel's arguments are plausible enough, there are other theories that are equally plausible. The factors involved are so ill defined that it is difficult to settle the issue by using historical or empirical evidence. The most that can be said is that no one has a clearly superior theory.

III Countries or classes as units of analysis?

If we accept, for the moment, the theory as presented, we may well ask: so what? Suppose that prices in international trade are systematically biased in favour of the high-wage countries and against the low-wage countries, why does it matter?

Starting with the basic model in which products and capital are freely mobile between two countries while labour is not, it is not clear that it matters at all. This basic model defines *three* classes: the working class in each country and a *single* capitalist class. It is clear that no distinct national capitalist classes with distinct interests can exist when capital is freely mobile between countries and a single profit rate is formed. If workers in one country succeed in raising their (equilibrium) wage, they do so at the expense of profits; this clearly follows from the idea (on which Emmanuel insists) that wages are the independent variable, so that a wage increase in one country cannot reduce the (given) wage in the other.

All that happens is that a wage increase *anywhere* harms capital on the world scale, and a wage reduction *anywhere* benefits capital. If capital were not freely mobile the effect would fall on the national capitalist class.

Can we say that the high-wage country benefits *as a country*? Clearly not, since there is no national interest but two diametrically opposed class interests. High wages benefit the workers, of course, but no one ever supposed otherwise. They are not gaining from unequal exchange, but from high wages.

IV Demand and development

Emmanuel, however, argues that *unequal exchange* acts as the basis for a process of *unequal development*. He argues this on two different counts. Firstly, capital is attracted to demand, so the high incomes generated by unequal exchange attract further investment and start a cumulative process of development. Secondly, he argues, high wages will lead to the use of capital intensive methods of production which raise productivity and promote development.

The argument that demand attracts capital investment is clearly out of place in the models discussed so far, which assume free movement of goods and a predetermined pattern of specialisation between countries. High incomes in a country as a result of high wages and the resulting unequal exchange may mean more demand, but this demand is just as likely to be demand for the products of the low-wage countries as for home produced goods. Correspondingly, the low-wage country's low level of demand will also be divided between both countries' products.

There is, in fact, one good reason to expect the opposite: that high wages and prices will repel capital. If the products of the high-wage country sell at high prices, as the theory requires, then this will generally mean that less will be sold, and, correspondingly, income and employment in the high-wage country will be reduced. The critical factor is the 'elasticity of demand' for the country's products: the percentage fall in the quantity demanded when price increases by one per cent. If this is greater than one, then the fall in the quantity sold will outweigh the increase in prices, and total sales revenue will be lower. If it is less than one, then a price increase will lead to increased receipts and an increase in national income. In the numerical example of section I, I assumed demand to be independent of price (elasticity of demand equal to zero) to get the result that a higher wage level corresponded to a higher level of national income and expenditure. Strictly speaking, there are complications (a change in output will also affect spending on imported means of production and, in addition, income changes will affect the composition of demand: increased demand for particular products from countries where income has increased does not necessarily exactly offset reduced demand where income has decreased), but the principle should be clear. Price increases have a double effect: they increase income for each unit produced, but they tend to reduce the number sold. The overall effect may go either way.

Is anything then left of Emmanuel's argument that high wages and prices generate increased demand which attracts capital? If we accept his (implicit) assumption that high wage and price levels mean increased incomes, then his argument can be rescued by a simple change in the assumptions, a change implicit in his arguments. We assume that some goods are traded internationally but that others are not. These non-traded goods would include perishable and bulky goods, together with construction and many services. Protective tariffs can also, artificially, ensure that certain goods are not traded which otherwise would be.

In this case, high incomes in a country will mean high levels of demand for non-traded as well as traded goods. Since non-traded goods can only be produced locally, capital will flow into a high-wage country to meet this demand, and this will generate more employment in these industries, more incomes and hence more demand. If, for example, half of income is spent on non-traded goods then each dollar of income from the production of traded goods will generate another dollar of income for the producers of non-traded goods, taking all the repercussions into account. This model, which Emmanuel does not set out explicitly, is reminiscent of a Keynesian foreign trade multiplier, or of the theory, in urban economics, of the relation between the economy of a city and its 'economic base' of 'exports'.

It is essential to the argument that each country should produce both traded and non-traded goods. Traded goods are necessary to the theory in order for unequal exchange to have something to bite on. You cannot benefit from trade without trading. Non-traded goods are essential to convert high incomes into an attraction to capital from outside. High prices reduce employment in the export industries by reducing the quantity sold, but the increased demand for non-traded goods may offset this.

If, on the other hand, the fall in sales as a result of increased prices outweighs the increased income per unit, the mechanism works the other way round and multiplies the reduction in income and employment through a reduction in demand for non-traded goods.

Non-traded goods must, of course, be produced by local labour and their prices are determined in the same way as those of traded goods. Identical non-traded goods will therefore have higher prices in high-wage than in low-wage countries, since their prices incorporate higher wage costs.

This introduces a complication, which Emmanuel discusses. If *real* wages in one country are to be, say, twice those in another, then *money* wages (translated at current exchange rates) will have to diverge much more, perhaps by four or even ten times, since high wages and a high cost of living (high price of non-traded goods) go together. To put it another way, if productivity in non-traded goods is the same everywhere, and so is the rate of profit, then higher standards of living in one country compared with another can only come from a high purchasing power in terms of traded goods (whose prices are the same everywhere), so if the fraction of traded goods in workers' consumption is rather low it will require a large difference in money wages to generate a moderate difference in living standards.

It is the divergence in *money* wages that will determine international prices, since capitalists' production decisions will be determined by money costs and not by what the money wages will buy. Relatively moderate divergences in real wages may thus be the foundation for extreme inequality in exchange.

In discussing the role of unequal exchange in creating local demand and attracting capital imports, I have so far assumed that demand depends on the total incomes generated locally. It is not clear that this is correct, since with international mobility of capital we cannot specify in advance where capital has come from, nor can we predict where profit incomes will be spent. Profits accruing to British capitalists from production in Africa may well be spent in the South of France.

Workers, however, must clearly spend the main part of their wages in the locality where they are employed. Emmanuel, rightly, stresses the importance of wage incomes as generating a local demand which attracts capital. His interpretation of the oil price rises of the 1970s (Emmanuel, 1974) seems, however, with hindsight, to carry this view to excessive extremes.

If the stress is laid on workers' demand for consumer goods, however, this alters the role of unequal exchange. It is high wages, rather than unequal exchange as such, which create this market. The role of unequal exchange, in this case, is to permit the equalisation of profits between countries, so that the effect of high wages falls on profits everywhere, not just in the high-wage country. Without this equalisation of profits, high-wage countries would be low-profit countries and could not attract capital.

I should stress that the model built up in this section is mine rather than Emmanuel's, though I think it embodies the essential points of Emmanuel's arguments. I have tried to indicate the points that I have taken directly from Emmanuel by linking his name clearly to them.

It is worth pausing to take a general look at the picture of the world economy built up in this section. It might appear at first sight to be an underconsumptionist model, in that development is made to depend on demand, and specifically on workers' consumption demand, but this is not in fact so. I have not specified the determinants of growth on a world scale, since the purpose is to discover why development occurs unevenly between different countries.

With free mobility of capital between countries, the critical factor in determining *where* growth will take place is the *division* of new investment between different locations. The assumption underlying the model presented here is that the division of investment between the production of different traded goods depends on the demand for those goods, in other words, on social needs as expressed through the mechanisms of a capitalist system. With a predetermined pattern of specialisation between countries in the production of traded goods (and this is basic to the theory, as presented so far) the scope for expansion in the production of traded goods is determined outside of any given country, on the world scale.

What the pricing mechanism of unequal exchange does, is to determine the *terms* on which a country participates in this world division of labour, and that, in turn, governs the scope for expansion in the non-traded goods sector.

In this model, then, unequal exchange does not generate a cumulative growth of inequality between countries unless there is a cumulative growth in wage differentials. Emmanuel does, however, argue for a cumulative enlargement of wage differentials, and this is crucial to his whole argument: again his theory of wages emerges as the heart of his whole theory.

V Methods of production and development

The second main argument that Emmanuel puts forward for linking unequal exchange to real development is also a consequence of high wages rather than of unequal exchange as such. Again, therefore, unequal exchange is important primarily as a mechanism that permits relatively high wages in one country without a relative depression of profits.

The argument here is that high wages lead to a high organic composition of capital and also a high 'organic composition of labour'. (The latter phrase is Emmanuel's own invention.) I will discuss these in turn.

As far as the organic composition of capital is concerned, the basic point is simple. Capitalists will try to minimise costs (and competition will force them to do this) by substituting means of production for labour where wages are high. In fact, the main effect must be to increase the use of those means of production produced in low-wage countries, since those produced in the high-wage area itself will also be increased in price. It therefore tends to reduce employment and wage incomes in the high-wage country in much the same way as substitution of lower-priced for higher-priced products does, and acts to *reduce* the attraction of capital to the production of non-traded goods.

It is not, then, at all clear why the mechanisation that may follow a wage increase should be beneficial to capitalist development in the country where the wage increase takes place. One can, of course, say that mechanisation *is* development, and thus define the problem away (I don't think Emmanuel does this, though he comes close to it at times), but the real question is whether it provides a further impulse for *sustained* or *cumulative* development.

The main way in which Emmanuel seeks to answer this is by arguing that mechanisation alters the social character of work and of production and thus lays the foundations for further wage increases. This links up both with his theory of wages (above) and with the organic composition of labour, to which I now turn.

High wages, according to Emmanuel, lead to a high 'organic composition of labour'. By this he means a high proportion of skilled workers, professionals and so on in the total labour force. Even if basic wage rates and the scale of wages were the same everywhere, areas with a large proportion of skilled workers, who receive higher wages, would have a higher level of *per capita* income and therefore larger markets.

Why should there be a connection between high basic wage rates and a high proportion of skilled workers? A casual comparison of rich and poor countries suggests that these two factors do, in practice, go together, but what has to be demonstrated here is a relation of cause and effect, not just a statistical association which might well be the result of a third factor which influences both.

It is possible to argue that mechanisation is the result of high wages (I have discussed this above), and that mechanisation, in turn, leads to the training and employment of engineers, technicians, and so on. However, Marx argued that mechanisation tends to eliminate skills, and Braverman has, recently, re-emphasised this aspect of Marx's thinking. Braverman, in fact, goes further in arguing that conventional classifications of skills are seriously misleading; farm workers and others usually classified as unskilled, are, in fact, highly skilled. This argument does not directly undermine Emmanuel's position, since Emmanuel is concerned with the proportion of socially recognised skills, recognised by being paid above the rates for other workers. It does, however, suggest the possibility that certain skills are recognised and rewarded because they are particularly important in high-wage countries, while traditional craft skills, for example, may be badly rewarded precisely because they are practised, in general, in areas where the wage is low. If this is so, then a high or low organic composition of labour becomes merely the way high or low wages are manifested, rather than being a distinct result of high or low wage levels with its own distinct effects.

I conclude that Emmanuel has not succeeded in demonstrating this particular part of his case.

VI Some special cases

Before going on to the main criticism of the theory, it is worth looking at some historical examples which Emmanuel regards as particularly favourable to his case, and which'show how the theory can be elaborated to deal with the complexities of the real world.

The first example is of England in the period of the industrial revolution. England made a decisive advance during this time, laying the foundations of a century of dominance in the world economy. Real wages, however, did not rise to any substantial extent until after the major advances had been made, so this appears to contradict Emmanuel's theory in which wages are the independent variable and high wages lead to development.

Emmanuel points out that wages in England were relatively high even before the industrial revolution got under way, and then argues that the Corn Laws (import restrictions on grain), by raising the price of subsistence goods, raised *money* wages even though *real* wages failed to rise, and the mechanism of unequal exchange depends, as we have seen, on relative levels of money wages. Instead of the workers being the beneficiaries of unequal exchanges, the benefits went to landowners in the form of a 'super rent'.

This is an ingenious argument, but there are still criticisms to be made. Firstly, it is widely agreed that it was the conquest of world markets for cotton textiles that provided a crucial opportunity for industrialisation in England, and this must have been the result of *reduced* prices, not *high* prices. The price cuts were made possible by technical advances, and while Emmanuel can say that the Corn Laws held prices higher than they would have been otherwise, this still leaves the technical advances, the increase in productivity stemming from mechanised production, as the main driving force of the industrial revolution. High money wages still followed, rather than caused, the breakthrough in development.

Secondly, it is not clear how the 'super rent' accruing to the landlords fuelled economic development. In so far as it was saved, and became a source of capital accumulation, it should not have contributed to a *relative* advance in England if capital were internationally mobile (which it probably was not at that date, but which the theory requires). In so far as the extra revenue was spent, it created extra local demand, though how much of landlords' extra revenue was spent on industrial products must be doubtful.

A second example is the colonies of European settlement. Emmanuel argues that the USA, Canada and Australia became rich, while Latin American countries did not, mainly because the social conditions under which migration took place, together with the form of appropriation of land (relatively freely available in the USA, etc., by comparison with Latin America), favoured high wages, and this set the mechanisms of unequal exchange into operation. South Africa, he argues, has developed to a lesser extent precisely because of the availability of cheap local labour. Tariff protection, according to Emmanuel, played an essential role, but only in excluding imported goods, especially industrial products, from the enlarged market created by high wages. This argument is attractive, since the relative success of the USA, Canada and Australia in developing as advanced capitalist countries is a major historical problem that calls out for a Marxist analysis.

There must, however, be doubts about this explanation. The major export products of the USA, Canada and Australia were also produced in other parts of the world where wages were much lower. Where countries with different wage levels produce the same commodities and trade them on the world market, the high-wage country must have correspondingly higher levels of productivity (or lower profits). So, again, advances in productivity appear as the driving force, with high wages the result rather than the cause of development. High productivity in agriculture, in these cases, must have been at least partly the result of favourable natural conditions and plentiful land. In any case, US exports in the early stages were quite largely produced by cheap labour in the plantations of the southern States.

VII Critique of Emmanuel's theory

Emmanuel's theory of unequal exchange can be viewed on two levels. One could argue simply that he has filled a gap in the Marxist analysis of the world economy by providing an analysis of the determination of international prices and by developing some of its consequences. This is my view of it, and it amounts to a substantial and important contribution. Emmanuel, however, makes a stronger claim:

> Even if we agree that unequal exchange is only one of the
> mechanisms whereby value is transferred from one group of
> countries to another, and that its *direct* effects account for only a
> part of the difference in standards of living, I think it is possible to
> state that unequal exchange is the *elementary* transfer mechanism
> and that, as such, it enables the advanced countries to begin and
> regularly give new emphasis to that *unevenness of development*
> that sets in motion all the other mechanisms of exploitation and
> fully explains the way that wealth is distributed. (*UE*, p. 265)

As Emmanuel recognises, the disparity in standards of living and in productivity between advanced and underdeveloped countries are far larger than can be explained by unequal exchange in itself. There are many commodities that are produced in both groups of countries and there are enormous differences in productivity between countries.

We must therefore look at the connection between unequal exchange and the process of capitalist development in a broader sense. I have argued that Emmanuel's arguments mainly come down to asserting that high wages are the key to development, so that unequal exchange is important in permitting wage disparities to exist without corresponding inverse differences in profit rates. High wages, we are told, promote development, firstly, by creating a larger local market and, secondly, by encouraging mechanisation. There is considerable merit in both of these arguments, though it is not clear that either would explain a *cumulative* growth of inequality between countries. Cumulative divergence can, however, be explained if we follow Emmanuel in saying that wages will increase further in high-wage countries as an indirect, long delayed response to industrialisation and that they will remain low in low-wage countries in the absence of this stimulus. His wage theory is therefore critical, and I have argued that it is plausible, but by no means beyond criticism.

I have, however, a further major criticism of Emmanuel's model. I have presented it throughout in terms of a *given* division of activities between countries, or groups of countries, so that high wages in a particular country mean a correspondingly high price of production for its products. The objection is very simple: why should the high-wage, high-price products go on being produced in the high-wage countries? *Given free mobility of capital between countries why should any investment go to the high-wage countries at all?* For some products the answer is clear: oil will be extracted from Alaska, the North Sea and so on because it is a scarce natural resource which must be extracted where it is found. But the advanced countries specialise mainly in the products which are *least* tied to the location of natural resources: manufactured goods, and especially 'high technology' products whose raw material content is very small in relation to their total cost.

Emmanuel is aware of this problem, and makes several attempts to meet it. One attempt is to argue that there are so many different products that 'a high wage country can never find itself in a position where it *cannot* discover a specialisation that . . . is free from competition on the part of the low wage countries' (*UE*, pp. 145–7). He illustrates this by saying that India, having moved into textile production, displacing Britain, could now move into producing textile machinery, and so on, but 'if India were to specialise one day in metallurgy and engineering . . . Britain would find no difficulty in taking up [textiles] again'.

This argument is, however, incorrect. *Countries* do not choose what to specialise in (and if they did, they could choose to do everything). In the model that Emmanuel has constructed, production is in the hands of many, competing, capitalist enterprises, which are free to move capital between countries. They will be driven by the blind forces of competition to produce wherever costs are lower. If they are free to produce all goods in low-wage countries with productivity and other costs equal, then they will do so.

Emmanuel meets this problem in a rather roundabout way: he recognises that according to his own arguments the underdeveloped countries would do better if they only traded amongst themselves, and considers whether they might decide, collectively, to do so. He concludes that they would benefit by not trading with high-wage countries and, instead, producing the goods that they (collectively) import at the moment. However, he says that this would involve monopoly of foreign trade (on the part of the states concerned) which goes outside the bounds of his theory, which assumes free competition. However, as I have argued above, the real problem is to explain why free competition itself should not produce the outcome which his foreign trade monopoly is intended to achieve. Free competition clearly has not done so, but it remains to explain *why*.

His strongest argument is presented almost as an afterthought. The rich countries are benefiting from an *existing* specialisation. If production is to start up in poor countries, it will have to suffer the handicaps of an infant industry: 'during this "acclimatization" period of the new branch, the ratio between the costs of the old producers and the new is not one that can be deduced from merely calculating the effect of the difference in wages' (*UE*, p. 151). During this time, he says, the high-wage countries have time to 'adjust their aim'. These points are still rather doubtful, since the establishment of 'prices of production', the theoretical basis of his whole argument, requires a sufficient timespan for the mobility of capital to take effect, and, in any case, if it is difficult and costly for a poor country to take up a new branch of industry, it should be equally hard for a high-wage country. In practice, it is probable that the advanced countries have more flexible economic structures, but this implies a greater technological capacity, not simply a difference in wages.

Emmanuel, however, produces a final argument which does carry conviction: the period of adaptation when a new branch of industry is introduced into a country is 'too long for the relatively short view taken by private capital, which under a competitive system is the exclusive agent of the introduction and establishment of the new branch' (*UE*, p. 51).

The foundation of the argument, then, comes down to this: to set up production in a new location takes longer than to alter the scale of production in areas where a line of business is well established. The period required is long enough for private capital to be unwilling to do the job, despite the profits it would reap at the end of the day. In theoretical terms, there is no doubt that this is a good argument (and a fairly well known argument too; it is the basic argument for tariffs to protect infant industries). It does not seem to me to be enough in itself to explain the pattern of development of the world economy over the last two centuries, though it may be an important part of the explanation (see chapters 10 and 12 below).

The first thing that has to be explained is the rapid development of areas of European settlement (the USA, Canada, etc.) in the nineteenth century. Private capital did flow into these areas, and established new industries there. Why were 'infant industry' problems overcome in some places, while in low-wage areas, where export production should have been very profitable, the problems of establishing new industries were insuperable?

Secondly, in Emmanuel's framework it does not matter what branches of production the high-wage countries specialise in, they will benefit from unequal exchange all the same. However, in practice, the rich countries are those which have a large, modern industrial sector, even where they may export primary products as well, while the poor countries are those which have a large peasant or pre-capitalist agricultural sector. The 'rich' countries are also those that are 'advanced' in a more general sense. This has to be explained, and I do not believe that wage differences are the primary cause.

Gathering the argument together, Emmanuel proposes a mechanism by which differing wage levels between countries can be compatible with equalisation of profits, provided that a definite pattern of specialisation exists in the production of traded goods. The high-wage country will then have a larger market for non-traded goods. He has not, however, fully accounted for the pattern of specialisation, and his account of wage determination is debatable.

Emmanuel's position has much in common with those of Frank, Wallerstein and the dependency theorists, in that it is an essentially static system in which the focus is on the redistribution of surplus rather than on production, and its main weaknesses stem from the way in which production is introduced as an afterthought (the social context of wage determination, the 'organic composition of labour', the difficulties of infant industries). I think it is best regarded as an analysis of *one aspect* of unequal *specialisation* in an interdependent world economy which is not wholly capitalist at the level of relations of production.

A final comment: Emmanuel only considers fully capitalist production, but a similar analysis can be applied to other cases. If wages and living standards in certain countries are low, then peasant producers, for want of any better alternative, may go on marketing cash crops even when the prices they receive yield very low incomes. Provided the goods concerned are wage goods or means of production, the low prices will raise the (world) profit rate. Similarly, nationalising an industry in a single country may not change anything if the commodity is produced in other low-wage areas as well. Competition will prevent price increases, and the profits of superexploitation will go on being transferred to the general profit rate through a low selling price.

VIII Summary

Emmanuel's essential contribution is to extend the analysis of prices of production (equilibrium prices in a capitalist system) to the determination of *international* prices when capital is mobile between countries and labour is not. This analysis hinges on the existence of a given and predetermined pattern of international specialisation. (In this, and in other aspects of his work, Emmanuel has much in common with the dependency theorists.) The major weakness in Emmanuel's arguments is that he is unable to explain why all capital does not flow into low-wage areas. He argues, on the contrary, that high wages attract capital (since markets are large) and induce the use of more mechanised methods of production. I have argued that this analysis can only be justified on rather special assumptions.

Appendix to chapter 9

In this appendix, I will briefly set out the algebra of prices of production, first with a single wage rate (the usual case) and then with different wages in different sectors (assumed to represent different countries). I will not use Emmanuel's notation (*UE*, appendix V), which is based on that of Sraffa and seems to me to be rather clumsy. Instead I will use my own notation, based on that of Morishima (1973) which is now fairly widely used.

I will also alter Emmanuel's model in some technical matters to simplify the exposition. I assume that all means of production are used up in a single period of production, in order to avoid complications connected with depreciation. Emmanuel does not make this simplifying assumption, and engages in a debate over the correctness of Sraffa's treatment of depreciation (in a note added to the English edition). As far as I can see, the method proposed by Emmanuel simply represents a different way of writing Sraffa's equations. I also assume that the purchasing power of the wage is given as a list of physical quantities of different goods. This is one alternative considered by Emmanuel, who seems to prefer a model in which wages are fixed as a quantity of the 'money commodity'. He notes that the commodities actually bought by workers will depend on prices, so that both of these devices are somewhat artificial.

The basic problem is as follows: given the technical conditions of production and the real wage, find a set of prices such that the rate of profit is the same in all industries.

Translating this into algebraic form, we number all goods, 1 to n. Let a_{ij} be the quantity of good i required as means of production in producing 1 unit of good j, and l_j the amount of labour. These coefficients are assumed to be fixed. Let the wage per hour of labour be w, and the prices (as yet unknown) p_1, p_2, ..., p_n. The wage, we assume, must be sufficient to buy quantities of goods given as b_1, b_2, ..., b_n, so that $w = p_1 b_1 + p_2 b_2 + \ldots + p_n b_n$. If, say, the ith good is used only as means of production, then $b_i = 0$; correspondingly, if it were used only in consumption then $a_{ij} = 0$ for all j. Luxuries, goods which do not enter into the real wage and are not used as means of production, can be ignored. Wages are assumed to be advanced at the beginning of the period of production (following Marx and Emmanuel, but not Sraffa). Let r stand for the rate of profit (as yet unknown).

We can now write down the equations. The capital advanced (per unit of product) is the same as the cost of production. Cost plus profit must be equal to price, and the profit must equal the capital advanced multiplied by the general rate of profit. Hence

$$p_1 = (p_1 a_{11} + \ldots + p_n a_{n1} + w l_1)(1 + r)$$
$$p_1 = (p_1 a_{12} + \ldots + p_n a_{n2} + w l_2)(1 + r)$$

$$\ldots\ldots\ldots\ldots\ldots\ldots\ldots\ldots\ldots\ldots\ldots\ldots\ldots\ldots\ldots\ldots$$

$$p_n = (p_1 a_{1n} + \ldots + p_n a_{nn} + w l_n)(l + r)$$

Incorporating the equation for the wage gives:

$$p_1 = [p_1 (a_{11} + b_1 l_1) + \ldots + p_n (a_{nl} + b_n l_1)] (1 + r)$$
$$p_2 = [p_1 (a_{12} + b_1 l_2) + \ldots \quad p_n (a_{n2} + b_n l_2)] (1 + r)$$

$$\ldots\ldots\ldots\ldots\ldots\ldots\ldots\ldots\ldots\ldots\ldots\ldots\ldots\ldots\ldots\ldots$$

$$p_n = [p_1 (a_{1n} + b_1 l_n) + \ldots + p_n (a_{nn} + b_n l_n)] (1 + r)$$

There are n equations with $n + 1$ unknowns (n prices and the rate of profit). However, only relative prices matter, so we can fix the price of one good arbitrarily and solve for the remaining $n - 1$ prices and the rate of profit.

Counting equations is a rather primitive method; any mathematician knows that it ensures neither that a solution will exist nor that it will be unique. Fortunately, it can be shown that if the real wage is set at a level that permits a profit to be made at all, then prices will indeed be determinate and positive.

The analysis can be written more compactly in matrix form. Let A be the matrix with elements (a_{ij}), B the real wage vector; L the vector of labour requirements and P the price vector. We can write the equations as

$$P = P(A + BL)(1 + r)$$

where BL is the matrix (not the scalar) product. This is a (slightly) disguised form of a standard problem, that of finding the eigenvalues and corresponding eigenvectors of a matrix.

Now we can modify the analysis to deal with Emmanuel's main subject: pricing with different wages in different sectors. Write w_j as the wage in the jth sector, and let it correspond to a real wage vector $B_j = (b_{1j}, b_{2j}, \ldots, b_{nj})$. The equation for good j must now be written as

$$p_j = [p_1 (a_{1j} + b_{1j} \, l_j \ldots + p_n (a_{nj} + b_{nj} l_j)] (1 + r)$$

The structure of the equations is not changed in any essential way. There is, of course, no need to have a different wage in each sector; there could be just two wages for two countries.

Notice that the b_{ij} coefficients enter into the equations in much the same way as the a_{ij}s. A change in the real wage affects the working of the system in the same way as a change in methods of production. An increased real wage in any sector is equivalent to a cost increasing change in technical coefficients. It can be shown (Himmelweit, 1974) that any change that reduces costs (at the prices ruling before the change) will increase the rate of profit, and conversely that cost increases reduce the profit rate. Hence increases in wages in any sector will reduce profits, and low wages anywhere raise profits.

10 · Amin

By the later 1960s and 1970s, the volume of Marxist writing on imperialism was growing very rapidly, and a stage was reached where writers could build on to an established tradition rather than having to set out a complete framework of their own, although there were still major differences between different writers. In this chapter I will examine the work of Samir Amin, who has tried to synthesise most of the major lines of thought into a single picture of a capitalist world economy.

Amin has written two major works of synthesis: *Accumulation on a World Scale* (1974, cited below as *AWS*) and *Unequal Development* (1976, cited as *UD*). These two works cover virtually identical ground, and *UD* is perhaps best regarded as a second edition of *AWS*. The later work shows some relatively minor theoretical developments, and contains rather more historical detail about particular areas, while the earlier work contains a more detailed discussion of orthodox economic theories of international trade and development. Substantial passages are taken virtually unchanged from *AWS* and incorporated in *UD*. *Imperialism and Unequal Development* (1977, cited as *IUD*) is a collection of essays, one of which, 'The End of a Debate', sets out Amin's main ideas very clearly, and he has subsequently published another work (1978) in which the emphasis is more methodological. Amin has also written a considerable amount about particular areas, notably North Africa (1966) and West Africa (1971).

To call Amin's work a synthesis may seem disparaging, as if he showed no originality; this would be quite unfair to him. He has made important contributions, particularly in his analysis of international (unequal) specialisation, and in any case the synthesis of various elements into a coherent whole is an essential original contribution in its own right. The whole is not simply the sum of the parts. There are, however, corresponding weaknesses. On many issues, Amin tries to reconcile ideas that are in fact irreconcileable, and is led into inconsistencies. I shall also argue that in one major respect, the analysis of wages in the advanced countries, he is simply wrong.

I will give an overall summary of Amin's theories (section I) and a brief survey of his historical account of the emergence and development of the capitalist world economy (section II), and then concentrate on the main theoretical issues involved: unequal specialisation (section III) and the determination of wages in the central social formations (section IV).

I Unequal development

Amin's guiding vision is summed up by the titles of his two main works: *Accumulation on a World Scale* and *Unequal Development*. The process of accumulation, of development, must be analysed as a single process on a world scale, but it takes place in a world divided into many distinct national social formations. Accumulation does not tend to create uniformity between these social formations, but divides them into two categories: those of the *centre* and those of the *periphery*.

His overall view of the relations between centre and periphery is similar to that of the dependency theorists. Accumulation at the centre is 'autocentric' (i.e. self-centred); it is governed by its own internal dynamic, as analysed by Marx. In the periphery, by contrast, accumulation is dependent or 'extraverted', constrained by the centre-periphery relation. The arguments that Amin uses to justify this distinction are very similar to those of the dependency theorists. I have argued (chapter 7) that the idea of dependence, in this context, is based on the assumption of a given pattern of *specialisation* between centre and periphery.

At the heart of Amin's synthesis, as I read it, is an explanation of *unequal specialisation*, which I will discuss in detail in section III of this chapter. Put very simply, he argues that international specialisation is determined by absolute cost levels (and not by comparative advantage, as Ricardo thought), and that cost levels depend on productivity and on wages. The countries of the centre developed capitalism earlier, or under especially favourable conditions, and got a huge lead in productivity during a period in which wages were held down to something close to physical subsistence levels in both centre and periphery. This established a pattern of unequal specialisation. Later, wages started to rise at the centre, but the centre's lead in productivity remained enough to ensure lower costs at least in most sectors of industry. Unequal specialisation is thus both cause and consequence of unequal development; both are anchored in the conditions of production and reflected in exchange relations.

Given this pattern of unequal specialisation and development, capitalism at the centre develops in the way that the classical Marxists analysed, driving out pre-capitalist modes of production, while capitalist development in the periphery was blocked, since the periphery could compete only in resource-based export activities (minerals, tropical agriculture), and there could only be limited development oriented to the narrow domestic market. The larger part of the population was excluded from the capitalist sector, so that pre-capitalist modes of production were not eliminated. This account provides an explanation for the 'typical' structure of underdeveloped countries as described by Baran and the dependency theorists. Amin calls this structure *'peripheral capitalism'*.

After a certain stage of development, wages started to rise at the centre, while in the periphery massive unemployment and the persistence of pre-capitalist modes of production (and exploitation) held wages down. Amin's explanations of increased wages at the centre are both obscure and inconsistent; I will criticise them in section IV. Whatever the reason, however, there can be no doubt of the fact. High wages at the centre and low wages in the periphery lead to *unequal exchange*, as analysed by Emmanuel (chapter 9 above). Some care is needed here; Amin argues that the centre has advantages in productivity that more than outweigh the higher wages there, so one might think that Emmanuel's analysis would not apply. However, he argues that although the centre has relatively high productivity in most lines of (industrial) production (thus maintaining unequal specialisation despite the wage gap), the periphery has relatively high productivity in the few lines of production that it specialises in. In its export industries, therefore, the periphery combines high productivity with low wages, the recipe, given international equalisation of profits, for unequal exchange.

Amin's criticism of Emmanuel is that he treats wages as an 'independent variable', without adequately explaining them. In Amin's words: 'Which is cause and which effect: the international prices, or the inequality in wages levels? The question is pointless. Inequality in wages, due to historical reasons (the difference between social formations) constitutes the basis of a specialisation and a system of international prices that perpetuate this inequality' (*UD*, p. 151). There are thus no independent variables, only a self-perpetuating process (see also Amin, 1977, p. 185).

The social formations of the periphery are characterised by *disarticulation* between sectors, since most of the industries producing means of production are absent. The links between departments I and II (producing means of production and consumer goods respectively), analysed by Marx in his schemes of reproduction, exist at the world level but are incomplete within the national economy. The periphery is also characterised by *unevenness of productivity*, in that export sectors operated by foreign capital on the most modern lines coexist with primitive pre-capitalist sectors. The capitalist mode of production is dominant but does not tend to become exclusive, and the tertiary sector becomes overexpanded as a result of the pattern of demand and the lack of opportunities for investment in industry. These features of peripheral capitalism are not at all characteristic of 'traditional' pre-capitalist societies, they are the product of the 'development of under-development'.

Amin does not have a great deal to say about the social formations of the centre (apart from his analysis of wage levels), since he concentrates on relations between centre and periphery. Much of the time he writes as though there were a single centre. He does stress that, after a certain stage of development, exchanges and capital flows between the formations of the centre grow in importance (relative to total production and to flows between centre and periphery), integrating them ever more closely together. Trade with the periphery is relatively marginal to the centre, even though it is large quantitatively and in its effects for the periphery. This clearly implies that the total level of production in the centre must be very large relative to that in the periphery as a whole; this is in fact the case, and is explained as the effect of unequal specialisation and unequal development.

How does Amin's account of the world system relate to those of other writers? He takes the analysis of international prices from Emmanuel, and provides his own account of unequal specialisation to complement it. Together these theories amount to the first serious analysis of international trade in the Marxist tradition. Other writers have, of course, described the destruction of industries in the periphery by foreign competition (Marx on the destruction of Indian handloom weaving, Baran, etc.), but Amin develops the idea more fully and makes it the centrepiece of his analysis. I shall, however, argue that he still leaves the job incomplete. Unequal specialisation provides a foundation for an analysis of peripheral capitalism that has much in common with Baran and with the dependency theorists. Amin takes little from Frank apart from the phrase 'the development of underdevelopment', though he does agree with Frank (and many others) that underdevelopment is caused by capitalism and that complete capitalist development in the periphery is no longer possible. He analyses social formations in terms of the interaction of different modes of production, and argues that the formations of the periphery are distinguished by the persistence of pre-capitalist modes, but his viewpoint is really rather different from that of Rey, in that it is the failure of capitalist development that causes the persistence of other modes, and not vice versa. In this he is close to Arrighi. Monopoly, as such, plays very little part in Amin's analysis, but the export (or rather the mobility) of capital is of central importance.

II Modes of production and social formations

Amin argues that 'economic laws' of the sort elaborated by Marx in *Capital* only apply to a pure capitalist system, while capitalism, in fact, coexists in the world system with other modes of production. An 'economistic' analysis which deals only with quantitative relations between narrowly economic variables can only be a subordinate part of the story. He argues, consistently and convincingly, that real history can only be understood by the analysis of concrete social formations, and cannot be reduced to a preordained succession of modes of production.

A major part of his work is therefore devoted to historical analysis (*UD*, chapters 1, 5). I cannot hope to give an adequate account of this aspect of Amin's writing here, and I will not try to do so; I will only pick out some points of theoretical interest and try to indicate the main outlines. Amin's discussions of the Arab world and of Africa are especially notable for their combination of wide-ranging knowledge and analytical insight.

Amin defines five modes of production, of which four are familiar: the primitive-communal, slave owning, simple petty-commodity and capitalist modes. The one that stands out as unusual is:

> the 'tribute paying' mode, which adds to a still existing village
> community a social and political apparatus for the exploitation of
> this community through the exaction of tribute; this tribute paying
> mode of production is the most widespread form of precapitalist
> classes, and I distinguish between (a) its early and (b) its developed
> forms, such as the 'feudal' mode of production, in which the

village community loses its *dominium eminens* over the soil to the feudal lords. (*UD*, p. 13)

The 'tribute paying' mode is clearly that old friend the 'Asiatic' mode, under another name, and Amin is, in effect, setting up a spectrum of social structures from African societies little removed from the primitive-communal mode, through the great Asiatic cultures to feudal Europe. The all-inclusive nature of this concept rather reduces its usefulness, though it has to be said that this is an area in which it is hard to make firm distinctions.

He insists that pre-capitalist societies must be analysed as social formations which may contain several modes of production and, as a result, a complex class structure. A formation dominated by the tribute-paying mode may contain commodity production and exchange, even though the tribute-paying mode by itself excludes these. Different social formations interact, in particular by long-distance trade, which can form the basis for societies living on a surplus produced elsewhere. The key to the analysis of any social formation is the production and circulation of surplus, defined, much as in Baran, as 'an excess of production over the consumption needed in order to ensure the reconstitution of the labour force' (*UD*, p. 18). This amounts to a rich and flexible framework for historical analysis.

Amin describes a pre-capitalist world made up of three 'central' tribute-paying formations (China, Egypt, India), with a 'periphery' around them which was much less stable and which was influenced more by the centre than the centre was influenced by it. In particular, the Mediterranean periphery produced a society dominated by the slave owning mode, dependent on its own periphery (Europe) for supplies of slaves, and the collapse of this society confronted by the barbarian invaders produced European feudalism and, finally, capitalism. On the far eastern periphery of China, Japan evolved a feudal society and thus an indigenous capitalism. One could note here that this bears a suspicious resemblance to Marx's (now usually derided) judgment that Asiatic societies have no real history, but with the reversal that these Asiatic societies are now called 'central'.

One point of this is to argue that progress took place on the periphery, and Amin argues that today the transition to socialism must start from the periphery. It is a nice thought, though the feudalism-capitalism transition is so different from the capitalism-socialism transition that this analogy cannot really be regarded as a proof of anything.

Amin's treatment of feudalism is somewhat inconsistent. He describes it as the most *developed* form of the tribute-paying mode, and says that 'when well developed [the tribute paying mode] nearly always tends to become feudal (this happened in China, India and Egypt)' (*AWS*, p. 140), so that it is the 'central' tribute-paying formations that are described as moving towards feudalism. On the other hand, he describes feudalism as *peripheral* because it is a borderline case analytically (*UD*, p. 16) and because it develops on the borders (geographically) in areas where natural conditions were less favourable and centralising tendencies weaker (*UD*, pp. 55–6). This may represent a shift in position between the two works cited, but I think that it is rather a reflection of the unsatisfactory state of the definitions. The point, of course, is that capitalism is going to emerge from this 'peripheral' feudalism, so that the erstwhile periphery becomes, in its turn, central.

The emergence of capitalism from its feudal origins is a familiar story, and Amin spends little time on it. It is explained both by the formation of a landless proletariat and by mercantile accumulations of loot; which is the determining factor is not clear. It is clear, however, that capitalism emerged where it did because it was preceded by feudalism. The 'new' capitalist centres of the USA, Canada, Israel, etc., are also explained in terms of modes of production. They were the by-product of proletarian-isation at the centre, which led to emigration and the formation in areas of settlement of societies which had an unusual predominance of petty commodity production. These were an unusually favourable environ-ment for capitalist development (cf. the explanations of the emergence of new centres proposed by Frank, p. 163 in this book, and Emmanuel, p. 225 in this book).

Amin divides the development of the capitalist world economy into three (familiar) stages. The first, the mercantilist stage, is marked by the emergence of capitalism in its homelands and by the establishment of a net of exchange relations connecting capitalist with pre-capitalist formations.

The next stage is that of fully developed pre-monopoly capitalism ('competitive' for short, though relations with the periphery were frequently monopolistic), and lasts from about 1800 to about 1900. This stage was, according to Amin, characterised by approximately equal exchange between centre and periphery (since wages were still low at the centre). Productivity increases were passed on as price reductions under competitive conditions. It was a 'pause' of a century while 'Europe and the United States withdrew into themselves' (*UD*, p. 187). Again, there are inconsistencies in Amin's phraseology, if not in his story, in that his 'pause' was also a period in which 'external extension of the capitalist market was . . . of prime importance as a means for realising surplus value' (p. 188, i.e. the following page). During this period, in any case, the foundations of a new pattern of international specialisation were laid, and the dividing line between centre and periphery was established.

It is the imperialist stage (from 1900 on) that is Amin's main concern. During this stage wages started to rise (along with productivity) at the centre, capital became fairly freely mobile and world markets became closely integrated, establishing the conditions for unequal exchange. Amin argues that the tendency of the rate of profit to fall comes into operation at the centre (since the rate of surplus value is not rising, while the organic composition of capital is), but is offset by high rates of exploitation in the periphery which sustain the profit rate through unequal exchange.

In the emerging periphery, capitalist development was blocked by competition from the centre, and pre-capitalist modes of production survived. These peripheral social formations developed in a great variety of ways according to the pre-existing social structure, the date of capitalist penetration, the opportunities for capital offered by natural conditions and so on. It is in the analysis of these different paths to peripheral capitalism that Amin's skills as a writer of analytical history are most evident, and I will not try to summarise.

All of these varied peripheral formations are, however, moving towards a common pattern of peripheral capitalism. Amin shows a certain ambivalence here; on the one hand he defines peripheral capitalism, in effect, by the persistence of pre-capitalist modes of production. On the other hand, he argues that these have become a mere 'shell, whose content has become the sale of labour power' (*IUD*, p. 191).

> We too often confine ourselves to looking for the capitalist relation at the 'microeconomic' level, that of the firm. . . . In peripheral capitalism . . . the petty commodity production mode may appear to be integrated within the capitalist market, but in reality capital dominates the direct producer. The latter is not a petty commodity producer. . . . In fact he is very like the cottage industry proletarian as he formerly existed in Europe; that is exploited by capital to which, in fact, he sold his labour power rather than his product. Here the failure to see that it is the sale of labour power

which gears the system is a failure to understand the unity of the world system. (*IUD*, pp. 90–1; see also *UD*, p. 361)

Amin argues that this absorption of precapitalist modes by capitalism (as opposed to an articulation between distinct modes) is something that has developed very rapidly recently. As we shall see, Amin also concedes that the rise of multi-national companies could change matters drastically, as they shift their activities to sources of low-cost labour. Taken together these hints could be the basis for a prediction that 'peripheral capitalism' is changing its nature very fundamentally and rather rapidly at the moment, but Amin is distinctly unwilling to draw this conclusion.

III Unequal specialisation

At the heart of Amin's argument is an *economic* process; the development of capitalism in the periphery is blocked by the superior competitive strength of the industries of the centre. This greater competitive strength is manifested in an ability to undercut the industries of the periphery or to establish a price level such that new industries cannot come into existence in the periphery. In saying that this is an economic mechanism, I am not asserting that it can be analysed on a narrowly economic basis. What I am asserting is that the social processes of development, and of the development of underdevelopment, must *manifest* themselves in these strictly economic terms.

This mechanism works, according to Amin, at *all* stages of development, both of the centre and of the various social formations of the periphery, at least from the stage at which fully developed capitalism emerged at the centre, i.e. from the industrial revolution onwards. (The mercantile stage, here, must be regarded as part of the prehistory of capitalism.)

Amin summarises this process:

> The distortion towards export activities (extraversion), which is the decisive one, does not result from 'inadequacy of the home market', but from the superior productivity of the centre in all fields, which compels the periphery to confine itself to the role of complementary supplier of products for the production of which it possesses a natural advantage: exotic agricultural produce and minerals. When, as a result of this distortion, the level of wages in the periphery has become lower, for the same productivity, than at

the centre, a limited development of industries focussed on the home market of the periphery will have become possible, while at the same time exchange will have become unequal. The subsequent pattern of industrialisation through import-substitution, together with the (as yet embryonic) effects of the new international division of labour inside the transnational firm, do not alter the essential conditions of extraversion, even if they alter the forms that it takes. (*UD*, p. 200)

As a result of the destruction of craft production and the blockage of capitalist industrialisation, the population is forced into pre-capitalist agriculture, in the first instance, and later into an overexpanded tertiary (service) sector. This forces wages down for those who do find jobs, and reinforces the hold of landlords and other pre-capitalist exploiting classes whose power is rooted in the agrarian sector. Low wages and the persistence of pre-capitalist modes are thus both the product of the absence of a fully fledged industrial sector.

There are, of course, other mechanisms at work. Capital never scorns extra-economic coercion when it is the most cost-effective means to maximise profits, and coercion is absolutely necessary to break into societies where commodity production is not well established. State power and the economic power of monopoly also play a role at all stages of development. However, Amin stresses the convergence of the formations of the periphery towards a common path, despite their very different histories, and the economic mechanism summarised above is his *general* explanation.

Amin's arguments are stated most clearly in *AWS*, where he distinguishes three mechanisms at work in the transition to peripheral capitalism. First, there is the transition from subsistence economy to commodity economy, whether this is achieved by purely economic means or by violence. 'Primary' money incomes are created by purchase of peasant harvests for export or by wage payments by foreign enterprises. These have a limited effect in monetarising the local economy because a 'large proportion of the primary money income is spent on imports' (*AWS*, p. 145). Once commodity production is established it 'will inevitably result in the ruin of some and the enrichment of others; in other words, in the formation of indigenous capital. This is an absolute law' (*AWS*, p. 146). But this capital formation will not generate capitalist development:

First, because the indigenous capital thus formed will come up against the competition of foreign industries. This will lead it to seek investment in the sphere of production for export and in the tertiary sector. . . . Second, competition will direct these investments into light industry. In other words, the local capitalism . . . will not compete with the dominant foreign capitalism but will be complementary to it. (*AWS*, p. 146)

Second, there is the impact of developed capitalism on commodity-producing formations in the periphery-to-be:

Whereas at the start of the development of European capitalism there was investment of indigenous capital, and the creation of manufactures that put on the market products that till then had been supplied by the crafts, we find that at the start in the economies that were to become underdeveloped, there was penetration by products of *foreign* industry. . . . In the colonial scheme overall demand was sharply reduced by the introduction of manufactured goods. The ruined craftsmen were doomed to unemployment. (*AWS*, p. 150)

Here we see another aspect of the process, adjustment of economic balance by income effects. The peasants switch from selling food to craftsmen to selling goods for export, leaving no place for the ruined craftsmen. Income, demand and production have all gone down together, leaving no mechanism to restore employment.

Thirdly, there is foreign investment. Amin argues that foreign investment as such does not block development. If a movement of capital were accompanied by no trade other than the movement of goods needed to transfer the capital, so that 'the craft sector of our precapitalist economy is disintegrated not by foreign trade . . . but by competition from industries set up locally by foreign capital' then 'the resulting capitalist development would be full and complete in character' (*AWS*, pp. 159–60). Foreign investment was in practice, however, super-imposed on an economy subject to foreign competition, and was thus directed into export production, the tertiary sector, and, later, light consumer goods industries, just as local capital was. In other words, it is the specialisation imposed by exchange in a world market that is the dominant mechanism, and capital flows conform to this pattern.

Amin's line of argument can be related to the theory of 'comparative advantages' or 'comparative costs'. There are two elements to it. Firstly, the peripheral formations have a comparative advantage in the production of 'exotic agricultural produce' and (certain) minerals. This is not difficult to accept. Secondly, Amin is arguing that the employment created by this export activity is not sufficient to absorb the whole labour force. Historical experience shows that he is right here, but the exact mechanisms involved are not clear from his account. To elucidate these questions involves a careful reexamination of the theory of international specialisation.

One fundamental point must be disposed of at the start. In the main tradition of bourgeois economics, the productivity of labour in different branches of production in different countries is taken as given. Amin, rightly, criticises this. The periphery is not ordained by nature to be a supplier of raw materials; the productivity of labour in different activities is the result of a historical process of development. What a theory of specialisation can do is to show how unequal development manifests itself in trade relations. These relations, in their turn, modify the subsequent pattern of development.

The standard post-Ricardian bourgeois theories of international specialisation are based on an assumption of full employment. This is not so obvious in the basic Ricardian example that is usually given, since with only two goods, if one country specialises in one, the other country must specialise in the one remaining good. In practice, of course, there are a multiplicity of commodities. Suppose there are two countries, A and B, with many commodities, all tradeable. If, say, A has twice the labour force of B, then it must specialise in the production of commodities that absorb $\frac{2}{3}$ of the total social labour of the two country system. If we think of a spectrum of commodities, arranged in order so that those in which A has the greatest comparative advantage are at one end, and those in which its comparative advantage is least are at the other end, then a dividing line must be established between A's specialisms and B's specialisms at a point that allows full employment of labour in both countries.

What mechanism can be proposed to bring about this providential allocation of activities between countries? The answer is simple. If there is unemployment of resources in A, then factor rewards (wages, profits, etc.) must fall there, until A is able to undercut B in some additional branches of production. The dividing line is moved along the spectrum of activities until full employment (or at least equal unemployment) is established everywhere.

Amin, by contrast, is arguing that a pattern of specialisation emerges in which the industries assigned (by the 'invisible hand') to the periphery are not enough to absorb the productive resources available there, so that there is massive unemployment and, at the same time, money capital is diverted away from productive uses. It seems that his argument is incomplete; falling wages (and other factor rewards) should restore the periphery's capacity to compete in enough areas to offset the fall in demand.

In fact, his analysis is in an even worse position. He wants to argue that contact with a more advanced economy will create unemployment. Ricardo's classic analysis (1971, chapter 7) is aimed at showing that trade will *raise* incomes in the less advanced as well as the more advanced economy, so there is no question of it being necessary to force down wages in order to restore full employment. The point of the Ricardian argument is simple: exchange of commodities can only transmit a structure of *relative* prices. If one country can produce every commodity with, say, a hundred times lower real costs than the other country this makes no difference at all provided that relative costs are the same. I will examine the analysis, to begin with, for the case where both countries are wholly capitalist; note, however, that the basic point that relative costs (or supply prices) are the determining factor does not depend on either country being wholly capitalist, since it applies to any commodity-producing system.

There are two quite distinct cases in which Amin's account can be rescued. Firstly, there is the case in which the comparative advantages are such that the less developed area is excluded from activities which are relatively labour intensive given the techniques used in that area. This is exactly the case that Amin considers, and is what happened in practice; the periphery was excluded from 'industrial' activities which were carried out by labour intensive (craft) methods, and forced to specialise in agriculture (land intensive). The result is to increase pressure on the land, raising rents and either forcing down wages or creating unemployment. (This analysis is an application, in different circumstances, of the famous Stolper-Samuelson (1941) argument.) In this case, then, it is the pattern of *comparative* costs that matters.

The second case is quite different. The Ricardian argument assumes that it is *only* commodities that are mobile between countries, so that only (relative) commodity prices are equalised. Suppose, however, that capital is mobile as well. Capitalists will set up production wherever profits are highest, and this will be where costs are lowest. Costs will depend largely on unit labour costs, and hence on wages relative to productivity. This is still not enough to ensure de-industrialisation and unemployment in the periphery. If the wage differential matches the (assumed) productivity differential, then the periphery's costs will not be higher. Amin does consider this possibility (new 'light' industries are established in the periphery once wages in the centre have risen far enough), but it plays only a subsidiary part in his argument. We therefore have to add the assumption that wages are, at least to some extent, fixed in real terms. This corresponds to Amin's description of the nineteenth century as a time when wages were close to subsistence in both centre and periphery, so that there was no scope for wage reductions of a sufficient size to allow the industries of the periphery to compete.

The second case, therefore, is where capital is mobile and productivity differences outweigh differences in wages. The more advanced country has the higher rate of profit (lower costs), so capital flows out of the less developed country, leaving unemployment. In this case, specialisation is determined by *absolute* and not *comparative costs*. Ricardo commented on this possibility in a passage cited by both Emmanuel and Amin (Ricardo, 1971, p. 154). Amin refers to the outflow of capital from the periphery to the centre, which fits in with this analysis, though he also argues that profits are higher in the periphery than in the centre as a result of higher exploitation there.

How must these arguments be modified if the periphery is partly or wholly pre-capitalist to begin with? We then have to consider the effects of trade on the nascent capital of the periphery and also on the profits and costs anticipated by prospective foreign investors. The pre-capitalist *milieu* may in itself be favourable or unfavourable to capitalist development; that is a rather different argument. The first case considered above applies fairly directly, with the addition that the destruction of the crafts destroys the part of the local economy which is most likely to generate an indigenous development of capitalist relations of production, while the enforced migration into agriculture reinforces pre-capitalist ruling classes and relations of production in that sector. Amin stresses this point.

Mobility of capital, the second case above, can only affect a capitalist sector. Nascent local capital will flow out (or shift into mercantile activities that enter into a world-wide equalisation of profit rates), and foreign capital will be repelled. Petty commodity production will not, however, be affected by capital mobility. The only thing that concerns an individual craftsman or peasant is the ratio between the prices of the goods he sells and those he buys. Emmanuel (1974) has noted that craft production in 'industrial' sectors of the economy persists on a large scale in the periphery, as, of course, does peasant agriculture.

The two cases considered above can, of course, be combined. If certain areas in the periphery have natural advantages in a few products (exotic agriculture, minerals), then their absolute costs may be low, and these sectors will develop, but they may not absorb all of the labour available. The exploitative grip of merchant capital can also be incorporated into the picture. It is, however, important to separate these different issues on an analytical level. Amin does not do this. I should emphasise, therefore, that the analysis set out above is mine, not Amin's; it is my attempt to relate his arguments to more orthodox theories. It may be relevant to the periodisation of the world economy that large-scale commodity trade (and hence transmission of relative prices) predated large-scale international capital flows.

The level of productivity in different activities, and its evolution, are clearly crucial to the argument as I have presented it. Amin discusses the pattern of relative advantages, under the guise of a discussion of 'sectoral unevenness of productivity' (in the periphery):

> It is not, of course, possible to compare productivities in the strict sense of the word except between two enterprises that produce the same product . . . Between one branch and another one can speak only of different *profitabilities*, as Emmanuel has reminded us. All the same, if, with a given price structure, conditions are such that labour, or capital or both, cannot be rewarded in one branch at the same rate as in another, I say that productivity is lower in that branch. In the capitalist mode of production . . . the effective tendency is for labour and capital to be rewarded in all branches at the same rates. If, however, this price structure [of the centre] . . . is transmitted to the periphery, the result will be that factors cannot be rewarded at the same rate in the different branches if the technical conditions (and so the productivity) are distributed other-wise than at the centre. (*UD*, pp. 215–16)

Note the assumption here that the price structure of the centre determines world prices. This rules out unequal exchange in Emmanuel's sense, since the point of unequal exchange is precisely that low wages in the periphery are incorporated in low prices for the periphery's products. Amin could argue that prices are intermediate between those corresponding to the costs of the centre and of the periphery, giving both unevenness of productivity (as defined) and unequal exchange.

In *IUD*, Amin has gone much further in rejecting Emmanuel's analysis, asserting that the same products are produced at the centre and in the periphery and even denying that 'the productions exchanged on the world market are specific, that they have irreducible use values' (*IUD*, p. 209). The point seems to be that it doesn't matter what is produced, since a demand can be created for anything, for example for plastic flowers. However, even if the goods produced are constantly changing, we must still regard them as distinct from each other, or there is no basis for commodity exchange or for a social division of labour. In particular, if use values are not 'specific', then there is no way we can talk of unequal specialisation, and the whole basis of Amin's analysis evaporates, along with the theory of unequal exchange.

If the periphery produces the same range of goods as the centre, then they must sell at the same prices, so that superexploitation in the periphery must be manifested as super-profits for firms producing there rather than through unequal exchange. There could, of course, be both super-profits and unequal exchange if capital were only partly mobile. Again, Amin does not clearly distinguish the cases he examines or specify the various assumptions involved.

Levels of productivity, and their evolution, remain to be explained. Amin largely takes these for granted rather than trying to give any connected theoretical explanation of them.

At an early stage in the evolution of the world economy, when commodity exchange was the only integrating factor, productivities in different areas would differ according to the level of development reached. Specialisation would depend on comparative (not absolute) costs. Given a pattern of costs such that the periphery was excluded from industrial activities, this pattern would tend to persist or to be reinforced, since there would be no opportunity to gain experience in industry.

Once capital becomes mobile, however, it is difficult to see why technology, and hence productivity levels, are not transferred, along with capital. Clearly they have been, for example in mining. I return to my central criticism of Emmanuel: why do any industries remain in the high-wage countries at all? Amin is aware of this problem (*IUD*, p. 212).

A major part of the answer must surely lie in *external economies*: those conditions of production that a particular branch of industry needs, but that an individual enterprise cannot provide for itself or, more commonly, that it need not provide for itself in a location where the industry concerned is well established. Examples are a skilled labour force, a network of suppliers, suitable transport services, and so on.

These are, of course, all reasons why it is difficult (i.e. in a capitalist context, costly and hence unprofitable) to establish production in a new location. The same arguments could be used to defend Emmanuel's assumption of a fixed pattern of specialisation, though they fit more easily into a context of unequal specialisation and unequal development than they do into Emmanuel's argument in which wage differentials are treated as the 'independent variable'.

In the earlier parts of the imperialist (i.e. post-1880–1900) stage, when wages in the centre were still fairly low and when technology was still quite largely in the hands of skilled workers rather than being systematised and brought fully under the control of capital (cf. Braverman, 1974), it is easy to see that there was little incentive for established capitalist firms in the centre to shift production to the periphery.

In the present stage of development, however, there are very large wage differentials, and multi-national firms have great experience of transferring technology, so that it is much harder to see why a productivity gap should persist. Without it, Amin's main arguments would collapse.

Amin disarmingly admits that transfer of industries from the centre to the periphery is indeed the tendency. He gives a number of reasons why this tendency does not dominate. Firstly, it takes time, and is only beginning. This is true, but why should it take much more than, say, the turnover time of capital equipment? Secondly, he argues that capitalism needs the high wages of the centre to provide a market (*IUD*, p. 213). I think this argument is false (see next section), but in any case he does not explain why it should affect the decisions of individual capitals. In other contexts he is very aware that capitalist competition and class struggle may produce outcomes that conflict with the system's 'needs' (see Amin, 1978, pp. 32–3). Thirdly, he refers to the need for balance of payments equilibrium (*IUD*, p. 213). This is no argument: large-scale capital outflows from the centre would not disturb its balance of payments if accompanied by exports of capital goods. Once industries have been transferred, the centre's capacity to pay for imports would be reduced, but so would the general level of activity and hence the demand for them. Amin is willing to accept this argument for the periphery; why not for the centre in its turn? Fourthly, he repeats that development in the periphery must be blocked and distorted in order 'to reproduce its own conditions of existence' (*IUD*, p. 218), but this simply restates the problem. Why and how does it reproduce itself?

It is fairly easy to see the ways in which internal development is blocked (balance of payments problems prevent large-scale import of modern capital goods, etc.), but these limitations do not apply to expansion of production by foreign enterprises, which is the case under discussion. Similarly, limitations of the local market do not limit production for the world market. Amin is not always consistent here, insisting sometimes on the global nature of the system and of markets, and appealing to the limits of the local market at other times. He finally, rather desperately, says that if, say, Mexico were to become a fully developed province of the USA, then 'the contradiction would shift from the economic to the cultural and political domains' (*UD*, p. 381). There is, of course, no reason to suppose that any migration of industry to the periphery would be evenly spread.

To sum up this section, Amin provides a convincing account of the evolution of a periphery which is integrated, by stages, into a world market, while retaining a distinct wage level, a distinct social structure (persistence of pre-capitalist modes) and a lagging productivity level, at least in some sectors. He does not, however, seem to me to work the analysis out fully, nor does he have an adequate explanation of the evolution of productivity, especially in the era of multi-national companies.

IV Wages and autocentric accumulation

We have seen that an important part of Amin's account of relations between the centre and the periphery rests on the fact that wages in the centre have increased roughly in line with productivity since about 1900 (I would say rather earlier). This is important to him in two ways. Firstly, rising wages in the centre and constant wages in the periphery bring into existence the mechanisms of unequal exchange. This has been discussed. Secondly, according to Amin, wages that increase in line with productivity generate a falling rate of profit that must be offset by increased exploitation in the periphery.

That real wages in the centre have, in fact, increased is not in doubt. I shall, however, argue that the reasons Amin gives for this and the conclusions he draws from it are thoroughly confused and in places quite wrong.

First, I will briefly examine his argument concerning the falling rate of profit. The rate of profit, according to Marx (see chapter 2 above), is determined by two ratios, the rate of surplus value (s/v in the usual notation) and the organic (value) composition of capital (c/v). Technical advance and accumulation tend to increase both of these, and so the effects tend to offset each other. The rate of surplus value is increased because wage goods are cheapened, reducing the value of labour power with a constant real wage. However, says Amin, if the real wage increases in line with productivity, this stabilises the rate of surplus value, so that the rising organic composition of capital makes the tendency of the rate of profit to fall 'necessarily get the better of the counter-tendencies' (*A WS*, p. 598).

It is now well known that a rising technical composition of capital can be offset by rising productivity in the production of means of production, so that the organic composition of capital need not rise (see chapter 2 above). This is, in fact, recognised in the formal models that Amin has constructed more recently (*IUD* and Amin, 1978). Amin does cite some empirical evidence, not on organic compositions, but on the ratio of capital to production (in price terms) which can be assumed to reflect the organic composition of capital. These show the ratio reaching a maximum in the USA in 1919 and in Britain in 1909, with a decline after that (*UD*, p. 166). In other words, almost as soon as wages rose, the organic composition started to fall. It seems we can forget the falling rate of profit.

Amin is more seriously concerned about the 'contradiction between the capacity to produce and the capacity to consume'. He elaborates this in many passages in all his main works. Here is one example (for others, see *UD*, pp. 73–4, 191; *IUD*, pp. 195–205, 239–52):

> It is clear that in a closed capitalist economy (the autocentric, central capitalist mode of production that Marx studied) there is a relation between the overall level of productivity . . . and that of wages. If wages fall below a certain level, the system's capacity to produce exceeds its capacity to consume. . . . This proof, which is of fundamental importance, accounts for the observed fact that the share taken by wages and by profits in national income is relatively stable. . . . I have shown, however . . . that for the extraverted capitalist economies of the periphery this necessary link is absent. Wages in the periphery can therefore be frozen at very low levels without extraverted development being hindered. This is the centrepiece of my demonstration that if the capitalist mode of

production is autocentric it tends to become exclusive, whereas extraversion blocks its development. (*A WS*, pp. 598-9)

To analyse this, we must first note that Amin treats the central capitalist economies as if they were closed economies, arguing that 'the essential relations of the system can be grasped without taking account of [external] relations' and that the flows between centre and periphery are marginal to the centre (*UD*, p. 75).

This line of argument raises some difficulties. Amin wavers between treating the world system as a system of distinct national economies, and as an integrated global system. If it is a global system, then the relations between sectors can only be analysed on a global level. (I think he is more consistent in this in his most recent work, *IUD*.) He argues that the economies of the centre are relatively integrated, so that an initial impulse of some sort stimulates the whole economy, while in the periphery, the stimulus leaks away abroad (*UD*, pp. 237-8). Here he is falling into the problematic of 'independent variables'. In fact there are no independent stimuli which then have a series of effects. There is only a single process of accumulation which carries both centre and periphery along to their (differing) destinies.

His key idea, however, is that 'the determining link in an autocentric capitalist system is . . . that which connects the production of consumer goods with the production of the production goods that are destined to make it possible to produce these consumer goods' (*UD*, p. 73). This seems to me to be both right and, crucially, wrong. The relationship between departments is an essential link in the system, but Amin views it in a unilateral way; means of production are used to produce consumer goods. So they are, but they are also used to produce further means of production. Amin sees consumption as being in some sense more fundamental than investment. The line of thought is related to that of Rosa Luxemburg (discussed in chapter 3), and that of Paul Sweezy (chapter 6). Some errors have an amazing capacity to survive.

Given this way of looking at things, it is easy to arrive at Amin's conclusions, at least as long as one sticks to vague verbal arguments. If investment must keep pace with the growth of consumption, and if the saving that finances investment comes from profits while consumption demand is determined by wages, then wages must grow in line with profits if investment demand is to be maintained. (See *UD*, pp. 73-4, 234, 236.)

Tugan Baronovski showed, long ago, that accumulation could go on with fixed real wages and rising productivity, provided that department 1 (production of means of production) expanded faster than department 2 (production of consumer goods). Amin rejects this for exactly the same reasons as Rosa Luxemburg, and I will not repeat the criticisms that I have made of her argument (see pp. 65–6 above).

Amin, however, presents a formal model which purports to support his argument (*IUD*, pp. 239–52). I will argue that the results he obtains from this model are wholly the result of mistakes in the formulation of the model, that there are two major mistakes and that the 'conditions for equilibrium growth' derived from the model are really the conditions for these two mistakes to cancel each other out.

The model is based on the schemas of expanded reproduction in Marx's *Capital*, vol. II. There are two departments, 1 and 2, producing means of production (Amin calls it 'equipment') and consumer goods, respectively. Goods are assumed to be exchanged at their values; a model in terms of prices of production would give similar results (*IUD*, p. 196). All of wages is spent on consumer goods, and all of surplus value is accumulated, again a simplification that could be relaxed (p. 251). Means of production are entirely used up in one period of production (Amin calls it a 'phase').

The essential part of Amin's argument is his assertion that there are two conditions for dynamic equilibrium (p. 242):

(1) that the wages distributed for each phase (in both Departments) enable the entire output of consumer goods produced during that phase to be bought;

(2) that the surplus value generated during one phase (in both Departments) makes it possible to purchase the entire output of Department I during that phase at the equilibrium price of the next phase.

It is the second of these conditions that is crucial and that I will concentrate on. Firstly, Amin has overlooked the part of the output of department 1 which goes to replace means of production used up during the cycle of production. This is not purchased out of surplus value, since a part of the value of gross output is already allocated to replacement of constant capital. Amin thus confuses gross and net output.

Secondly, if means of production are bought by capitalists at the prices of the following period, they must also be sold at those prices. We are dealing here with conditions for equilibrium in exchange, and only surplus value actually realised by sale of products can be available for spending on additional means of production. Amin counts the revenue received from the sale of means of production at their value in the present period in reckoning surplus value, but the expenditure on their purchase is reckoned at a different price. Since the exchange of capital goods is internal to the whole class of capitalists (one capitalist buys from another), this simply throws his equations out.

Neither of these criticisms seem to me to be a debatable matter of theory; they are entirely a matter of consistency in the accounting framework that is used. They are not simply verbal slips either; I shall show that Amin's results follow from these mistakes. A possible source of this confusion is that Amin has omitted one form of 'depreciation' (the using of constant capital) and inserted another (the devaluation of constant capital). Apart from the name, however, these have nothing in common. (This interpretation was suggested to me by Ben Fine.)

Amin's notation is somewhat difficult to follow; I think I can make my point more clearly using standard Marxist notation. (For a presentation of Amin's equations in his notations see the appendix to Brewer, 1980.) Here I shall write c, v, s, for constant capital (means of production used up), variable capital (the wage bill) and surplus value, respectively, with subscripts 1, 2 for departments 1 and 2.

Writing down his two conditions in the standard notation we have
$$v = c_2 + v_2 + s_2 \qquad (1)$$
$$s = (c_1 + v_1 + s_1)p \qquad (2)$$
where p is the price of department 1 output in the second phase relative to the first.

Amin assumes that labour required per unit of output in department 1 is multiplied each period by a constant δ ($\delta < 1$). The productivity of labour, in other words, is multiplied by $1/\delta$ per period, so that low values of δ represent higher rates of technical change, and $\delta = 1$ represents no change in technology. Since he assumes that the means of production required per unit of output in department 1 remains unchanged, the value per physical unit of output is multiplied by δ from one period to the next.
Hence:
$$p = \delta \qquad (3)$$
Amin, in effect, adds (1) and (2) together, incorporating (3).
Since $c + v + s = (c_1 + v_1 + s_1) + (c_2 + v_2 + s_2)$, this gives:
$$v + s = c + v + s - (1 - \delta)(c_1 + v_1 + s_1) \qquad (4)$$
Equation (4) makes it very obvious what is happening. Because of Amin's confusion of net and gross magnitudes, we have net output on

the L.H.S. and gross output on the R.H.S. Because of the inconsistency over the prices at which means of production are sold, we have an extra term on the right.

If we reckon capitalists' gross receipts and spending consistently in current values, (2) would be replaced by

$$c + s = c_1 + v_1 + s_1$$

and adding to (1) would give

$$c + v + s = c + v + s$$

a totally uninteresting identity: gross output = gross output. This is, in effect, Say's law, which applies because Amin assumes that all receipts are spent. Reckoning in terms of net investment, or at the following period's value, for all or part of output would require equal alterations to both sides: the identity would remain true.

Returning to equation (4), we can see how Amin gets his result. This equation can only hold if the effects of the two mistakes cancel out, i.e. if:

$$c = (1 - \delta)(c_1 + v_1 + s_1)$$

That is, if the discrepancy between net and gross output exactly equals the devaluation of the output of department 1 between one period and the next. There can be no question of giving any sensible economic interpretation to so bizarre a result. He is able to show that there is one, and only one, division of resources between the two departments that will satisfy this equation, and since department 1 output is sold to capitalists while department 2 output is sold to workers, there is only one rate of exploitation that is consistent with this division of resources. The required real wage rate turns out to increase over time when productivity is increasing. Hence his result, asserted in all of his main works, that 'there is a relation between the overall level of productivity and that of wages' (1974, p. 598) in a closed capitalist economy.

What are the consequences for Amin's analysis of rejecting his argument that wages must increase in line with productivity in order to maintain demand? To see this, we must first see how this particular argument fits in to his analysis.

The level of wages must obviously be explained somehow. Fortunately Amin has an alternative explanation: they are determined by class struggle, and the outcome of the struggle depends on the balance of forces. He himself prefers this explanation, saying that if wages fail to rise because of the strength of the bourgeoisie, who will individually try to force down wages despite the fact that (according to him) the system needs increasing wages, then 'the system suffers crisis, that's all' (Amin,

1978, p. 33). This treatment of wages at the centre is consistent with his analysis of wages in the periphery.

The analysis of the 'contradiction between the capacity to produce and the capacity to consume' does not, in fact, provide an explanation of wages at all, because Amin provides no mechanism whereby a divergence of wages from the required level can be corrected. If wages are too high there is a crisis, and if they are too low there is a crisis. In either case wages will be forced down (presumably – Amin fudges this; see *UD*, p. 74), so that there is no remedy if wages are too low.

Amin's discussion of the role of the periphery in this context also seems to me to be confused. He argues that high wages are needed at the centre (to stimulate demand) while low wages on the periphery hold up the rate of profit. But a combination of high and low wages in different sectors is essentially equivalent, for the world economy, to an intermediate level of wages throughout, both from the point of view of demand, and from the point of view of profit. So the difference between centre and periphery solves none of these problems.

Amin also tries to connect his analysis to that of Baran and Sweezy by arguing that the problem of demand is solved by excess consumption or waste paid for out of profits. In the periphery this excess consumption is carried out by local capitalists (and /or landowners, etc.). However, if the profits of superexploitation in the periphery are consumed locally, they cannot be transferred to the general (world) profit rate by unequal exchange.

Finally, Amin is faced with a problem in that his own historical analysis shows that wages in the centre did not rise during the century-long competitive stage of capitalism. This should have been impossible, on his own arguments. Amin answers this by saying that in his period 'external extension of the capitalist market was . . . of prime importance as a means for realising surplus value' (*UD*, p. 188). This is a return to Rosa Luxemburg's arguments, which elsewhere he rejects. Export of goods cannot solve his problem (since there must be corresponding imports) and nor can export of capital (since where will the products of the new establishments find a market? The relocation of investment does not alter anything).

Altogether, the argument that capitalism must overcome a 'contradiction between the capacity to produce and the capacity to consume' is a source of massive confusion in Amin's work. A surgical excision of all of this material seems to me to be both necessary and possible.

V Summary

Amin argues that the capitalist world economy is divided into two distinct types of social formation, those of the centre and those of the periphery. In the centre, the capitalist mode of production eliminates other modes, and generates a process of development of the sort analysed by the classical Marxists. In the periphery, capitalist development is 'blocked' by the competition of the more advanced industries of the centre, so that pre-capitalist modes persist for a long time, and an economic and social structure quite distinct from that of the centre arises. The explanation that Amin presents for the central mechanism of unequal specialisation hinges on the development of productivity in the industries of the centre and of the periphery, and he gives no adequate explanation for it. He also presents an analysis of the 'contradiction between the capacity to produce and the capacity to consume', which he uses to explain the evolution of wages in the centre and to link his arguments to the 'falling rate of profit' and to the Baran/Sweezy discussion of surplus absorption. I have argued that this part of his argument is untenable.

Gathering together my criticism, it may appear that there is little left of Amin's analysis. I think, nevertheless, that there is a great deal to be gained from a (critical) reading of his work. His is the only serious attempt to tackle what is surely the central problem, that of analysing accumulation on a world scale, a dynamic process involving social formations of very divergent structures linked into a single world capitalist economy. In the process, he has tried to link together a range of subjects that had previously been studied in virtual isolation from each other: modes of production, class structures in the periphery, the pattern of international trade and specialisation, the formation of international prices, the (economic) problems of national development in the periphery, the periodisation of capitalist development, and so on. To pose the problem is often the most important step.

Part IV

Current debates

11 · The 'modes of production' debate

It is almost an axiom of Marxism that international relations (political or economic) can only be understood in terms of the internal structure of the states concerned, conceptualised by Marxists in terms of modes of production. The story of the emergence and subsequent evolution of capitalism in the advanced centres is relatively common ground among Marxists, at least in outline, but there have been a series of debates, especially in recent years, about the appropriate way to analyse social and economic structures in underdeveloped countries. These debates have been surveyed by Foster-Carter (1976). I shall concentrate on those aspects of the debate relevant to theories of imperialism.

I The Marxist tradition

The main tradition of Marxism, until recently, conceived of modes of production as successive stages in the evolution of human society, following each other in a predestined order and linked to each other by 'transitions'. In a transitional period, the old mode was in a state of decay, while the new mode first grew up within the previous system, and then replaced it. The development of the new forms of organisation actively undermined the old and accelerated their decay. At some stage in this process a revolution would be necessary to sweep away the political and legal superstructures corresponding to the old mode of production and reconstruct them to fit the needs of the new. The relation between the two modes was therefore one of contradiction, and the new ruling class had to establish itself through class struggles in which it was irreconcileably opposed to the old order. Each nation had to go through the sequence of stages, though external influences might accelerate or slow the process or even allow a whole stage to be skipped. This brief summary is, of course, a caricature, but I think it brings out the key ideas that underlie more sophisticated accounts. There is some warrant for it in Marx's own writings (especially the *Preface to the Critique of Political Economy*).

Trotsky had a somewhat different view. Although his thinking remained in essence bounded by a 'stages' perspective, he stressed the importance of (relative) backwardness, and argued that the structure of societies that started to develop late was not the same as those that had led the way. This thesis, as applied specifically to Russia, is to be found scattered through his works: see Knei-Paz (1978) for an exposition of Trotsky's views and for detailed references. Russia, he argued, came under pressure, military and economic, from the more advanced West, and the Russian state, reacting to this pressure, took the initiative in promoting both industrial development and (limited) measures of social and administrative modernisation designed to increase the military efficiency of the state. The result was a society in which the relative weight of the state machine was far larger than in west Europe, and that of the bourgeoisie much smaller, in which massive disparities existed between the industrial cities and the impoverished and backward countryside. This is summarised in the phrase 'uneven and combined development', meaning that nations, sectors, areas develop at different rates, but do not do so in isolation from each other. What is distinctive about Trotsky's view is his emphasis on the role of the state. As it stands it is difficult to think of many areas except Russia, Japan and parts of south-east Europe to which it is relevant; in other areas national states went under when confronted with western pressure. Ex-colonial territories frequently exhibit a rather similarly enlarged state apparatus, though they have reached this condition by a quite different route.

The classic account of a transition from feudalism to capitalism is Lenin's *The Development of Capitalism in Russia* (1974). Russia at the time was in the middle of the transition, and Lenin, grappling with the real problems of political strategy in a relatively backward country, looked in detail at the actual process of transition and at the transitional forms created. The issues he focused on are substantially the same as those that concern Marxists in the underdeveloped world today: the prospects for capitalist development and the class struggles and possible class alliances inherent in the situation.

Lenin identified four main processes at work in the countryside. Firstly, commodity production and exchange were emerging through the progressive separation of successive 'industrial' activities from agriculture. These activities formed distinct industries, perhaps at first organised on a craft basis, but rapidly penetrated by capitalist relations of production, linked to each other and to agriculture by exchange relations, creating a social division of labour and a 'home market' (cf. Marx's similar analysis). Secondly, there was a progressive differentation of the peasantry, with the breakdown of the 'middle peasantry' of relatively self-sufficient family units into a rural bourgeoisie (the 'kulaks') and a rural proletariat. Thirdly, the role of the landlord was transformed by the replacement of the (feudal) *corvée* or labour service system by capitalist agriculture based on the employment of wage labour. Capitalist agriculture emerged simultaneously by two routes: the rise of a rural bourgeoisie from the peasantry and the reconstruction of the land-lords' economy into capitalist estates. Finally, there was a developing pattern of specialisation within agriculture itself, and thus a development of commodity exchange within agriculture as well as between agriculture and industry.

In this process a great variety of transitional forms were created; 'the systems mentioned are actually interwoven in the most varied and fantastic fashion' (Lenin, 1974, p. 197). Taken in isolation these would be incomprehensible. Lenin is able to make sense of them only by setting them in the context of a process of transition from one fairly well-defined system (feudalism) to another (capitalism). I suspect that at least part of the debate about contemporary underdeveloped countries is bedevilled by a desire to link immediately observable features of society (the 'fantastic forms' that Lenin described) directly to the defining features of various modes of production without setting them adequately in the context of a historical process.

Lenin's analysis, though not neglecting the international dimension, places the emphasis heavily on an internal evolution of economic and social structures driven by forces internal to the Russian economic and social system. This emphasis was no doubt correct as applied to Russia at that date, but would be harder to defend if carried over to contemporary underdeveloped countries, which have suffered direct colonial occupation, and are much more closely tied to a world economy dominated by the advanced capitalist centres.

II Contemporary debates

The classical Marxist analysis proved brilliantly successful in analysing European history (when applied in a creative and undogmatic way, as in Marx's own historical writings). It has not had the same success in dealing with non-European societies. I will not discuss here the difficulties in analysing non-European history before European (capitalist) penetration. The essential problem in discussing the expansion of capitalism outside its homelands in terms of modes of production is to characterise the societies created in underdeveloped countries by their incorporation into a world system dominated by the centres of capitalism.

In a 'stages' perspective, one must either say that underdeveloped countries are pre-capitalist, that they are capitalist, or that they are in transition (thus implying that they are becoming capitalist). In the orthodox Marxist view, the capitalist stage has three main characteristics: commodity production, the relation between wage labour and capital, and the pressure to accumulate and to introduce new methods of production. In underdeveloped countries, however, the general penetration of commodity production has gone along with very slow development of material production, and wage labour has been confined to small sectors of the economy. Either these areas are not becoming capitalist (in which case what are they?) or capitalism has quite different laws of motion in underdeveloped areas (in which case, what use is the concept of capitalism?).

The main attempts to solve these problems have already been discussed. I will survey them briefly as they relate to the modes of production debate.

Frank and Wallerstein take the most drastic line. Capitalism, they argue, can only be defined as a world system. It must be defined in terms of production for exchange on the world market, regardless of whether wage labour is employed or not. This is a fundamental shift of definition. Its laws of motion, too, are quite unlike those analysed by Marx. Capitalism does not promote general development; it promotes the development of some areas at the expense of others.

This line of argument seems to me to contain an essential truth: the world system can only be analysed at a global level. This is not the same thing as saying that the capitalist mode of production can only be analysed at a world level, since modes of production can be conceived of as abstract concepts which do not exist in a directly observable form on a global, national, or any other, scale. I have criticised Frank and Wallerstein for the lack of any well-worked-out theoretical analysis to back up their sloganistic generalisations.

An alternative approach, and one that is more faithful to Marx, is to concentrate on the wage relation as the defining feature of capitalism, as

Laclau suggested. Since wage labour has remained confined to relatively small sectors in underdeveloped countries, this requires one to argue that different modes of production can coexist within a single society, either permanently (abandoning the 'stages' perspective) or over a very long-drawn-out transition. Various phrases have been used in this context; one can talk of a 'conservation-dissolution' relation (between capitalism and the subordinated mode) of a 'blocked' transition (preserving a 'stages' view, at least verbally) or, as Bettelheim does in another context, of a transition 'between' two stages without implying movement in one direction or another, All of these devices seem to me to be essentially semantic; what matters is the substance of the analysis.

Abandoning a 'stages' approach raises questions about what a mode of production is. I will not go into the high theory debates on this question; the discussion of the general properties of 'doubly articulated complex structures' seems to me to have become a sort of conceptual sculpture that should be discussed by art critics rather than social scientists. I will only say that it seems best to me to regard modes of production as abstract constructions showing how a particular set of relations of production can be reproduced in a 'pure' form. The problems of analysing real societies, then, can be seen in terms of analysing the reproduction of a complex of relations of production characteristic of more than one mode. Whether we call this an 'articulation' between different modes or a 'transitional social formation' is relatively unimportant.

The case for focusing on the relation between the direct producers and their exploiters, and thus on the wage relation as the defining characteristic of capitalism, has been put most forcefully by Brenner (1977), in the context of the origins of capitalism. He argues that it is the production of *relative surplus value*, and thus the tendency to increase productivity, that differentiates capitalism from all previous modes of production:

> The logic of [Wallerstein's] position . . . is that capitalist under-development is as much the cause of capitalist development, as capitalist development is the cause of capitalist underdevelopment. Such an argument is not compatible with the view of capitalist economic development as a function of the tendency toward capital accumulation via innovation, built into a historically developed structure of class relations of free wage labour. For from this vantage point, neither economic development nor under-

development are *directly* dependent upon, caused by, one another.
Each is the product of a specific evolution of class relations, *in part*
determined historically '*outside*' capitalism, in relationship with
non-capitalist modes. . . . Wallerstein resorts to the position that
both . . . are essentially the result of a process of transfer of
surplus. . . . He must thus end up by . . . ignoring any *inherent*
tendency of capitalism to develop the productive forces. (pp. 60–1)

Why is the existence of free wage labour crucial? For two reasons.
Firstly, because only in a system of free labour can labour be reallocated
from one task to another and gathered into ever larger and more complex
productive organisations. Capital can only be genuinely mobile where it
can gather labour and means of production freely in the market.
Secondly, and perhaps more important, in a wage labour system all the
needs of reproduction have to be bought in the market and competition
then acquires a coercive force. Any enterprise that fails to keep up with
the socially established levels of productivity will be driven out of
business; the process of concentration and centralisation, an essential
part of the development of the forces of production under capitalism, is
thus dependent on the wage relation. A labour saving innovation enables
wage costs to be reduced, by simply making some workers redundant, an
option not open, for example, in feudal systems in which peasants are
tied to a particular estate. Competition will force capitalists to minimise
labour costs in this way, thus constantly recreating a mobile reserve
army of labour. (Rey argues a rather similar point, contrasting the
latifundia system with capitalist production.) Fine (1978), commenting
on Brenner, argues that capitalist production, in its early stages, relies
primarily on absolute surplus value until legislative/political pressures
limit working hours, and thus compel a turn to relative surplus value. In
underdeveloped countries the weakness of working-class organisation
postpones this development.

In a feudal forced labour system, by contrast, the essential needs of
reproduction are met by peasant plots, so that the *demesne* product,
which may be sold on the market, is a surplus product only. A feudal
lord, maximising his short-run profit, will attempt to intensify his hold
over the peasantry, to restrict their mobility, and to reduce both the land
and labour time devoted to the needs of reproduction on the peasants'
plots, not by increasing productivity, but by increasing absolute surplus
value, even to the point where the long-run reproduction of the system is
threatened. An extension of market opportunities can intensify feudal

exploitation and promote a regression in the forces of production. Brenner gives a telling example; in the Poland of the 'second serfdom' (one of Wallerstein's favourite examples), 'despite the orientation of the entire economy to exports, it could send out at best 5 per cent to 7 per cent of its total grain produce' (pp. 69–70). Serf peasant plots had a higher productivity than did the *demesnes*, and could generate a larger marketable surplus per acre, but they were ruthlessly cut down to expand the lords' profits. Here profitability (for the rulers) generated regression. A switch to wage labour would only be profitable for the lords in the very long run, if at all. Wage labour was only used where serfdom had already decayed beyond possibility of restoration.

An alternative system in agriculture is small peasant proprietorship. Here again the market lacks coercive force so long as peasants can produce their own subsistence (cf. Luxemburg and Rey), and here again the attachment of producers to the means of production inhibits flexibility and thus technological advance. England was the one place in Europe where serfdom had been eliminated (as a result of previous class struggles), but small peasant proprietorship had not replaced it. There are also cases in which the producers are wholly dependent on the market for their subsistence without labour power, as such, becoming a commodity. Peasant producers of non-subsistence agricultural goods, such as industrial raw materials, are an example. In these cases fully capitalist production can penetrate relatively easily.

The mode of production, defined by the relation between the direct producers and the owners of the means of production, is thus not a purely formal characteristic of the social system, nor does it define classes opposed to each other in purely distributive terms. It is of crucial importance in determining the evolution of the forces of production, and thus in determining development and underdevelopment. What Brenner does is to show the mechanisms which connect the *structural* features of the mode of production to its *dynamics*, and thus to demonstrate their relevance rather than merely asserting it; in this, of course, he follows Marx. Development and underdevelopment are the product of class structures which are themselves the outcome of class struggles and a historical process of development that cannot be analysed in the abstract.

Rey's analysis follows somewhat similar lines. It predates Brenner's work, and is more directly aimed at the analysis of contemporary underdeveloped countries. The distinctive feature of Rey's approach is that he seeks to build his analysis on the reproduction of the defining relations of production of the modes involved, and on almost nothing else (though the second, later, essay in *Alliances* modifies this, placing greater stress on class struggle). The concept of a mode of production is central to Rey's work in a way that it is not for any other writer. The slow pace of capitalist development in underdeveloped areas is a result of the persistence of pre-capitalist modes, which thus play an active role in determining the development of the societies in which they are 'articulated' with capitalism (see chapter 8 above).

Brenner and Rey thus both stress the survival of pre-capitalist modes of production, determined at least partly by causes internal to the under-developed countries, as the major factor in underdevelopment.

By contrast, most other recent writers (Amin and Arrighi are good examples) explain the slow development of capitalism in some areas in terms of forces internal to capitalism ('unequal specialisation' in Amin's analysis). Pre-capitalist modes of production survive essentially as a residual sector which capitalism is unable to penetrate because of its reduced vigour. The coexistence of different modes of production is then a result, not a primary cause, of underdevelopment, and is important mainly to elucidate the complex class structure that results. In the analysis of capitalism, therefore, these writers follow Frank and Wallerstein in arguing that capitalism produces both development and underdevelopment, but with the advantage (at least in Amin's case) that they have a positive theory to explain underdevelopment.

At about the same time as the Frank-Laclau debate, and the other developments surveyed above, there was a debate in India over rather similar ground. Rudra (1969, 1970) provoked the debate with a rather naive statistical survey of large farms in the Punjab, from which he concluded that there was no clearly defined class of capitalist farmers. U. Patnaik (1971a, b; 1972) criticised this conclusion, and Chattopadhyay (1972a, b) criticised both for being insufficiently Marxist. A general *melée* ensued (Banaji, 1972, 1977; Frank, 1973; Sau, 1973; Alavi, 1975). The debate has been surveyed by McEachern (1976) and Foster-Carter (1976). The main point at issue was whether Indian agriculture should be described as capitalist, a question which seems to me to be essentially semantic and rather uninteresting, but some important substantive points did emerge.

The context of the debate was the 'green revolution', the introduction of new strains of wheat and other grains which permitted large increases in output when used in conjunction with irrigation and fertilisers. There is general agreement that this development was associated with increased differentiation among the peasantry (whether as cause, effect or both is less clear) since the richer farmers were better able to take advantage of it. All the participants in the debate (except Rudra, who was generally ignored) seem to have agreed that this represented a development of capitalism in agriculture. The main point at issue was whether agriculture in India had been capitalist already during the colonial (pre-1949) period (as Chattopadhyay argued), so that the 'green revolution' was a development within capitalism, or whether agriculture had not previously been capitalist (as Patnaik and others claimed).

The basic facts were common ground. It was agreed that Indian agriculture had been generally engaged in commodity production (producing for the market) for a long time, that a fraction (30–40 per cent) of the rural population consisted of agricultural wage labourers, and that development in methods of production had been very slow, with little reinvestment of surplus. Alavi (1975) has a useful review of the facts and their historical context.

It is convenient to start with Chattopadhyay (1972a, b), ignoring the chronological order of debate. He argues that since commodity production and wage labour are the defining features of capitalism, Indian agriculture must be regarded as substantially capitalist, though still in transition. India, in fact, is in substantially the same position as Russia was in Lenin's time. He does not regard the slow pace of development as a problem (for analysis) since the early development of capitalism was slow everywhere else as well. In short, he restates a traditional Marxist analysis in which each nation, in its turn, passes through substantially the same stages of development. He hardly mentions external factors in his analysis, though he does discuss the colonial period (p. A–189) in terms strikingly (and no doubt deliberately) reminiscent of Marx's article on the results of British rule in India. Altogether, he sees no need for new analytical concepts; what is needed is a return to the ideas of Marx and Lenin.

Chattopadhyay's approach may be just about plausible for India since independence, but it can hardly be applied to any other underdeveloped country, since most are patently very different in structure from Europe at an early stage of capitalist development.

McEachern (1976) generally supports Chattopadhyay's diagnosis of India in terms of a classical Marxist analysis of transition, while placing much more emphasis on the external dimension. He is generally unwilling to accept any idea that modes of production may be 'combined', except during relatively brief periods of transition, and argues that the pre-capitalist forms that survive in India conceal the real (capitalist) relations of production.

U. Patnaik (1971a, b; 1972), along with Sau (1973) and Banaji (1972, 1977), also draws a distinction between apparent forms and underlying reality, but uses it to support the opposite conclusion. The existence of wage labour, she argues, is not conclusive evidence that Indian agriculture was capitalist, since workers were not really free given the lack of employment opportunities. More centrally, she insists that one should not speak of capitalism unless the surplus was productively invested within the same sector or even the same enterprise. There are two issues here. The first is whether to *define* capitalism in terms of accumulation, the third major characteristic of capitalism in the classical Marxist view (the others being commodity production and wage labour), and the second is whether the definition applies at the level of a firm or farm, or at some higher level. Frank (1973) has pointed out the connection between these issues by commenting that the surplus was indeed invested, but in England.

The question of definition seems to me to be semantic. What matters is to discover the necessary and sufficient conditions under which accumulation will take place, and the forms that it takes. Patnaik does have an explanation for the stagnation of Indian agriculture in the colonial period, and it is very similar to the explanations proposed by Arrighi and Amin. Industry failed to develop because of British competition, backed by the colonial state, so that markets for agricultural products were stagnant. Agriculture was exploited by 'antidiluvian forms of capital' (merchant capital, usury) and 'generalised commodity production . . . led to a prolonged disintegration of the precapitalist mode without its reconstitution on a capitalistic basis' (Patnaik, 1972, p. A–149). Independence has led to a certain amount of (state-sponsored) industrial development, and hence to scope for investment in agriculture.

Patnaik, then, argues that Indian agriculture, in the colonial period, was not capitalist, but she does not offer any definite alternative classification. Baraji (1972) and Alavi (1975) have proposed a new concept of a 'colonial mode of production' to cover colonial India and other colonial territories. Since Banaji has subsequently abandoned the idea, I will concentrate on Alavi's arguments. It is worth noting that this concept has nothing, apart from the name, in common with Rey's 'colonial mode'.

Alavi argues that colonial India was neither feudal (since there was widespread commodity production) nor capitalist (since there was little accumulation). He is unwilling to talk of a combination of modes, because different modes of production can only coexist in a state of contradiction, and the agrarian structures in India were not in conflict with the interests of capital. No one, he says, has 'demonstrated that there is any conflict between the rural "capitalist" class and the "feudal" landlords'. (One could, however, say the same of England.) His main idea, then, is to restore the classical conception of modes of production as stages of development. Colonialism does not correspond in any simple way to either a capitalist or feudal stage, so it must be something else, a 'colonial' stage.

The colonial mode, he argues, is characterised by colonial bourgeois state power, internal disarticulation, generalised commodity production, a transfer of surplus to the metropolis, and a lack of accumulation. These are, of course, the features that characterise Baran's 'typical' underdeveloped country or Amin's 'peripheral capitalism'.

Alavi is entitled to call this a mode of production if he wishes, but it is not remotely like any other Marxist concept of a mode of production. It is not an abstract conceptual construction, it has no defining relation of production, it does not define any specific class opposition. It is difficult to see what can be gained by calling this a 'colonial mode of production'. The conclusion I draw is that a 'stages' conception of modes of production, in which different modes are incompatible, and succeed each other with the new always destroying and driving out the old, is not adequate to deal with the experience of colonialism and underdevelopment.

Banaji (1977) has developed the idea that capitalism is to be identified with capital accumulation. He argues that modes of production are 'a definite totality of historical laws of motion' which must be discovered by analysis, and cannot be reduced to 'simple abstractions' (such as commodity production or wage labour). Any given mode of production may be compatible with a variety of 'forms of exploitation'. Capitalism, for example, has operated with serf labour or slaves, as well as with wage labour.

How then are the 'laws of motion' of the various modes to be distinguished? Banaji seems to reduce them to different (socially determined) motivations or purposes on the part of those who control production. Capitalism is production directed to accumulation, feudalism is directed to meeting the (socially determined) luxury consumption needs of the landlords, and the 'patriarchal-peasant' mode is governed by the subsistence needs of the peasant family. The *latifundias* of Latin America are, he argues, feudal estates, while superficially similar production units in plantation agriculture are capitalist, since they are oriented to the accumulation of capital, albeit 'only in the long run, as a relatively slow and mainly sporadic tendency dominated by feudal modes of consumption' (p. 16). I find this distinction hard to grasp.

Although there are many incidental felicities in this provocative article, such as the demonstration of the prevalence of wage labour in thirteenth-century England, which Banaji suggests was very like present-day rural India (p. 23; p. 39, n. 25), the main argument seems to remain very much up in the air. Where do these 'laws of motion' come from? The political economy of consumption and the social bases of motivation are certainly important and neglected topics, but they must be explained, not introduced as a *deus ex machina* to define modes of production. To trace these things back to their roots in relatively permanent features of social structure would, I suspect, lead us back to relations of production.

Two major issues emerge from the Indian debates. Firstly, there is the place in the analysis of 'forms of exploitation' (wage labour, serfdom, etc.). This is also, of course, the central issue in the Frank-Laclau-Wallerstein-Brenner debate. Many writers have pointed out that superficial or juridical relations may be misleading; a nominally independent peasant, for example, may depend on advances from a merchant and receive a price for his product that is more like a piece-rate wage than a genuine market price. This is no problem; Marxists are accustomed to distinguishing between juridical and real relations. It is a quite different matter to claim, for example, that a slave plantation can be capitalist, when the slaves are really slaves who can be bought and sold in slave markets. This issue is not settled, though there are strong reasons, as explained by Brenner, for thinking that the (real, not juridical) relation between the direct producers and their immediate exploiters is crucially important.

Secondly, there is the question of the appropriate level of analysis: world system, nation state, unit of production, or whatever. This is a non-problem. There can be no question of choosing to analyse at one of these levels, and ignoring the others; any adequate account of the world system must incorporate all of them, and their interrelations. There is only a problem if one asks the purely semantic question: to what kinds of entities can the adjectives 'capitalist', 'feudal', and so on be attached? Can one, for example, talk of a capitalist farm, or a feudal nation? Taken in isolation these are meaningless questions.

III Summary

Much of the debate over modes of production has been about the use of words and no more. As such it is of little interest. The substantive questions are about the way the world system works, and how it can be changed.

The classical Marxists defined modes of production in terms of the relation between the direct producers and their immediate exploiters, and simultaneously treated them as successive stages of social development. This approach does not work well when applied to underdeveloped countries. One answer is to redefine modes of production as stages of development on a world level and to deny the relevance of production relations as they are usually defined, but this leaves little to put in their place. The alternative is to modify the conception of modes of production as successive stages by arguing that a variety of relations of production can coexist within a single society. In itself, this step only provides a framework for analysis. Most of the elements of a substantive analysis are discussed in other chapters.

Two main questions emerge from the debate. Firstly, how important are relations of production in explaining development or under-development? For some authors they are central, while others explain underdevelopment in terms of factors, such as the extraction of surplus, that could apply to a variety of social systems or, like unequal exchange, in a wholly capitalist world. My own view is that a single explanation is unlikely to apply to all cases at all stages of development, so that a complete theory may draw on both views. Secondly (and this is a very closely related issue), how can we analyse changes in the relations of production? Some writers regard them as very durable, only subject to alteration as a result of catastrophic events (such as conquest) or of protracted class struggles. Others regard production relations ('forms of exploitation' or 'modes in which labor is recruited and compensated') as fairly easily altered in response to economic conditions. Again, it is not clear to me that one can safely generalise about this question.

12 · Central and peripheral capital

The classical Marxists thought of capitalism as an engine of change, advancing in a generally predictable direction through a series of crises and disturbances. There was no presumption that whoever was on top at any particular stage would stay on top (although as long as class societies persisted, someone would be on top, and most would be at the bottom). Capitalism generates *uneven* development. In Lenin's view, in particular, there were strong reasons to expect that the centres of accumulation would shift from more advanced to less advanced areas in search of cheap labour, accessible natural resources and higher profits, and that any division of the world would be disrupted by changes in the relative strengths of different imperialist powers.

By contrast, recent Marxist theorists have tended to assume that capitalism always acts to accentuate existing differences in levels of development. This is most obvious in Frank's picture of a chain of metropolis-satellite relations which ensures development for the metropolis and underdevelopment for the satellites, thus reinforcing the chain. In Frank's account, there has been no really fundamental change in this system in the whole history of capitalism. As applied to the contemporary world, this approach leads to a prediction that the United States, as the most powerful imperialist centre, will continue to dominate the system and that underdeveloped countries are bound to remain subordinate unless they break away from the capitalist world system altogether by socialist revolution. This view can be called 'Third Worldist' since its adherents see the fundamental contradiction of the system as being between the United States bourgeoisie and the masses of the Third World.

It was, perhaps, inevitable that Marxists should lose sight of the idea of uneven development in exploring the principle of cumulative causation as an explanation of the opening up of the huge gap that exists between advanced and underdeveloped countries. (See Barratt-Brown, 1972, p. 62. The principle of cumulative causation in this context was first explicitly stated by Myrdal, 1957.) However, the classical Marxist view is now being reasserted. The modes of production debate (discussed above), with its emphasis on internal causes of underdevelopment, is part of the revival of a classical perspective. This chapter deals with present trends in the development of capitalism (as opposed to any surviving pre-capitalist modes). The first section is a brief discussion of the multi-national corporation, the latest form of capitalist enterprise. The second section surveys debates about the future of central capital; is US domination assured, or is a return to rivalry between relatively equal capitalist centres likely? The final section is concerned with the future of capitalism in the periphery; is it doomed to remain underdeveloped, or is the complete capitalist industrialisation of the world a real possibility?

I Multi-national corporations

Multi-national corporations are capitalist firms that operate in more than one country. There is no clear line between multi-national and national firms, since all multi-nationals have started as national firms and expanded their operations abroad by degrees. Multi-nationals are generally thought of as large; this need not necessarily be so, but most of the world's largest firms are multi-national and it is large multi-nationals that are the principal subject of concern. Many discussions of multi-nationals restrict attention to firms which have production activities in several countries, thus excluding commercial and financial companies, which are also rapidly becoming multi-national. Multi-nationals may alternatively be referred to as transnational or international firms; in general the terms are synonymous, though Michalet (1976) makes a distinction between multi-national and transnational firms.

By far the most important fact about multi-nationals is that they are *capitalist* firms. Both national and multi-national firms sell products and buy means of production in markets that are by now usually fairly well integrated on a world scale, and both buy labour power at wages substantially determined by local labour markets. Both are subject to the same competitive imperative to minimise costs and to accumulate. Not surprisingly these circumstances, determined by the working of the capitalist *system* on a world scale, place close limits on their behaviour. Consider, for example, a system without multi-nationals in which firms in several different countries compete in selling, say, raw materials. The lowest cost supplier will generally succeed, while the others fail.

Knowing this, all will try to reduce costs to the minimum by, for example, depressing wages. Now consider, for comparison, a situation in which a multi-national firm operates in all the different countries concerned. It, too, will concentrate production in the lowest cost location, and try to minimise costs. It is pointless to attack foreign firms for 'disregarding the needs of the national economy' when there is no reason to suppose that domestic capital would behave any differently. Criticism must be directed at the system. This example also suggests that nationalisation or state control of industry is likely to be relatively ineffective as long as the imperatives of competition in a world market remain.

The second most important fact about (large) multi-nationals is that they are large, and generally have a substantial degree of monopoly power. The development of multi-national firms has generally followed on from the emergence of monopoly capital on a national scale simply because large firms have the organisational resources to control operations scattered over several countries and to deal with the legal and financial complications involved. Much of the literature, especially on multi-nationals in underdeveloped countries, conflates the effects of capitalism, of monopoly capitalism, and of foreign capital under the single heading of the impact of multi-national companies. This is understandable, since these firms often represent just about the first appearance of modern industrial capitalism in underdeveloped areas; it does not, however, make for analytical clarity.

It would be a mistake to overstate the novelty of multi-nationals. Merchant capital has operated internationally since its beginnings. The organisation and financing of mines, plantations, etc., abroad also goes back to the beginnings of capitalism. By the late nineteenth century, international flows of capital were occurring on a large scale, and a noticeable part of this flow of capital took the form of direct investment, that is the investment of capital in productive activity abroad by a firm already engaged in production in its home territory. Multi-national firms today generally (though not always) have the bulk of their activities located within the boundaries of the state where they have legal domicile and their head office. Nevertheless, it is possible to speak today, even if only as a tendency rather than an established fact, of companies which look over the whole world for potential locations for production, which have a 'global perspective'.

The emergence and significance of multi-national corporations cannot be adequately analysed at the level of the firm; it must be seen as part of a much wider process of internationalisation of production and of capital (see Palloix, 1973). Multi-national firms can be seen as organisations that channel the international movement of goods, of capital, of technical knowledge and organisational capacity, and of skilled personnel. They are not by any means the only channel for any of these flows. Relations between capitalist firms (within a single country or in different countries) can range across a whole spectrum from impersonal market exchange to incorporation under a single ownership; there are, for example, licensing arrangements for the use of technology, brand names, etc., joint ventures, management contracts, and 'turnkey' contracts for the supply of complete industrial plants together with the necessary training for those who are to operate them.

More specifically, the emergence of multi-nationals is the result of the process of concentration and centralisation of capital on a world scale, in the context of this continuing internationalisation of capitalism. It would be very surprising if the formation of giant monopoly firms were restricted within national boundaries; in fact, of course, it has not been. Bukharin analysed these processes (chapter 5 above), but made a judgment, based on the situation at the time when he wrote, that the formation of national blocs of capital would be the dominant tendency; it has not turned out quite that way. The multiplicity of linkages between capitalist firms across national boundaries represents the internationalisation of the 'relations of mutual dependence and domination' described by Hilferding at the level of a single national economy (see chapter 4 above).

Michalet (1976) argues that the development of multi-nationals is the defining feature of the imperialist stage of capitalism. He starts by opposing two conceptions of the world economy. Neo-classical theory deals with relations between distinct nation states, assuming free mobility of capital and labour within but not between nations. This approach he calls 'international economics'. Many Marxists (Marx, Luxemburg, Amin) have adopted this approach. The alternative approach, 'world economics', conceives of production and capitalist relations of production as international, or rather world-wide.

Lenin is found not guilty of adopting the first of these approaches (where even Bukharin does not completely escape the charge) but is, instead, found to be incomplete and ambiguous in his analysis. Michalet thus feels free to 'reread' (rewrite?) Lenin. He argues that it is capital export that is the fundamental characteristic of Lenin's imperialist stage, but he insists that the essential thing is not the export of *capitals* (money capital) but the export of *capital* (i.e. of capitalist relations of production). He thus has much in common with Rey. Capitalist relations of production on a world scale are created by *direct investment* by firms or financial groups which create subsidiaries abroad (as opposed to *portfolio investment* through loans or the purchase of shares as purely financial assets). The emergence of large monopoly firms and of finance capital is a necessary precondition for the creation of overseas subsidiaries. Michalet thus identifies imperialism (in Lenin's sense) directly with capital export and the emergence of multi-national firms. He dates the start of this trend to around 1900, though it was held back by depression and war, so that it appears even now as a novel phenomenon.

Capital export takes three main forms, each of which predominates in successive stages in the formation of a world economy. Firstly, capital export in Lenin's time was aimed mainly at obtaining raw materials. This is of declining relative importance now. Secondly, it may be aimed at penetrating markets that cannot be effectively penetrated by exports. This is the dominant form today, as a result of oligopolistic rivalry (and possibly general 'realisation' problems; Michalet is unclear on this). This form of capital export generates a structure in which production facilities are replicated in several different countries. Thirdly, and of increasing importance, capital export may be aimed at exploiting cheap labour to produce goods for re-export to the 'home' country or to third markets. This leads to the creation of integrated production organisations cutting across national boundaries, and is the form that Michalet stresses.

Michalet describes and emphasises a real movement to transfer production to the low-wage periphery, not merely by way of 'import substitution' (the second motive above) but to produce for the large markets of the centre and the whole world. I have already mentioned this possibility and argued that it has been neglected by most Marxist writers. Michalet, however, argues that it will not eliminate the centre-periphery gap, since capital intensive methods of production will keep employment in the periphery low and hence keep wages down. He does not, however, except in passing (p. 154), note the possibility that wage and/or employment levels in the centre might be dragged down towards those in the periphery.

Like many other writers, Michalet argues that the growth of multi-national companies and of relations of production on a world scale represents a lessening of the importance of the nation state. Here I think he falls into confusion. It is true that the internationalisation of capital makes the neo-classical conception of the world system in terms of distinct national economics increasingly irrelevant, but this is quite different from arguing the irrelevance of the nation as a site of class conflict, of political integration, and of a state apparatus that has at its command more potent weapons than those of monetary and fiscal policy. I will argue below that the nation state in this sense is a very important and durable institution.

I shall not give a complete survey of the literature on multi-nationals; it is rather scrappy and much of it is irrelevant to the topic of imperialism. It is better to look at the effect of multinationals, along with other aspects of capitalism, in the context of more specific problems. Perhaps the most influential writer on the subject has been Hymer, who started out writing from a critical and objective standpoint within the bourgeois tradition and then adopted a Marxist standpoint not long before his tragic death (see Hymer, 1972, 1976; Hymer and Rowthorn, 1970). Radice (1975) provides a useful collection of articles, which also has a bibliography.

The most important result of the emergence of multi-nationals is that the expansion of the *national capital* of a particular country (i.e. of the firms based there) is no longer tied directly to the expansion of the *national economy*. The implications of this are explored in the next two sections.

II Central capital: unity or rivalry?

Multi-national corporations, by definition, operate in several nation states. Other capitalist firms may be involved in the world economy through production for export, use of imported materials or components, through the use of technology on licence from abroad or through the export of technology, and so on. Commercial and financial capital is also internationalised. None of this means that capital exists that does not have a nationality, a definite base in a particular capitalist nation state. The idea that multi-national firms are somehow above the petty conflicts of nation states is an ideological fiction designed to defuse nationalist opposition to foreign capital.

Virtually all multi-nationals have in fact a very clear national base; not only does the parent company have a legal domicile (the use of tax havens may make legal registration misleading), but the company has originated within a particular country, and in almost all cases its top management is recruited there and the largest part of its capital and production is still located in its home country. The few exceptions consist of firms based in very small countries (e.g. Nestlé of Switzerland) and the two Anglo-Dutch giants (Shell and Unilever), which have a dual nationality.

Capital and the nation state have grown up together. The *analytical* primacy, in Marxist theory, of the economic over the political does not imply a *historical* order, nor does it imply that the division of the world into distinct nation states and the determination of their boundaries can be explained at the economic level. At the beginnings of capitalism, and for a long time after, the productive activities of industrial capital were locally based while the markets it served were as often local or international as national. It would be a mistake to think of an integrated national economy or national 'social formation' coming into existence and then conjuring up a state to suit its needs. Rather, the existence of a state (and the extension of its boundaries to the point where the resistance of other nation states limited further expansion) created and delimited national interests, national markets and so on. Each capital looked to its 'own' state for support against other capitals forming in other nation states and, through the common need for state support, formed an alliance with other regional capitals within the same nation. The need for compromise between different sectional interests within the capitalist class, and the need to contain conflict with other classes, has created a dense network of political and ideological links which is what constitutes a 'nation'.

As capital extends outside national boundaries, it must, of course, create links with other states as well, at least to the extent that it needs conditions that can only be provided by state action (a legal framework, a monetary system, infrastructure, etc.). Murray (1971) has discussed these questions, and drawn the general conclusion that internationalisation weakens the nation state *vis-à-vis* private capital, a conclusion contested by Warren (1971) and (briefly but cogently) by Rowthorn (1971). Rowthorn argues, in my view rightly, that the key question is not about the power of the state *vis-à-vis* particular capitals, but about how a state can support its own capital when it operates abroad.

The essential point is that capital that operates internationally needs the support of a home state to protect its interests. The whole range of needs that are met internally by the state (protection of property, enforcement of contracts, etc.) are met internationally by interstate negotiations and agreements. A large part of the diplomatic apparatus through which nation states deal with each other (in time of peace) has grown up precisely to negotiate the regulation of commercial activities. A stateless corporation, while not perhaps in principle impossible, would be at a crushing disadvantage, since it would have no representation in the system of legalised coercion.

Rowthorn (1971) has taken the analysis further, looking at the particular example of Britain. British capital is relatively strong, while the British national economy is relatively weak. Individual firms respond by shifting more of their activities abroad, where growth prospects are better, thus further weakening the British economy. In the end, however, this weakens the British state's capacity to defend their interests, and 'nationalist' policy measures to improve the performance of the national economy are blocked by the threat of retaliation against the vulnerable foreign interests of British capital. 'Leading sections of the British bourgeoisie have been effectively ''denationalised'', not through their own weakness, but through the weakness of the British state and their own home base' (Rowthorn, 1971). This accounts for the anxiety of British capital that Britain should join the EEC, which may provide, ultimately, a more substantial home base. The strength of a particular nation state and its capacity to defend the interests of its national capital thus depends on the strength of the national *economy* as well as the national *capital*.

The history of the capitalist world economy has seen periods of acute rivalry between capitalist powers, separated by periods of relative peace. Marx wrote at a time when it seemed reasonable to predict the obsolescence of the nation state, while Lenin and his contemporaries analysed a period when inter-imperialist rivalry was at its most violent. After the Second World War, the United States emerged as very much the strongest capitalist power, and when Marxist discussion of imperialism revived it was generally assumed, almost without debate, that inter-imperialist rivalry had been superseded by US dominance. This seemed particularly obvious to those American writers who took a special interest in Latin America, the area most clearly within the American sphere of influence.

However, the rapid recovery of the European and Japanese economies, the weakness of the US dollar and the American defeat in Vietnam raised doubts about this view of the present stage of imperialism, and opened up the debate again.

The question, then, concerns the kind of relations between the national capitals of the advanced capitalist countries that exist and the future developments that are to be expected. There seem to me to be two issues involved here. Firstly, what are the relative strengths of the different national groups and, in particular, is American capital increasing its lead over other national groups or being overhauled by them? Secondly, are national capitals remaining distinct from each other, or are they tending to merge together with the progress of internationalisation?

If a fusion of national capitals is taking place, one possibility is that it might take place on a relatively equal basis. This is the only case in which the nationality of capital might give way to genuine supra-nationality, raising questions about the future of the nation state. No one, to my knowledge, has asserted that such a fusion is taking place, or could take place in the foreseeable future, on a global basis; the strength of US capital is such that any fusion would be US dominated. However, a number of writers have anticipated such a fusion on a smaller scale within the EEC, to form a unified European capital. Mandel (1967, 1975) predicts such a development, which is also discussed, more cautiously, by Rowthorn (1971). It must be said that the formation of truly European companies (as opposed to the takeover and absorption of a company from one country by another from a different country) has not progressed at the pace that these authors expected; the Pirelli-Dunlop merger has not been a success, and has not been copied. Fusion of capital on a European scale would strengthen European capital *vis-à-vis* that of America, while continued divisions in Europe correspondingly favour American capital. The prediction of Europe-wide fusion of national capitals is of course bound up with the possible evolution of the EEC into something closer to a nation state, where it is, at the moment, little more than a loose alliance. The slow development of European unity reinforces the argument above that nationality is a very deeply rooted thing; the dense network of political links that constitutes a nation state represents the institutionalisation of a multitude of compromises between classes, fractions of classes and other interest groups, which is very difficult to reconstruct on a new basis.

An alternative possibility is that national capitals are merging together under US dominance by the absorption of enterprises from other capitalist states by American multi-nationals or by their subordination through licensing agreements, subcontracting arrangements and so on. This seems to be Poulanzas's position (1975, chapter 1). This case, however, differs little from one in which national capitals remain distinct, but in which other imperialist nations accept a role subordinate to that of the US simply because they know that any challenge to American domination would be sure to fail; this argument has been stated forcefully by Nicolaus (1969). Many writers have taken the general position that US capital is overwhelmingly dominant in modern imperialism without spelling out the details (for example, Magdoff and Sweezy, 1969; Magdoff, 1969). This belief in the effective unity of the imperialist centres is generally combined with the view that the struggle against capitalism and imperialism is, and will be, centred in the under-developed periphery and will not arise from contradictions within the imperialist centres.

Prima facie evidence for the dominance of American capital is easy to find. American corporations predominate in any listing of the world's largest firms. American domestic production and overseas investments are much larger than those of any other country, and the American lead is largest in the most advanced branches of production (computers, micro-electronics, automation, aerospace, etc.). The size and growth of American investments in Europe are particularly significant. The breaking up of European colonial empires has enabled American capital to penetrate and, in some cases, dominate areas of the world formerly denied to it (hence American 'anti colonialism' in the post-war period). American military dominance in the non-communist world is obvious. These facts are not in dispute.

What is in dispute is the *trend* of development. America clearly enjoyed a quite exceptional superiority immediately after the Second World War and one would expect some relative recovery by other powers. Some writers argue that the more rapid recent growth in Europe and Japan as compared to America is no more than a return to the trend (e.g. Poulanzas, 1975), while others argue that it represents a real threat to US dominance, and presages an epoch in which there will be relative equality between the main capitalist powers. Mandel (1967, 1975) and Rowthorn (1971) both predict a narrowing of the gap between America and other imperialist centres and a consequent intensification of rivalry.

Rather oddly, on both sides of the debate attention has focused on the relative strength of American and *European* capital. The relative failure (to date) of movements towards European unity has hampered the competitive strength of European capital, and it has been justly remarked that the largest beneficiary of the formation of the EEC has been American capital in Europe, which has been much quicker to treat Europe as a unified market. However, on present trends it is *Japanese* capital which looks the more formidable rival; it is not divided on national lines, and has maintained a rate of growth quite unprecedented in the history of capitalism for some three decades.

The debate centres on the interpretation of the large flow of capital from America to Europe and the consequent rapid growth of American capital in Europe. Poulanzas (1975) regards this as decisive evidence of American hegemony, on the grounds that the export of capital is the dominant factor in the expansion of capital in the imperialist period; he offers little evidence for this particular assertion other than a reference to Lenin. Rowthorn, drawing on his work with Hymer (Rowthorn and Hymer, 1971), counters this ingeniously. American capital still operates predominantly in America, European capital in Europe; since European economies were expanding more rapidly than the American economy, American capital had to increase its penetration of the European market simply to maintain its relative position. (Expansion in other markets could not offset the loss of ground relative to Europe, since the Japanese market proved difficult to penetrate, and other markets were very small by comparison.) This could be done either by export or by investment in Europe; since lower European wages gave the edge to producers located in Europe, export of capital was chosen. A large net expansion of exports to Europe unaccompanied by capital export would be difficult in any case, since it would upset the European balance of payments and force corrective action (as indeed happened during the post-war dollar shortage). Combining the effects of relative market growth rates and changing market shares, 'big American firms are having and will have increasing difficulty in keeping ahead of their foreign rivals' (Rowthorn, 1971, p. 163).

Rowthorn thus accepts the view that American investment in Europe represents, in itself, a gain by American capital relative to its rivals, but argues that it is offset by the fact that European companies still had the larger share of the more rapidly growing European market. Mandel (1967) similarly argues that American expansion in Europe is a 'defeat' for European capital. However, the relative rate of growth of different markets cannot be taken as given. Not only is the more rapid growth in Europe the result as well as the cause of the greater dynamism of European capital, but the inflow of investment from America may well have contributed to European growth. American investment may thus have helped rather than hindered the expansion of European capital. In more general terms, the expansion of one capital may be complementary to, rather than competitive with, the expansion of others. This is relevant to the question of rivalry.

If we accept that there is a trend towards relative equality between a small number of imperialist centres, as Mandel and Rowthorn argue, we must ask what kind of relation between them is likely. Rowthorn seems to take it for granted that there will be rivalry and antagonism: 'Relations between capitals are always to some extent antagonistic, the degree of antagonism depending both on the area of actual or potential competition and on its intensity' (Rowthorn, 1971). This is undoubtedly true of individual capitals at a micro-economic level; the overall rate of expansion of the market in which they are competing with other firms is beyond their control, and they are struggling over shares of a given market. However, it is not clear that similar antagonism must exist between capitalist *states*. As I have pointed out above, once the overall rate of expansion of the whole economy is treated as a variable, the expansion of one capital may be complementary to that of another. The state is in a position to try to reconcile the two aspects of the relation between capitals, complementarity and antagonism. It may thus be possible to resurrect Kautsky's notion of 'ultra-imperialism', that imperialist powers could agree to cooperate and exploit the world jointly. We do not have to make a simple choice between predicting inter-imperialist rivalry on the one hand or ultra-imperialism on the other; it is more relevant to ask how far the recognition of some common interests can contain the antagonisms generated by other, divergent interests.

That some degree of co-operation, some limits to antagonism, are taken for granted is indicated by the fact that few recent writers consider the possibility of inter-imperialist war (which Lenin and Bukharin regarded as inevitable). Sutcliffe (1972) mentions this possibility in passing, as do one or two others. My own opinion is that if states really did act rationally in the interests of their national capital as a whole, as some rather simple Marxist analyses have assumed, then it would not be difficult for them to co-operate; Kautsky would be proved right. However, this is not an adequate analysis of the state. State policies are the outcome of real political practice (this is what the 'relative autonomy' of the state means) which has constantly to compromise between the interests of different groups and is deeply affected by a long history of such compromises and the ideologies that go with them. As a result, state policies are not necessarily rational in any simple sense.

Since the date of the main writings discussed here, the world capitalist system has been subjected to a very severe test in the oil crisis and the subsequent world recession. Although co-operation between the major capitalist states has clearly not been perfect, I think that most commentators would have predicted far more severe rivalry than in fact occurred. The measures taken by the oil companies to redirect supplies during the period when some oil importing states were embargoed by Arab suppliers, and the surprisingly successful expedients taken to preserve the world monetary system from potentially disruptive movements of 'petrodollars', are examples of private sector adaptability based on inter-state co-operation. I would conclude that although the dominance of the United States is coming to an end, it would be unwise for revolutionaries to expect inter-imperialist rivalry to lead to any immediate breakdown of the world capitalist system.

III Capitalist development in the 'Third World'

The classical Marxists assumed that each country must go through successive stages of development; the capitalist stage performed the historic task of creating a proletariat and laying the material basis for the succeeding stage of socialism. Lenin and Trotsky argued that the bourgeoisie in Russia (then a relatively backward country) was too weak to carry through the political tasks of the bourgeois revolution, so that the proletariat had to take the lead and could then carry straight on to the socialist revolution. The evolution of a relatively backward country differed from that of the more advanced centres. This argument, however, still presupposes the existence of a proletariat adequate to the task, and thus a certain degree of capitalist development.

However, in the first half of the twentieth century, there were few signs of capitalist development in underdeveloped countries, and many Marxists came to argue a position almost diametrically opposed to that of the classics. Where it had been argued that capitalist development had to come first to create the *possibility* of a socialist revolution, it was now argued that the absence of capitalist development made socialist revolution *necessary*. Frank is the leading exponent of this view, summed up in the title of one of his books, *Latin America: Underdevelopment or Revolution*. This shift of perspective entails a shift to a more voluntaristic concept of politics and to treating the peasantry or lumpenproletariat, rather than the industrial proletariat, as the revolutionary class. This trend in political thinking was encouraged by the success of the Chinese and Cuban revolutions.

What are the issues? At the time when Britain, followed by western

Europe and North America, industrialised, the world economy was relatively unintegrated. Transport was expensive and risky, so that goods were traded only where production costs were very different in different areas. Most basic subsistence goods and means of production were produced locally, initially by craft techniques. There was therefore scope for local development of capitalist production at the expense of older methods, while competition from more advanced centres was limited. Capital was relatively immobile, and technology was largely embodied in the skills and experience of the labour force. Thus any capitalist development that did take place created an independent local bourgeoisie and a local concentration of skills and technical knowledge. Independent capitalist development in many centres was possible, and its progress was determined largely by local conditions (except where it was suppressed by a colonial state). Frank and Wallerstein would not accept this analysis; they argue that an integrated capitalist world economy has existed from an early stage. I think that the facts are against them. Up to the industrial revolution the bulk of intercontinental trade was in luxuries such as sugar (slaves are an exceptional case), and the impact of European colonial dominance was primarily through its effects on the mode of production in the subordinated areas.

During the later part of the nineteenth century transport costs fell dramatically, organisational forms were found that permitted large scale international capital flows, and the separation of mental from manual labour led to a systematisation of technical knowledge that permitted international transfers of technology. All of this, of course, is the result of capitalist development, and in its turn it led to the progressive creation of a relatively integrated world capitalist economy. The situation facing an underdeveloped country today is therefore quite different from that of earlier periods. One can ask whether industrialisation on the pattern set by, say, Britain is possible today. One can also ask whether industrialisation on that pattern is a relevant standard to set in present day conditions.

On the one hand, underdeveloped countries industrialising now face competition from advanced centres with centuries of capital accumulation and technical progress behind them. As a result, a world pattern of specialisation has been established in which the underdeveloped areas export mainly primary products and import industrial products. Industrialisation means displacing these imports (or breaking into export markets) rather than displacing primitive craft industries. On the other hand, capital and technology can now be imported, and rising wages in the advanced countries offset the advantages they gain from high productivity.

It is generally agreed that there has been a substantial amount of industrial development in the Third World in recent years. Typically this has taken the form, to begin with, of import substitution, starting with the production of relatively 'light' consumer goods using imported capital equipment, often using at least some imported funds and with some sort of involvement of multi-national companies (wholly or partly owned subsidiaries, joint subsidiaries, licensing arrangements, etc.).

The central issue in debate is whether this sort of industrialisation merely reproduces relations of dependence between centre and periphery in new forms (as Amin, Frank, Sutcliffe and others argue) or whether it marks the beginning of a breakdown of the centre-periphery division (as Warren argues).

Sutcliffe (1972) is one of the few writers who have tackled the question of the prospects for development in the present underdeveloped countries explicitly, and who have recognised clearly how different the present Marxist orthodoxy is from classical Marxism. (Barratt-Brown, 1972, covers some of the same ground.) Sutcliffe recognises the facts of industrial growth in the periphery, but argues that these are not enough to answer the two critical questions: can there be a full independent industrialisation like that of Japan, or failing that, can there be enough development to create 'progressive socio-political forces', i.e. a proletariat like that of Russia in 1917? Apart from some problems of measurement (the figures may overstate the extent of development) he gives two reasons for discounting the observed industrial growth. Firstly, growth has often been by import substitution concentrated in the production of luxury consumer goods for which the demand is limited, and this type of industrialisation reinforces the income distribution and social structure which limit demand. This is the argument of the 'dependency theorists' (see Furtado, 1973); to be acceptable it needs to be supported by some explanation of the failure of industrialisation to penetrate into other branches of the economy or into export markets. Secondly, growth of industrial output may not be matched by growth in employment, since high productivity, capital intensive methods are used. With production in the hands of foreign capital, the result is 'the absence of a bourgeoisie and the absence of a proletariat'.

Hence capitalist development may not create the kind of class structure that Marx described, while the great majority of the population are left unaffected or even worse off. This 'marginalisation' of masses of people has been stressed by many writers. It should be remarked that Marx in fact predicted a growing 'relative surplus population', and it could be said that the underdeveloped countries fit Marx's model of capitalist accumulation more closely than do the advanced countries.

Sutcliffe proposed various criteria for 'independent' industrialisation. This, he says, 'does not mean autarky, but carries with it the idea that industrialisation is not merely "derived" from the industrialisation of another economy' (p. 174). I cannot see why the origins of industrialisation matter: the results are surely more important. His criteria for economic independence are that production should be oriented principally to the domestic market, that investment funds should be raised locally or at least should be under local control, that there should be a diversified industrial structure, and that technology should, in some (not very clearly defined) sense, be independent. The basis of these criteria is not clear; they seem to me to show up the rather nebulous character of the concept of dependence.

Economic independence also has its 'social and political counterparts'. Here Sutcliffe's argument seems stronger:

> Economic development only happens when the surplus gets into the hands of those who will use it productively. . . . This partly implies the need for an industrial bourgeoisie supported by a state that is capable of defending its interests. . . . The state must be largely independent both of those local social interests opposed to industrialisation and also of foreign interests. (Sutcliffe, 1972, pp. 176–7)

This seems to me to be the nub of the matter: is an independent national bourgeoisie formed? Independence in this sense does require that development be financed locally and under local control, but it requires 'technological independence' only in the sense that use of foreign technology may lead to effective foreign control through conditions attached to licensing agreements, and the like. (P. Patnaik, 1973, gives a detailed case study of the kind of dependence that can result from reliance on imported technology through joint subsidiaries.) I see no reason why an independent capitalist class should not be formed on the basis of export led industrialisation or copying of techniques; in an interdependent world economy a considerable degree of specialisation and large scale exchanges of goods, capital and technology are to be expected.

Sutcliffe's concern with technological independence seems to stem mainly from a different concern. He evidently considers that 'foreign' technology (can technology have a nationality?) is unsuitable because it is too capital intensive (p. 176). This is a line that has been widely argued; capital intensive technology means relatively little employment, which has further consequences for the structure of demand. However, it is likely that capitalist firms, whether foreign or national, will adopt the technique that maximises profits. Underdeveloped countries constitute a large enough market for capital goods for it to be profitable to adapt technology to the prices (and in particular, wage rates) that prevail there. It is thus unlikely that national capital using locally devised techniques would make very different choices. There are, in any case, reasons to think that a choice of technique that maximises reinvestible surplus may be the optimum choice from the point of view of long-run growth (Dobb, 1955, 1960; Sen, 1968; Amin, 1976, p.230).

Sutcliffe argues that independent development (in the sense in which he has defined it) is unlikely, unless the links between metropolis and satellite are disrupted by inter-imperialist war or acute capitalist crisis. The prospects of development are limited by the relative backwardness of the underdeveloped countries, by monopolistic control based on technological superiority, and by the pumping of surplus out of under-developed countries by repatriation of profits and by unequal exchange. These are all familiar arguments.

Warren (1973) makes a frontal assault on the present radical or 'Third Worldist' orthodoxy represented by Sutcliffe. He sums up his conclusions as follows:

> empirical observations suggest that the prospects for successful capitalist development . . . of a significant number of major underdeveloped countries are quite good; . . . that the period since the Second World War has been marked by a substantial upsurge in capitalist social relations and productive forces (especially industrialisation) in the Third World . . . that the imperialist countries' policies and their overall impact on the Third World actually favour its industrialisation; and that the ties of dependence . . . have been and are being markedly loosened. . . . None of this is meant to imply that imperialism has ceased to exist. . . . What we wish to indicate are elements of change. (Warren, 1973, pp. 3–4)

Warren puts forward a considerable amount of empirical material to substantiate these claims; it would be impossible to summarise it here. It is, in any case, somewhat beside the point, since many writers have conceded (if somewhat grudgingly) the fact of a certain degree of industrialisation; what is really at issue is the interpretation of these facts. Warren shows that industrial production has mainly been for the home market, and that capital is substantially raised within the country concerned, but it has been frequently argued that 'import substitution' (by definition directed to the home market) carried out by multi-nationals using local finance simply reproduces ties of dependence. The empirical facts cited are therefore not decisive.

Warren's essential argument is that development based on foreign (or foreign controlled) capital is complementary to the development of national capital (p. 39), given a state apparatus which exerts pressure on foreign business and promotes national capitalist development. He argues this largely in the context of resource based international enterprises (fuel and minerals), showing that local governments have successfully extracted greater shares of revenue and greater control. Since the date at which he wrote, of course, the OPEC countries have gone much further in this direction. The same developments, he argues, are taking place in manufacturing. In particular, the position of the 'host' country is strengthened as its nationals acquire greater experience and knowledge in particular industries, which they inevitably do as a result of the simple presence of the industry and even more as a result of government pressures to employ and promote local residents. Partly owned subsidiaries of multi-national companies tend to come more and more under the control of local shareholders, who thus form the basis of a national capitalist class. Multi-nationals serve, in fact, to transfer technology (p. 29), and, more generally, modern capitalism into the Third World.

Warren argues strongly that socialists have implicitly *defined* development in such a way that capitalist development is effectively ruled out. If development is defined by reference to the 'needs of the masses', then Marxists are unlikely to accept that capitalist development can fit the bill, but this leaves us unable to distinguish between continued stagnation, and development that is successful, in capitalist terms, in that it creates conditions for continued reproduction of capital. On this point Warren seems to me to be absolutely right.

What of imperialism as a system for draining surplus value from the periphery to the centre? Warren argues forcefully that even if the outward flow of repatriated profit exceeds the inward flow of investment this does not demonstrate that the economic effect is harmful, since 'what exactly is done with the capital "in between", so to speak, is ignored . . . under capitalism exploitation is the reverse side of the advance of productive forces' (p. 39). Capitalism both exploits and promotes development:

> If the extension of capitalism into non-capitalist areas of the world created an international system of inequality and exploitation called imperialism, it simultaneously created the conditions for the destruction of this system by the spread of capitalist social relations and productive forces throughout the non-capitalist world. Such has been our thesis, as it was the thesis of Marx, Lenin, Luxemburg and Bukharin. (Warren, 1973, p. 41)

There is an obvious objection to this view of imperialism. In the time since Lenin wrote, there has hardly been a single example of successful capitalist industrialisation. (Japan was well on the way before the First World War.) Over this whole period, the gap between advanced and underdeveloped countries has been widening, and it was precisely in response to this massively important fact that Marxists turned away from the classical theories. Warren's reply is that the period since the Second World War has seen the breakup of colonial empires and the establishment of independent states in the Third World. We must presumably see the history of imperialism in stages: first the creation of a basis for national (political) independence, and then full capitalist development.

National independence is crucial, according to Warren, both because it provides a political framework for popular pressures for higher living standards, which compel governments to follow policies of industrial development, and also because it breaks the monopoly hold of the colonial power, thus permitting the newly independent state to take advantage of inter-imperialist and East-West rivalries to bargain for favourable treatment. Capitalist development does not require the prior existence of a 'national bourgeoisie'; other ruling classes can and must promote industrialisation. 'These "industrialisers" may themselves become industrial bourgeoisies or may be displaced by the industrial Frankensteins they have created or they may become fused with them' (pp. 42–3). In addition, imperialist states have positively supported development (by right-wing, nationalist regimes) in order to contain socialism.

Warren has been criticised by Emmanuel (1974) and by McMichael, Petras and Rhodes (1974). Emmanuel is mainly concerned to reiterate his own argument that changes in the pattern of specialisation will have no effect without an alteration in relative wages (the 'independent' variable). This view ignores the growth in employment (if at low wages), and the transformation of social relations of production that flow from a change in the pattern of specialisation. McMichael, Petras and Rhodes complain, with justification, that Warren does not have a complete theoretical framework, and that he selects his empirical data rather capriciously. Unfortunately, one could make exactly the same criticisms of their reply. This interchange shows how much remains to be done to construct an adequate analysis of the present world system.

My main criticism of Warren is that he is too ready to generalise and to argue that industrial development is likely throughout the Third World. His own evidence shows that this development is proceeding very unevenly, and there are good reasons to expect increasing, rather than decreasing, unevenness. If large-scale modern industry establishes itself in a number of centres (and this seems to me to be likely), there will be intense competition between them. The successful 'new centres' will have a tremendous competitive edge, since they will combine the advantages of modern levels of productivity across a wide range of industries with low wages. This situation differs from those discussed by Emmanuel and Amin (chapters 9, 10 above), who assume that modern levels of productivity in low-wage areas are confined to a few lines of production. The advantage of low wages can persist for a long time, since capital intensive methods of production keep the demand for labour low and the persistence of mass unemployment holds wages down. In these circumstances, both the existing advanced countries (handicapped by high wages and by the costs of safety measures, social expenditures, etc., won by the working class) and the remaining underdeveloped countries (held back by a backward and incomplete industrial structure) would be at a competitive disadvantage and could be faced with severe problems. The prospect thus seems to me to be not of a simple reduction in inequality between nations (as Warren predicts), but rather of a shifting of the relative positions of different areas within a system of inequality that is likely to persist for a very long time (unless it is ended by revolution).

Warren's political conclusions, however, are valid and important. We must recognise that opposition to the dominance of the major imperial powers is not necessarily genuine anti-imperialism, and may represent no more than a desire by a newly formed bourgeoisie to establish itself within a world system that it does not wish to change. Socialists have frequently been deceived by anti-imperialist rhetoric into supporting viciously reactionary regimes. In any Marxist analysis the fundamental division must be that between classes, between capitalists and workers and not between nations.

IV Summary and conclusion

Marxist writers since the Second World War have generally predicted continued United States dominance in the capitalist world, and have argued that there is little prospect of underdeveloped countries improving their relative position without a complete break with the world capitalist system. Neither of these propositions has been supported with conclusive arguments, and there are good reasons for expecting that European and, especially, Japanese capital may challenge American dominance, and also that established industries in advanced countries could be seriously threatened by the development of major new industrial centres in low-wage areas. At the present stage of development of Marxist theory it is not possible to make firm predictions.

It will inevitably take some time to sift through the very large volume of work published in the 1970s, but considerable progress has been made and there is a real prospect of creating an integrated Marxist analysis of the world economy. This book is intended as a contribution to that essential task.

Bibliography

Adam, G. (1975), 'Multinational firms and worldwide sourcing', in
Radice (1975), originally published 1973.

Alavi, H. (1975), 'India and the colonial mode of production', in
R. Miliband and J. Savile (eds), *The Socialist Register 1975*, Merlin,
London.

Althusser, L. and Balibar, E. (1970), *Reading Capital*, New Left Books,
London, originally published in French, 1968.

Amin, S. (1966), *L'Economie du Maghreb*, 2 volumes, Editions de Minuit,
Paris.

Amin, S. (1971), *L'Afrique de l'ouest bloquée*, Editions de Minuit, Paris.

Amin, S. (1974), *Accumulation on a World Scale*, Monthly Review Press,
New York, originally published in French, 1970.

Amin, S. (1976), *Unequal Development*, Harvester Press, Hassocks, and
Monthly Review Press, New York, originally published in French, 1973.

Amin, S. (1977), *Imperialism and Unequal Development*, Harvester Press,
Hassocks, and Monthly Review Press, New York, originally published in
French, 1976.

Amin, S. (1978), *The Law of Value and Historical Materialism*, Monthly
Review Press, New York, originally published in French, 1977.

Anderson, P. (1974), *Lineages of the Absolutist State*, New Left Books,
London.

Andreff, W. (1976), *Profits et structures du capitalisme mondial*,
Calmann-Lévy, Paris.

Arrighi, G. (1966), 'The political economy of Rhodesia', *New Left
Review*, Sept.–Oct.

Arrighi, G. (1970a), 'International corporations, labour aristocracies
and economic development in tropical Africa', in Rhodes (1970).

Arrighi, G. (1970b), 'Labour supplies in historical perspective: a study
of the proletarianisation of the African peasantry in Rhodesia',
Journal of Development Studies, 3, originally published in Italian, 1969.

Arrighi, G. (1978), *The Geometry of Imperialism*, New Left Books,
London.

Arrighi, G. and Saul, J. S. (1968), 'Socialism and economic development
in tropical Africa', *Journal of Modern African Studies*, 2.

Arrighi, G. and Saul, J. S. (1969), 'Nationalism and revolution in
sub-Saharan Africa', in R. Miliband and J. Savile (eds), *The
Socialist Register 1969*, Merlin, London.

Arrighi, G. and Saul, J. S. (1973), *Essays on the Political Economy of Africa*, Monthly Review Press, New York.

Avinieri, S. (1969), 'Introduction' to Marx (1969).

Banaji, J. (1972), 'For a theory of colonial modes of production', *Economic and Political Weekly*, Bombay, VII, 52, December.

Banaji, J. (1977), 'Modes of production in a materialist conception of history', *Capital and Class*, 3, Autumn.

Baran, P. (1973), *The Political Economy of Growth*, Penguin, Harmondsworth, originally published 1957.

Baran, P. and Sweezy, P. (1968), *Monopoly Capital*, Penguin, Harmondsworth, originally published 1966.

Barratt-Brown, M. (1972), 'A critique of Marxist theories of imperialism', in Owen and Sutcliffe (1972).

Barratt-Brown, M. (1974), *The Economics of Imperialism*, Penguin, Harmondsworth.

Bleaney, M. (1976), *Underconsumption Theories: A History and Critical Analysis*, Lawrence & Wishart, London.

Bradby, B. (1975), 'The destruction of natural economy', *Economy and Society*, IV, 2.

Braverman, H. (1974), *Labor and Monopoly Capital*, Monthly Review Press, New York.

Brenner, R. (1977), 'The origins of capitalist development: a critique of neo-Smithian Marxism', *New Left Review*, 104, July/August.

Brewer, A. (1980), 'On Amin's model of autocentric accumulation', *Capital and Class*, 10, Spring, also corrections, 11, Summer.

Bukharin, N. (1972a), *Imperialism and World Economy*, Merlin, London, originally published in Russian, 1917.

Bukharin, N. (1972b), *Imperialism and the Accumulation of Capital* (edited by K. Tarbuck), Allen Lane, London, originally published in Russian.

Chandler, A. and Redlich, F. (1961), 'Recent developments in American business administration and their conceptualisation', *Business History Review*, Spring.

Chattopadhyay, P. (1972a), 'On the question of the mode of production in Indian agriculture, a preliminary note', *Economic and Political Weekly*, Bombay, VII, 13, Review of Agriculture, March.

Chattopadhyay, P. (1972b), 'The mode of production in Indian agriculture, an anti-kritik', *Economic and Political Weekly*, Bombay, VII, 53, Review of Agriculture, December.

Cutler, A., Hindess, B., Hirst, P. and Hussain, A. (1977), *Marx's Capital and Capitalism Today*, 2 vols, Routledge & Kegan Paul, London.

Dobb, M. (1940), *Political Economy and Capitalism*, 2nd edition, Routledge & Kegan Paul, London, first edition published 1937.

Dobb, M. (1955), *On Economic Theory and Socialism*, Routledge & Kegan Paul, London.

Dobb, M. (1960), *Economic Growth and Planning*, Routledge & Kegan Paul, London.

Dobb, M. (1963), *Studies in the Development of Capitalism*, Routledge & Kegan Paul, London, originally published 1946.

Dos Santos, T. (1970), 'The structure of dependence', *American Economic Review*, LX, May, reprinted in Wilber (1973).

Dumont, R. and Mazoyer, M. (1973), *Socialisms and Development*, Deutsch, London, originally published in French, 1969.

Emmanuel, A. (1972), *Unequal Exchange, A Study of the Imperialism of Trade*, New Left Books, London, and Monthly Review Press, New York, originally published in French, 1969.

Emmanuel, A. (1974), 'Myths of development versus myths of underdevelopment', *New Left Review*, 85, May/June.

Fann, K. and Hodges, D. (eds) (1971), *Readings in U.S. Imperialism*, Porter Sargent, Boston.

Foster-Carter, A. (1976), 'From Rostow to Gunder Frank: conflicting paradigms in the analysis of underdevelopment', *World Development*, IV, 3, March.

Foster-Carter, A. (1978), 'The modes of production controversy', *New Left Review*, 107, Jan./Feb.

Frank, A. G. (1969a), *Capitalism and Underdevelopment in Latin America*, revised edition, Modern Reader Paperbacks, New York, and London, first edition published 1967.

Frank, A. G. (1969b), *Latin America: Underdevelopment or Revolution*, Monthly Review Press, New York.

Frank, A. G. (1972), *Lumpenbourgeoisie: Lumpendevelopment*, Monthly Review Press, New York and London.

Frank, A. G. (1973), 'On feudal modes, models and methods of escaping capitalist reality', *Economic and Political Weekly*, Bombay, VIII, 1.

Frank, A. G. (1978), *Dependent Accumulation and Underdevelopment*, Macmillan, London.

Friedman, A. L. (1977), *Industry and Labour*, Macmillan, London.

Furtado, C. (1973), 'The concept of external dependence', in Wilber (1973).

Hay, D. and Morris, D. (1979), *Industrial Economics: Theory and Evidence*, Oxford University Press.

Hilferding, R. (1970), *Le Capital Financier*, Editions de Minuit, Paris, originally published in German, 1910.

Himmelweit, S. (1974), 'The continuing saga of the falling rate of profit – a reply to Mario Cogoy', *Bulletin of the Conference of Socialist Economists*, 9, Autumn.

Himmelweit, S. and Mohun, S. (1978), 'The anomalies of capital', *Capital and Class*, 6, Autumn.

Hobson, J. A. (1938), *Imperialism – a Study*, 3rd edition, Allen & Unwin, London, first edition published 1902.

Hodgson, G. (1974), 'The falling rate of profit', *New Left Review*, March/April.

Howard, M. C. and King, J. E. (1975), *The Political Economy of Marx*, Longman, London.

Hymer, S. (1972), 'The multinational corporation and the law of uneven development', in J. Bhagwati (ed.), *Economics and the World*

Order from the 1970s to the 1990s, Collier-Macmillan, New York. Reprinted in Radice (1975).

Hymer, S. (1976), *The International Operations of National Firms*, MIT Press, Cambridge, Mass., originally submitted as a PhD thesis, 1960.

Hymer, S. and Rowthorn, R. (1970), 'Multinational corporations and international oligopolies: the non-American challenge', in C. P. Kindelberger (ed.), *The International Corporation*, MIT Press, Cambridge, Mass.

Jalée, P. (1972), *Imperialism in the Seventies*, Okpaku Publishing, The Third Press, New York, originally published in French, 1970.

Kautsky, K. (1970), 'Ultra-imperialism', *New Left Review*, 59, Jan./Feb., originally published in German, 1914.

Kay, G. (1975), *Development and Underdevelopment*, Macmillan, London.

Kemp, T. (1967), *Theories of Imperialism*, Dobson, London.

Knei-Paz, B. (1978), *The Social and Political Thought of Leon Trotsky*, Clarendon Press, Oxford.

Krader, L. (1975), *The Asiatic Mode of Production*, Van Gorcum, Assen, Netherlands.

Laclau, E. (1971), 'Feudalism and capitalism in Latin America', *New Left Review*, 67, May/June, reprinted, with postscript, in Laclau (1977).

Laclau, E. (1977), *Politics and Ideology in Marxist Theory*, New Left Books, London.

Le Bris, E., Rey, P. P. and Samuel, M. (1976), *Capitalisme négrier*, Maspero, Paris.

Lenin, V. I. (1950), *Imperialism, the Highest Stage of Capitalism*, in *Selected Works*, vol. I, Foreign Languages Publishing House, Moscow, originally published in Russian, 1917.

Lenin, V. I. (1974), *The Development of Capitalism in Russia*, Progress Publishers, Moscow, originally published in Russian, 1899, second edition 1908.

Luxemburg, R. (1951), *The Accumulation of Capital*, Routledge & Kegan Paul, London, originally published in German, 1913.

Luxemburg, R. (1972), *The Accumulation of Capital – an Anti-Critique*, in Bukharin (1972b), originally published in German, 1921.

McEachern, D. (1976), 'The mode of production in India', *Journal of Contemporary Asia*.

McMichael, P., Petras, J. and Rhodes, R. (1974), 'Imperialism and the contradictions of development', *New Left Review*, 85, May/June.

Magdoff, H. (1969), *The Age of Imperialism*, Monthly Review Press, New York.

Magdoff, H. and Sweezy, P. (1969), 'Notes on the multinational corporation', *Monthly Review*, Oct./Nov., reprinted in Fann and Hodges (1971).

Magdoff, H. and Sweezy, P. (1975), 'The economic crisis in historical perspective', *Monthly Review*, March/April, reprinted in Magdoff and Sweezy (1977).

Magdoff, H. and Sweezy, P. (1977), *The End of Prosperity*, Monthly Review Press, New York.

Mandel, E. (1967), 'International capitalism and "supranationality"', in R. Miliband and J. Savile (eds), *The Socialist Register 1967*, Merlin, London.

Mandel, E. (1975), *Late Capitalism*, New Left Books, London, originally published in German, 1972.

Marx, K. (1957), *Capital*, vol. II, ed. F. Engels, Foreign Languages Publishing House, Moscow, originally published in German, 1885.

Marx, K. (1961), *Capital*, vol. I, Foreign Languages Publishing House, Moscow, originally published in German, 1867.

Marx, K. (1962), *Capital*, vol. III, ed. F. Engels, Foreign Languages Publishing House, Moscow, originally published in German, 1894.

Marx, K. (1969), *On Colonialism and Modernisation*, ed. with introduction by S. Avinieri, Doubleday Anchor, New York; collection of published and unpublished extracts, various dates.

Marx, K. (1976), *Preface and Introduction to a Contribution to the Critique of Political Economy*, Foreign Languages Publishing House, Pekin, preface originally published in German, 1859.

Marx, K. and Engels, F. (1971), *On Ireland*, Lawrence & Wishart; collection of published and unpublished extracts, various dates.

Marx, K. and Engels, F. (no date, a), *Manifesto of the Communist Party*, Foreign Languages Publishing House, Moscow, originally published in German, 1848.

Marx, K. and Engels, F. (no date, b), *On Colonialism*, Foreign Languages Publishing House, Moscow; collection of published and unpublished extracts, various dates.

Matthews, R. C. O. (1959), *The Trade Cycle*, Nisbet, London, and Cambridge University Press.

Meillassoux, C. (1964), *Anthropologie Economique des Gouro de Côte d'Ivoire*, Mouton, Paris.

Michalet, C. A. (1976), *Le Capitalisme mondiale*, Presses Universitaires de France, Paris.

Morishima, M. (1973), *Marx's Economics*, Cambridge University Press.

Morishima, M. (1974), 'Marx in the light of modern economic theory', *Econometrica*, XLII, July.

Morishima, M. (1976), 'Positive profits with negative surplus value – a comment', *Economic Journal*, September.

Murray, R. (1971), 'The internationalisation of capital and the nation state', *New Left Review*, 67, reprinted in Radice (1975).

Myrdal, G. (1957), *Economic Theory and Underdeveloped Regions*, Duckworth, London.

Nicolaus, M. (1969), 'Who will bring the mother down?', *Leviathan*, I, 5, reprinted in Fann and Hodges (1971).

Owen, R. and Sutcliffe, B. (eds) (1972), *Studies in the Theory of Imperialism*, Longman, London.

Palloix, C. (1969), *Problèmes de croissance en économie ouverte*, Maspero, Paris.

Palloix, C. (1973), *Les Firmes multinationales et le procès
d'internationalisation*, Maspero, Paris.

Patnaik, P. (1973), 'Imperialism and the growth of Indian capitalism',
in Owen and Sutcliffe (1973).

Patnaik, U. (1971a), 'Capitalist development in agriculture, a note',
Economic and Political Weekly, Bombay, VI, 39, Review of Agriculture,
September.

Patnaik, U. (1971b), 'Capitalist development in agriculture, further
comments', *Economic and Political Weekly*, Bombay, VI, 52, Review
of Agriculture, December.

Patnaik, U. (1972), 'On the mode of production in Indian agriculture,
a reply', *Economic and Political Weekly*, Bombay, VII, 40, Review of
Agriculture, September.

Poulanzas, N. (1975), *Classes in Contemporary Capitalism*, New
Left Books, London, originally published in French, 1974.

Radice, H. (ed.) (1975), *International Firms and Modern Imperialism*,
Penguin, Harmondsworth.

Rey, P. P. (1971), *Colonialisme, néo-colonialisme et transition au
capitalisme*, Maspero, Paris.

Rey, P. P. (1973), *Les Alliances de classes*, Maspero, Paris.

Rey P. P. (1975), 'The lineage mode of production', *Critique
of Anthropology*, 3, Spring.

Rhodes, R. I. (ed.) (1970), *Imperialism and Underdevelopment, a
Reader*, Monthly Review Press, New York.

Ricardo, D. (1971), *Principles of Political Economy and Taxation*,
Penguin, Harmondsworth, originally published 1817.

Rowthorn, R. E. (1971), 'Imperialism in the 1970s – unity or rivalry',
New Left Review, 69, reprinted in Radice (1975).

Rowthorn, R. E. and Hymer, S. (1971), *International Big Business
1957–67: a Study of Comparative Growth*, Cambridge University
Press.

Rudra, A., *et al.* (1969, 1970), 'Big farmers of the Punjab', in three
parts, *Economic and Political Weekly*, Bombay, IV, 39 and 52, and
V, 26, Reviews of Agriculture.

Sau, R, (1973), 'On the essence and manifestation of capitalism in
Indian agriculture', *Economic and Political Weekly*, Bombay, VIII, 13,
Review of Agriculture, March.

Sen, A. K. (1968), *Choice of Techniques*, 3rd edition, Blackwell, Oxford.

Steedman, I. (1975), 'Positive profits with negative surplus value',
Economic Journal, March.

Steedman, I. (1976), 'Positive profits with negative surplus value: a
reply', *Economic Journal*, September.

Steedman, I. (1977), *Marx after Sraffa*, New Left Books, London.

Stolper, W. and Samuelson, P. (1941), 'Protection and real wages',
Review of Economic Studies, IX.

Sutcliffe, B. (1972), 'Imperialism and industrialisation in the Third
World', in Owen and Sutcliffe (1972).

Sweezy, P. (1942), *The Theory of Capitalist Development*, Oxford

University Press, New York.

Terray, E. (1972), *Marxism and Primitive Societies, Two Studies*, Monthly Review Press, New York.

Turner, B. S. (1978), *Marx and the End of Orientalism*, Allen & Unwin, London.

Wallerstein, I. (1974a), *The Modern World System*, Academic Press, New York.

Wallerstein, I. (1974b), 'The rise and future demise of the world capitalist system', *Comparative Studies in Society and History*, 16, 4, reprinted in Wallerstein (1979).

Wallerstein, I. (1979), *The Capitalist World Economy*, Cambridge University Press and Editions de la Maison des Sciences de l'Homme, Paris.

Warren, B. (1971), 'How international is capital?', *New Left Review*, 68, July/August, reprinted in Radice (1975).

Warren, B. (1973), 'Imperialism and capitalist industrialisation', *New Left Review*, 81, September/October.

Wilber, C. K. (ed.) (1973), *The Political Economy of Development and Underdevelopment*, Random House, New York.

Wright, E. O. (1979), 'The value controversy and social research', *New Left Review*, 116, July/August.

Index